Defense and Dependence in a Global Economy

Defense and Dependence in a Global Economy

Edited by
Raymond Vernon
Ethan B. Kapstein

Congressional Quarterly Inc.
Washington, D.C.

Cover design: Ben Santora

These articles originally appeared in the Fall 1991 issue of
Daedalus, vol. 120, no. 4, from the Proceedings of the
American Academy of Arts and Sciences.

Copyright © 1992
Congressional Quarterly Inc.
1414 22nd Street, N.W.
Washington, D.C. 20037

Printed in the United States of America

Library of Congress Cataloging-in-Publication Data

Defense and dependence in a global economy / edited by
   Raymond Vernon, Ethan B. Kapstein.
        p.   cm.
   Includes bibliographical references and index.
   ISBN 0-87187-751-1 (hard) — ISBN 0-87187-750-3
   (pbk.)
   1. National security. 2. Defense industries. I. Vernon, Raymond, 1913–   . II. Kapstein, Ethan B.
UA10.5.D425   1992
355'.03--dc20
                                                92-13194
                                                   CIP

Contents

Preface

THE SOVIET UNION IS NO MORE. And with its departure from the roster of nations, military experts and foreign affairs specialists find themselves obliged to rethink the premises that have guided them through four decades of tension. One consequence of that development is the weakening of one of the ties binding Western Europe and Japan with the United States. The loss of a common external threat has tended to turn governments inward and to raise new questions about the relevance of existing military alliances and common defense policies.

While military experts and foreign affairs specialists have pondered the implications of these weakening ties, scientists, engineers, and business managers have moved in a contrary direction. Revolutionary improvements in the international means of communication have driven them relentlessly toward a global perspective; the movement toward a global economy, long in the making, has continued unabated through the period of political turmoil and restructuring. As a result, the international flow of technology, services, money, and goods has burgeoned. Enterprises have continued to develop their multinational networks of subsidiaries and affiliates and have continued to build business alliances with leading firms from other countries.

For defense planners, these developments have posed major problems. Increasingly, they have had no choice but to reach outside their national boundaries in their efforts to acquire the most efficient instruments of war at the lowest possible price. Increasingly, the temptation to sell their products and services to other countries in an effort to help finance their own defense costs has proved hard to resist. The usual objectives of such planners, the desire to achieve autonomy with efficiency, have been increasingly imperiled.

Some of the consequences of these developments have been particularly evident. As the policies of Iraq have graphically illustrated, the movement toward a global economy has been occurring at a time when weapons of mass destruction are no longer a monopoly of the advanced industrialized countries. Improvements in communication have greatly eased the task of governments determined to acquire the technological capacity to threaten their neighbors. Efforts to deal with the issue by the familiar devices of the past, such as export restrictions, can have only a limited transitory effect.

In an effort to define these issues more sharply, a group of us came together in 1989 under the auspices of the John M. Olin Institute for Strategic Studies at Harvard University. We recognized at once that the issues we had identified would be with us for a long time. To deal with them effectively required a much deeper understanding of the forces that were producing the existing national policies, as well as of the forces that were generating the trend to globalization. Accordingly, in a carefully coordinated effort, we developed a structure of studies that we believed would help to increase that understanding. These studies appeared originally as an issue of *Dædalus*, the official publication of the American Academy of Arts and Sciences.

In the chapters that follow, various authors have acknowledged financial and intellectual support from numerous sources. For the project as a whole, however, the principal sources of support came from several institutions at Harvard: the Olin Institute, the Center for International Affairs, and the Center for Business and Government of the John F. Kennedy School of Government.

Raymond Vernon

Raymond Vernon and Ethan B. Kapstein

National Needs, Global Resources

I N THE FOUR DECADES SINCE THE END of World War II, two
objectives have been high on the agenda of the rich industrialized
countries of the world: to increase the opportunities for their
national enterprises to roam the world in search of lucrative markets
and profitable investment; and to protect their national interests from
external threats, ranging from Moscow's nuclear capabilities to the
menacing gestures of petty tyrants such as Saddam Hussein and
Muammar Khaddafi.

By 1991, these countries appeared to have made giant progress on
both fronts. Yet it was apparent to any observer that there were
increasing tensions between the two objectives, that their successes in
opening up the world to their national enterprises seemed to be
nibbling away at their capacity to protect their own national security
interests. For the very factors that have helped to spread industry
around the world have speeded the diffusion of military technology.
That diffusion has rapidly diminished the possibilities for controlling
the spread of defense-related hardware to potential enemies and
terrorists, and has increased the dependence of the advanced industrialized countries, including the United States, on foreign suppliers of
technology for the components of major weapons systems and, in
many cases, for the weapons themselves. For some countries, such as
Denmark and Italy, the resulting tensions have been of no great
importance. But for others, such as France and the United States, the
disjunction between the globalization of industry on the one hand,

Raymond Vernon is Professor of International Affairs, Emeritus at Harvard University.

*Ethan B. Kapstein is Assistant Professor of International Relations at Brandeis University and
Codirector of the Economics and National Security Program at the John M. Olin Institute for
Strategic Studies at Harvard University.*

and the imperatives of national security on the other, have been acutely troubling.

PLANNING FOR DEFENSE

For forty years, national security officials in the West focused their attention on the Soviet Union. With both sides holding huge nuclear arsenals capable of untold destruction, the defense policy of the West emphasized deterrence. At the same time, national security officials saw a need to maintain forces sufficient to deal with the possibility that deterrence might fail.[1]

The postwar contest with the Soviet Union in effect provided the basis for an industrial policy in the United States and throughout the Western alliance. Between 1970 and 1988, the US government accounted for one half of the nation's total spending on research and development; and more than half of the nation's total R&D spending went to defense-related activities. With advanced R&D concentrated in a small number of countries, most of those in the NATO alliance, it was relatively easy to win agreement on multilateral export controls to keep technology out of enemy hands.[2]

It is ironic that the alliance-based policies of the United States also helped to hasten the decline of this seeming monopoly of defense technology. To promote the production of its weapons systems throughout the alliance, the United States entered into partnerships with Germany, Japan, Israel, South Korea, and various other countries for the production of aircraft, armaments, and ships. By the late 1980s, the United States had engaged in licensed production of major systems with over twenty-five countries.[3] Many countries eventually were able to develop their indigenous capabilities not only to arm themselves at home but also to contribute to a thriving export market. Added to that market were the Soviet Union's heavy shipments of arms, aimed at winning allies and strengthening their capabilities in the competition with the West.

With the globalization of "high-tech" industry, defense planners in the West found that they were no longer self-sufficient when it came to the production of advanced weapons systems and needed components. The defense industries saw component parts, and even completed systems, following a pattern that is common in the life of high-tech products—first manufactured at home for domestic consumption, then exported, then produced overseas. These developments seemed to threaten some of the major objectives of the defense planners in a number of countries, including the United States.

Defense planners with a passion for brevity often identify their objectives under two headings: achieving superiority and maintaining autonomy. So stated, they are deceptively simple and incomplete, a fact that the essays in this volume will amply demonstrate. Incomplete or not, however, it is evident that the increasing outreach of national enterprises has deeply affected both objectives.

When defining "superiority," defense planners have been faced with the necessity of changing that concept of mission with the times. Until the liquidation of the Soviet Union in 1991, US planners continued to see their prime defense requirements as countering a nuclear threat and supporting a conventional war in Europe. According to the US Joint Chiefs of Staff speaking early in 1991, "Soviet strategic nuclear forces . . . continue to represent the most compelling potential threat to our national survival and Soviet conventional capabilities remain an important force to reckon with. . . ." Despite the dismemberment of the Soviet Union, that preoccupation has not wholly evaporated. Still, with the Persian Gulf affair fresh in their minds, the United States and other countries can be expected to place added weight on a capacity to suppress blackmailers and provocateurs of the Saddam Hussein variety.[4]

The desire for autonomy, on the other hand, has been based on much more complex considerations.[5] All governments have wished to guard against the lack of a horseshoe nail in wartime. But governments have also sought autonomy for less tangible reasons: to be able to pursue their national interests as they saw fit, without the fear of being denied some critical resource by other governments. From the viewpoint of military and political leaders in the United States, for instance, the galling aspect of the country's dependence on imported oil has been not only the threat of actual shortage in wartime but also the restraint it has imposed on the country's foreign policies even in the absence of any hostilities.

The emphasis that different countries have placed upon superiority and autonomy has of course depended on their perceptions of their resources and their roles. As long as a bipolar rivalry existed, for instance, the passion of Soviet and US defense planners for autonomy stemmed from their common perceptions of their roles as the ultimate bastion for their side. Moreover, both had their political and military interests that extended well beyond those of their allies in Europe to distant corners of the world. In the US case, the possibility that some other countries, within or without the alliance, might try to deter the United States from the exercise of its interests in these distant areas has never been far from the minds of US defense planners. For the French, autonomy has also been pursued in the name of the national interest, as Gaullist visions of "grandeur" have animated both economic and military policies. In contrast, neither Germany nor Japan could see much purpose in striving for autonomy as long as they were obliged to rely on the United States for their military salvation.

The latent tension that has existed between the desire of defense planners for autonomy and their desire for superiority hardly requires explanation. Whatever the contingencies and threats that defense planners foresee, their hope is to maintain the largest possible measure of superiority over the enemy. That objective is partly served by denying the enemy access to the technology and instruments of war. Even more important, however, is amassing the largest quantity and highest quality of firepower that the country's resources can buy—acquiring the proverbial biggest bang for a buck. In the short run, with the outbreak of hostilities expected for the day after tomorrow, defense planners can best serve that objective by shopping the international field, buying from sources, domestic or foreign, that offer the highest quality and largest quantity for a given expenditure. Their obvious fear, however, is that over the long run such a policy will imperil the autonomy objective.

The tension between the autonomy goal and the superiority goal, always present in some degree, has been measurably increased by the intertwining of national economies in the past few decades, which has been accompanied by the increasing differentiation of products and processes. These have led to an increasing proliferation of niches and specializations in the productive world, and an increasing traffic across national borders of differentiated goods and services.

Hand-in-hand with the mushrooming of these differentiations has come a basic change in the character of the products and services required by the armed services. It was not so long ago in military history that the fighting man had only to check his sword, his horse, and his armor to be certain he was ready for battle. Today, the performance of a ship, a plane, or a missile depends upon the qualities of a thousand inputs, including hardware and software, metals and chemicals and composites. The fighting machines that are finally produced from these materials require assembly from many sources, in a process that builds up by layers, with each assembler relying upon subassemblies and materials delivered from a supply network below. Indeed, in the Gulf War, effective delivery systems sometimes consisted of several different systems—aircraft, ground vehicles, and satellites—working in close conjunction.

With so many different technological pools to be drawn upon in the creation of an effective system, the prime contractors for major military products have had little choice but to rely upon the capabilities of many different firms located around the world. Though no reliable data exist on the size and distribution of such networks, informed guesses suggest that as much as 20 percent of the ingredients in US weapons systems come from sources outside the United States, much of them buried in the black boxes of subassemblies.[6] For European defense industries and those found in the developing world, the reliance on foreign ingredients is certainly higher.

The extraordinary increase in the complexity of military hardware and the mounting number of inputs in any item ready for use on the battlefield pose numerous problems for those charged with defense acquisition. One problem is to find suppliers that are capable of developing and delivering the exotic materials, subassemblies, and software that the military services are constantly demanding, to be available in the various contingencies that procurement planners envisage. With different niches of the technological spectrum dominated by different firms all over the globe, procurement officers or their prime contractors commonly find themselves obliged either to accept a foreign source or to settle for second-best. During Operation Desert Storm, for example, US acquisition officials found themselves scrambling in the markets of foreign countries to get increased production of needed components and spare parts.[7]

To reconcile the need for superiority with the need for autonomy, some observers have suggested that defense officials should concentrate on developing multiple sources for their critical needs without concerning themselves whether the sources were domestic or foreign; autonomy could then be preserved by having alternatives available in times of crisis.[8] But military planners have not been comfortable about contributing to the capability and efficiency of sources beyond their control, lest that capability and efficiency be used eventually to put greater firing power in the hands of the enemy.

The dilemma for public officials in most countries has been sharpened by the fact that the pressure—or the temptation—to export some of their own weapons of war has been unremitting. Some of the pressure for such exports has been political, using sales and gifts of weapons to make friends and build alliances; the US arming of Israel and Saudi Arabia falls into this category. But in most countries there has been an economic incentive as well; policy makers have seized eagerly upon export opportunities in order to finance their own domestic production capabilities. Brazil, Italy, Israel, China, and France have long responded to the economic incentive on a large scale.[9] And in the early 1990s, it appeared that the United States was also moving in that direction, as the country's budgetary constraints bit deeply into the financial prospects of the US armaments industry.[10] The effect of these trends, as the Gulf War has so dramatically illustrated, has been to enhance both the armaments and the technological capabilities of a widening circle of countries.

The choice of defense planners between superiority and autonomy is now being complicated by another problem as well, namely, managing the choice between off-the-shelf components available to all comers and made-to-order components available only to a procuring service.[11] With a proliferation of inputs, a layering of subassemblies, and a widening net of suppliers in the production of military products, the number of cases in which an off-the-shelf item can be used to satisfy military needs has been rapidly on the rise.[12] Indeed, in an increasing number of cases, the pressures of competition in the commercial market have been to produce items superior in performance to anything that the slow-moving military market has been capable of devising and procuring. The speed with which the commercial market has pushed the development of memory chips, for instance, suggests that off-the-shelf chips may be well ahead of anything the military could have commissioned. Yet, with greater reliance upon the commercial market, defense planners are bound to feel a loss in autonomy as well as in their capacity to withhold superior technology from hostile nations.

The uncertainties of defense planners have been exacerbated by the fact that the business organizations responsible for future flows of technology, bearing such names as Siemens and Toshiba, along with IBM and Motorola, are constantly restructuring their organizations to cover new areas of the globe. Even the enterprises headquartered in their own national territory may, if they see good reason to do so, develop their new generations of products and processes in foreign laboratories; and many, including such key organizations as IBM and Texas Instruments, already do. All such issues have been sharpened very much further by the prospect of rapidly declining defense budgets, especially in the United States. Defense planners in the 1990s face the prospect that their contribution to R&D expenditures will be falling, further eroding their ability to control the pool of technology.[13]

Although developments such as these have posed difficult issues for defense planners bent on maintaining superiority in the short run, they have posed even greater difficulties for planners who have focused on some distant date, years or even decades ahead, when superiority must be assured. One reason for so distant a focus has been technological: the fighter aircraft or the amphibious tank planned in 1990 will not be in service until the twenty-first century. Another reason for a long perspective, however, has been the nature of the perceived threat: as long as defense planners in the West saw the Soviet Union as the ultimate enemy, as long as the nuclear stalemate seemed likely to hold for the medium term, a critical element in the defense planners' package of strategies was to present the Soviet Union with repeated evidence of their continued high resolve over the longer run. In the 1990s, however, the targets for long-term planning are much more obscure. As the 1991 assessment of the Joint Chiefs of Staff puts it, "the growing complexity of the international security environment makes it increasingly difficult to predict and estimate the circumstances under which US military power might be employed."[14]

Meanwhile, Iraq has brought yet another concern into much sharper focus, the fear of the destructive power of an outlaw nation. The challenge such nations pose, to be sure, is not that of global superiority; rather it is whether countries determined to blackmail their neighbors into political and economic concessions can gain enough killing power to present a credible threat.

Facing this nascent issue, national security officials find the increasing globalization of markets, technologies, and enterprises presenting an especially formidable problem. The technologies that are required to develop a mass killing capability, such as those necessary for the production of missiles and chemicals, are sophisticated in some respects, but they can readily be mastered by a small cadre of technicians. Moreover, they may retain their power to terrorize neighboring countries, even when they are based on technologies that are widely available and easily mastered. With the genie out of the bottle, defense planners must ponder how to contain such unprecedented threats.

As the multinationalization of enterprises and markets progresses, defense planners are being pushed to the realization that the trade-offs between superiority and autonomy are growing more acute, and that defense production based entirely on national facilities controlled by nationals is becoming increasingly implausible. That ineluctable conclusion affects planning for practically every military contingency. To gain a sense of the dimensions of the challenge, it helps to review the growth of the role of international trade, the widening of the technological pool, and the changes in the structure of large international firms.

THE SHIFTS IN INTERNATIONAL TRADE

The fact that international trade now occupies a critical place in the economies of some major countries is not new. Indeed, in the decades before World War I, Britain depended heavily on Argentina and Canada for its bread and beef, and Germany was importing large quantities of foodstuffs and other raw materials.[15]

But the dependence of industrialized countries that developed after World War II has been profoundly different both in magnitude and in kind from anything experienced in earlier decades. In the case of Germany, the United Kingdom, and France, about half of their consumption of manufactured goods came from foreign sources, including partners in the European Community. The United States lagged well behind the Europeans, but still had a fifth of its consumption of manufactured goods coming from foreign countries. Only Japan among the industrialized countries failed to show a strong increase in imports, with foreign products representing only about 5 percent of its requirements of manufactured goods.[16]

Industrialized countries were exhibiting their increased links to foreign markets through the growth of their exports as well: in the case of the United States, exports in 1986 embodied about one-seventh of the resources that went into the making of industrial products.[17] In Japan, the comparable proportion was about one-quarter, and in Germany, the United Kingdom, and France, about one-half.

Trends such as these, to be sure, say nothing conclusive about the degree of dependence of the nations concerned. Such judgments depend in part on the costs that would be involved to any nation in shifting its sources of supply or in diverting its production to other markets. Where those costs are perceived to be very large, the nation's dependence is high; but where the costs of a shift are seen as easily bearable, a high level of trade may not generate a high degree of dependence. In this instance, however, the sheer orders of magnitude of the growth in trade point conclusively to a heightened degree of vulnerability on all sides.

More important than the sheer size of the trade component in the economy, however, has been the change in the composition of the goods and services being traded. The dependence on trade that some industrializing countries exhibited in the nineteenth century was palpable and transparent, concentrated in some key raw materials such as cotton, oil, and grain. Some of these products, such as coal and iron ore, could be stockpiled against emergencies without great difficulty; others, such as oil and grain, could not be as readily stored. But in most instances, the existence of the dependence was easily identified, allowing for the possibility of effective countermeasures.

By the 1990s, however, the dependence of countries on goods and services emanating from foreign sources was of a wholly different kind. In the case of oil and a few rare metals, it is true, the United States, Europe, and Japan were still dependent in traditional ways. But during the 1970s and 1980s, the most rapid increases in international trade were in products closely linked to battlefield capabilities. Data processing equipment, transistors, telecommunication equipment, and engines headed the list, while measuring instruments and artificial resins were not far behind.[18] Because these products were of such complexity, a more subtle type of dependence was affecting all those countries.

On the surface, what economists and politicians saw was the pervasive growth of so-called intraindustry trade, that is, trade in which two countries exchange products or services in what seems to be the very same industry.[19] Below the surface, a revolutionary change was taking place in the logistical patterns by which producers of goods and services were fabricating and packaging their products for sale in the market. With the real cost of international communication and transportation declining precipitately over the decades, with dramatically new facilities coming on stream for the speedy movement of blueprints, components, and troubleshooters, managers were reaching across international borders to develop global logistical networks. And of the goods and services that moved across international borders, a large and growing share represented movements between parties with organic connections of some sort, usually represented by ownership, license, or long-term contract.

These new logistical networks put military planners on notice that they could no longer count on the obvious factor endowments of their country to provide a guide to its likely patterns of dependence. With machine tools being exchanged for machine tools, the basic skills and capabilities of the various industrialized countries showed striking similarities. Yet with the continuous refinements and differentiations in components, materials, and software that went into the finished products, it was increasingly difficult for planners to guess at whether the use of foreign resources was adding much to their country's vulnerability.

The rapid growth of services in all industrialized countries has been adding another major uncertainty to national patterns of dependence. Official data on the trade in services are notoriously incomplete. But in the years from 1976 to 1988, when the total US workforce rose by about 30 percent, employment in the seemingly exportable services, including engineering, finance, and air transport among others, rose by about 70 percent.[20]

It is the nature of some of these services more than their sheer volume, however, that is bound to create questions of dependency in the minds of defense planners. Some of these services, for example, are critical for the continued functioning of major installations. Picture, for example, the operation of a supercomputer of foreign origin installed in the control center of a national electric power grid. Repairs on the supercomputer are normally handled by a specialized engineering firm domiciled in the country. But the engineering firm may be relying on diagnostic protocols developed by the foreign manufacturer that are stored in the country of manufacture. Dependencies of that sort are not visible to the casual observer. When finally they emerge, their late discovery is sure to magnify the anxieties that they evoke.[21]

The trade patterns of the industrialized countries in the 1990s, therefore, differ in major respects from anything that military planners have previously encountered. In raw volume terms, national economies are probably more reliant on one another than ever before. Moreover, the diversity and range of that reliance have broadened to such an extent that monitoring the implications in terms of national security would require measures on the part of government agencies that would be far too costly and intrusive to be tolerated in a situation short of war.

THE POOL OF TECHNOLOGY

In the decades following World War II, the international flows of technology responded to some of the same factors that had so greatly influenced the postwar flows of trade. With international communication and travel facilities vastly improved, foreign students flocked to the science and engineering programs of Europe and North America, foreign technical licensing agreements proliferated, and foreign subscriptions to technical journals expanded. These developments eventually helped to produce several closely linked results.

By the 1990s, the US economy could no longer be counted on to supply the most advanced technology in every major branch of industry. By then, other countries had carved out numerous niches on the technological frontiers. And where US production could match foreign production in quality, it sometimes could not do so in price. That development explains why a substantial fraction of the content of US military hardware was coming from abroad, incorporated in the subassemblies and black boxes that went into the making of such hardware.

The phenomenon of increasing reliance on foreign technology was not, of course, unique to the United States. Other countries that were already much more heavily dependent on access to foreign technology were increasing their dependence. A hint of that trend can be seen in the data in Table 1. As the data show, not only the United States but also Germany, France, and the United Kingdom were experiencing a persistent increase in the relative importance of the patents applied for by foreigners; only Japan managed to resist the

TABLE 1 Patent Applications by National and Foreign Applicants, Five Countries, 1976–1987 (percent)

	1976–1979	1980–1983	1984–1987
United States			
Foreigners' applications as percent of all applications	38.6	42.9	47.2
Nationals' applications to foreign countries as percent of their total applications	60.6	67.0	71.1
Germany			
Foreigners' applications as percent of all applications	50.6	55.5	57.7
Nationals' applications to foreign countries as percent of their total applications	66.9	72.1	75.4
France			
Foreigners' applications as percent of all applications	71.8	76.6	78.5
Nationals' applications to foreign countries as percent of their total applications	67.9	75.1	76.5
United Kingdom			
Foreigners' applications as percent of all applications	62.4	67.2	71.4
Nationals' applications to foreign countries as percent of their total applications	54.3	60.8	67.5
Japan			
Foreigners' applications as percent of all applications	15.2	12.4	10.1
Nationals' applications to foreign countries as percent of their total applications	18.3	20.6	21.0

Source: OECD

trend. And as a corollary of that dominant tendency, the patent applications of the nationals of these countries addressed to foreign jurisdictions were increasing at a faster rate than their applications at home.

The reaction of defense planners in the United States to the increased reliance on foreign technology was especially acute. In most countries, the military had long grown accustomed to relying on foreign sources for significant elements of their military hardware; only in the case of the United States was this a comparatively novel experience.

Apart from the increasing interdependence of practically all countries in the procurement of advanced technological products and services, however, another development could be detected that gave US policy makers even greater concern. The relative position of the United States in the increased exchange appeared to be slipping, presaging even greater dependence for the future. For instance, factories in the United States, having supplied 95 percent of home market needs in high-tech products in 1970, supplied only 82 percent of US needs in such products in 1986. US factories, having produced 51 percent of the total high-tech output of the advanced countries in 1970, were producing only 42 percent of that output by 1986. And having provided 28 percent of world exports in high-tech products in 1970, factories in the United States provided only 22 percent of such exports in 1986.[22]

Just how much the US economy was in decline as a technological leader became a matter of furious debate, as various measures provided conflicting indications of the trends. Those who saw no great cause for alarm pointed to a number of trends over a period of twenty-five years that seemed to suggest that the US economy was holding its own: the fact that, measured in terms of real output, the US manufacturing sector had not shrunk in relation to the US economy as a whole, that the proportion of US output and of US exports falling in high-tech categories even had been growing over the years, and that the unique US capacity for planning and creating large industrial systems remained essentially unchallenged in international competition.[23] Still, with relative declines in the educational performance, literacy, and health of the US workforce, US policy makers saw little room for complacency.[24] There was also the fact—already adumbrated by the changing patterns of trade—that a considerable number of countries had acquired the technological capabilities for the mass killing of populations, and the number was bound to grow in time; however a policy of denying petty tyrants access to lethal technologies appeared increasingly difficult to execute.

THE CHANGING STRUCTURE OF ENTERPRISE

From the viewpoint of national officials charged with defense planning, however, the most significant development in the last four decades has been the profound changes in the structure of their national enterprises. Everywhere, large enterprises that had once been content to concentrate their production, their research, and their exports in their home economies have been developing multinational networks composed of affiliates, subsidiaries, and licensees. As with other developments in the globalization of the world economy, defense planners have viewed the multinational spread of large enterprises with mixed reactions. On the one hand, that spread has exposed national enterprises to the pressures and promises of many sovereigns, making their actions less responsive to the demands of national authorities. On the other hand, the spread of the national enterprise into foreign locations could enhance the strength of the national economy, allowing for more access to foreign resources and technologies. Of particular concern to authorities in the United States and Europe was the possibility that the dispersion of the activities of their multinationals to other countries might weaken their historical advantage as early industrializers. When dealing with multinational enterprises, defense officials have often seen themselves as engaged in an implicit competition with other countries for the location of the newest activities of an enterprise. Despite the fact that the telephone, fax, containerized freight, and commercial aircraft have vastly reduced the economic meaning of distance, the unique power of face-to-face communication still influences the locational decisions of multinational enterprises. As a result, some of the most important functions of these enterprises, such as research, development, and control, continue to be located in agglomerations such as Silicon Valley and downtown Manhattan. And, in the international competition for industry, these agglomerations continue to tip the scales in favor of existing centers.

Accordingly, planners in the industrialized countries see part of their rivalry as a contest among attractive poles, a struggle to maintain the attractiveness of existing agglomerations. As some technical activities are drawn away to foreign locations, they see the agglomerations on their home territories as losing some of their attractive force.[25] And, with HDTV and the hologram rapidly coming on stream to facilitate long-distance teleconferences, they see powerful new forces that will accelerate the decline in the attractive power of existing agglomerations.[26]

With multinational enterprises contributing to the stability of these agglomerations, planners have looked on their new locational decisions with some anxiety. Their analysis has been handicapped by the fact that there is not even a set of consistent statistics that depicts with reasonable accuracy the appearance and spread of multinational enterprises during the postwar period.[27] Still, the main trends are clear enough.

In the 1950s and 1960s, large firms based in the United States set up subsidiaries abroad in great numbers. Between 1950 and 1970 the number of manufacturing subsidiaries established in foreign countries by leading US manufacturing firms rose from about one thousand to nearly four thousand.[28] By the mid-1960s, Jean-Jacques Servan-Schreiber was warning Europeans, in a widely publicized tract, that American business might soon engulf the European economies, using their European enterprises as outposts but keeping their cerebral activities in the United States.[29] But already by that time, firms headquartered in Europe were extending their own networks outward from their home bases, setting up subsidiaries not only in other European countries but also in North and South America. As a consequence, by 1970, firms headquartered in Europe had established close to five thousand manufacturing subsidiaries outside their home countries.

By the late 1980s, it was evident that the multinational network had become the dominant form by which enterprises of any size conducted their business in world markets;[30] even firms headquartered in late-industrializing countries such as Brazil, Korea, Taiwan, and India were beginning to develop multinational networks.[31] And in practically all countries, the trend toward multinationalization seemed strongest in enterprises with advanced technological capabilities.[32]

The growing importance of multinational enterprises was reflected in numerous ways, including their domination of US export trade. By the last half of the 1980s, for example, it appeared that US-based multinational enterprises were responsible for about 65 percent of total US merchandise exports, while the US subsidiaries of foreign-based firms may have been accounting for another 25 percent of US merchandise exports.[33] Moreover, by the 1980s, the multinational-izing trend was not limited to manufacturing but was prominent in the service industries as well, including international banking, construction, management consulting, engineering, accounting, and insurance.

Numerous studies have confirmed that one of the factors driving enterprises toward a multinational structure is their desire to exploit a technological lead.[34] With that in mind, enterprises usually have a choice among several strategies, including exporting their products or services, licensing their technologies to others in foreign markets, or setting up their own subsidiaries abroad to produce and market the products or services. But exports can be slowed down by tariffs and quotas, and licenses can be abused by licensees who violate the quality control provisions of the license or sell in markets not covered by the license. Experienced enterprises, therefore, have tended to establish their positions in foreign markets through subsidiaries in preference to exports or to independent licensees.

However, when the foreign subsidiary approach has proved insufficient in providing the required linkage to foreign markets, foreign technology, or foreign capital, large firms also have resorted to various kinds of alliances with potential foreign competitors. Boeing, for example, has participated in a series of joint ventures in Europe and Japan to underwrite the development and to promote the sales of its various aircraft; Texas Instruments, IBM, AT&T, and Motorola have followed suit in their respective lines.

Reflecting the ambivalence of national defense planners, many of the new multinational links established in the 1980s have had the blessing—indeed, the urging—of planners. Faced with escalating costs, and with an increasing need to gain access to foreign technologies, planners have suppressed their misgivings over the leakage of technologies under their national control and have tolerated or sponsored various international teaming arrangements. Teaming among the European members of NATO of course has been commonplace. But transatlantic teaming between US and European firms has also achieved considerable importance; 70 such major arrangements were reported in the four years from 1986 to 1989 alone.[35]

Once they have established firm links in a foreign country, US-based enterprises have tended to widen and deepen those links over time. For instance, the foreign subsidiaries of US-based enterprises expanded their aggregate shares of the networks' total exports from 38 percent in 1966 to 52 percent in 1986.[36] Meanwhile, the expenditures of such networks on R&D undertaken outside the United States have grown a little faster than R&D expenditures in the home base, enough to stir apprehensions; the R&D expenditures of the foreign subsidiaries of US-based parents mounted from 6.9 percent of the total R&D expenditures of their parents in 1966 to 8.7 percent in 1982.[37] Since then, there have been strong hints that US-based firms have continued to build up their foreign R&D facilities, particularly in Japan;[38] by the end of the decade, seventy-one US-based firms had been identified with R&D facilities established in that country, and about half were less than ten years old.

The spread of R&D activities, however, has not been all one way. At the same time that US-based firms were discovering reasons for pursuing innovation and development activities abroad, some firms based in other countries were also discovering the advantages of engaging in such activities outside the home base. Glaxo and Philips, based in Europe, established research laboratories in Singapore as did Japan's NEC. And Philips, Unilever, and Imperial Chemicals, among many others, had long since discovered the advantages of conducting research in the United States. More recently, southern California has become a major center for the design of Japanese automobiles.

Defense agencies, however, have not taken kindly to the idea that the R&D activities of foreign-owned firms on their national soil might be regarded as an addition to the national industrial base or as an offset to similar activities being conducted by their own enterprises in foreign countries. Even when development activities are being undertaken by American engineers on US soil, the foreign ownership of their employing firms has been seen as a hindrance to maintaining secrecy or to ensuring access for the US military establishment to the results. From the viewpoint of the military, therefore, the movement of the activities of multinational enterprises across national borders has been asymmetrical in effect, always eroding the industrial base.

Yet, for all the uncertainties created by multinational networks and alliances, all signs point to the likelihood that they will remain a dominant form of business organization in the future, a major conduit for the international movement of goods, services, and technology. A basic issue for defense planners is how best to adapt to a world in which such enterprises occupy a dominant position.

AND WHAT NEXT?

The decline in the capacity of countries to rely on national resources alone as the basis for their military capabilities comes at a time when the military objectives themselves are undergoing intensive reexamination. With the Warsaw Pact dissolved, governments urgently need to reexamine their security needs and to assess the place that an industrial base plays in the fulfillment of those needs. At the same time, they must grapple with the prospect of a sharp decline in the resources available to implement any strategic change.

In the past, one could have detected a number of different purposes at work in governments' policies toward the production and procurement of military goods. Some of these purposes were economic, aimed at reducing the cost of military hardware. Some were strategic, aimed at maintaining a technological lead, irrespective of economic consequences. Some contained elements of both strategies. With the evaporation of the bipolar threat, the objectives are bound to change. In the chapters that follow, various authors will be sorting out and clarifying the objectives of a number of key countries, looking for connections between the changes in those national strategies and changes in national policies for the procurement and production of weapons of war.

In addition to changes in national objectives, another variable that will profoundly affect the procurement policies of governments in the future is the direction of the development of technologies most relevant to military capabilities, as well as the evolution of industries that are relied on to develop and apply those capabilities. A central question is whether new locational patterns in these industries are creating added difficulties for planners who hope to maintain a self-sufficient industrial base under national control. The industry studies that appear in the following chapters are designed to throw light on that critical question.

A number of conclusions, the reader will discover, are strongly suggested by these studies.

First, any nation that is determined to rely upon its own products, its own technologies, and its own enterprises to fulfill its defense needs will pay a far higher premium for such a policy than in years past, costs that will be expressed not only in terms of money but also in a sacrifice in the quality of its military equipment. Second, most countries are likely to accept a heavy reliance on foreign technologies and foreign components as an inescapable condition for maintaining their defense establishments. The United States, however, will have much more difficulty than other countries with accepting that state of dependence. Under pressure from various quarters inside and outside of government, the country will engage sporadically in programs aimed at developing unique technological defense capabilities and at holding down its dependence on foreign sources of technology and components. Third, driven by the desire to win friends and hold down defense costs, both the United States and other industrialized countries will continue to contribute to the lethal capabilities of other countries through the export of technology, know-how, and hardware. This trend will swamp the various bilateral and multilateral efforts to limit such capabilities.

As a consequence, the ability of the leading industrialized countries to withhold weapons of mass destruction from selected target countries will continue to decline. A critical question for the future is whether the international community can develop more effective responses, such as threats of reprisal or other strategies of deterrence, in order to make the world a safer place.

ENDNOTES

[1]US Office of the President, *National Security Strategy of the United States* (Washington, D.C.: US Government Printing Office, March 1990), 2.

[2]Council on Competitiveness, *Gaining New Ground: Technology Priorities for America's Future* (Washington, D.C.: Council on Competitiveness, 1991), 20.

[3]US Congress, Office of Technology Assessment, *Global Arms Trade* (Washington, D.C.: US Government Printing Office, June 1991), 1–6.

[4]US Department of Defense, *1991 Joint Military Net Assessment* (Washington, D.C: Department of Defense, 1991), 2–1.

⁵Our thinking on autonomy and efficiency benefited from Andrew Moravcsik's early drafts of his paper on the European experience.

⁶Ethan B. Kapstein, "Losing Control—National Security and the Global Economy," *The National Interest* (18) (Winter 1989/1990): 85–90.

⁷John Eckhouse, "Japanese Firms Reportedly Withheld Key Parts of U.S. G.W. Weapons," *Baltimore Sun,* 30 April 1991, 1.

⁸An eloquent elaboration of this approach appears in Theodore H. Moran, " The Globalization of America's Defense Industries," *International Security* 15 (1) (Summer 1990): 57–99.

⁹For a superb summary of the global armaments trade, see US Congress, Office of Technology Assessment, *Global Arms Trade.*

¹⁰See, for instance, Eric Schine, "The Casualties of Peace: Wounded Weapons Makers Will Get Strafed," *Business Week,* 8 January 1990, 70.

¹¹For an elaboration of this issue, see Jacques Gansler, *Affording Defense* (Cambridge: MIT Press, 1989).

¹²US Congress, Office of Technology Assessment, *The Defense Technology Base* (Washington, D.C.: US Government Printing Office, March 1988).

¹³Carnegie Commission on Science, Technology, and Government, *New Thinking and American Defense Technology* (New York: Carnegie Commission, August 1990).

¹⁴For an elaboration of planning difficulties, see US Department of Defense, *1991 Joint Military Net Assessment,* 1–5.

¹⁵United Nations (Geneva), *Economic Bulletin for Europe* 6 (1) (4th quarter 1953): 43–44; Ibid., 8 (3) (November 1956): 79.

¹⁶Precise data would require national input-output tables; these estimates are built up from cruder data provided from OECD sources.

¹⁷"Annual Input-Output Accounts of the U.S. Economy, 1986," *Survey of Current Business* 71 (2) (February 1991): 35–50.

¹⁸General Agreement on Tariffs and Trade, *International Trade 88–89,* vol. 2 (Geneva: GATT, 1989), Table IV–2, 38.

¹⁹Studies reflecting the rapid growth of intraindustry trade: for 1959–1967, Herbert G. Grubel and P. J. Lloyd, *Intra-Industry Trade* (London: Macmillan, 1975), 40–52; for 1953–1970, H. Hesse, "Hypotheses for the Explanation of Trade between Industrialized Countries, 1953–1970," in H Giersch, ed., *The International Division of Labor* (Tübingen: J. C. B. Mohr (Paul Siebeck), 1974), 39–59; for 1961–1978, J. M. Finger and D. A. DeRosa, "Trade Overlap, Comparative Advantage and Protection" in H. Giersch, ed., *On the Economics of Intra-Industry Trade* (Tübingen: J. C. B. Mohr (Paul Siebeck), 1979), 213–44.

²⁰Ronald E. Kutscher, "Outlook 2000: Industry Employment," in *The Service Economy* 4 (2) (April 1990): 5.

²¹For indications of the trend toward machinery repair from remote locations, see "Repairing Machinery from Afar," *New York Times,* 30 January 1991, D–6.

[22]National Science Foundation, *Science Indicators-1989* (Washington D.C.: National Science Foundation, 1989), 371, 375, 377; app. Tables 7–1, 7–2, and 7–10 are compiled from OECD sources.

[23]For a summary of these trends, see chapters by Raymond Vernon and Subi Rangan in I. Yamazawa and A. Hirata, eds., *Industrial Adjustment and Its Implications for Developing Countries* (Tokyo: Institute of Developing Economies, 1992).

[24]Michael L. Dertouzos et al., *Made in America: Regaining the Productive Edge,* (Cambridge: MIT Press, 1989), 83–93.

[25]Stephen S. Cohen and John Zysman, *Manufacturing Matters: The Myth of the Post-Industrial Economy* (New York: Basic Books, 1987), 12–27; Michael Borrus, Laura D'Andrea Tyson, and John Zysman, "Creating Advantage: How Government Policies Shape International Trade in the Semiconductor Industry," in Paul R. Krugman, ed., *Strategic Trade Policy and the New International Economics* (Cambridge: MIT Press, 1986), 91–113.

[26]For a striking account of the state of these developments, see Derek Leebaert, ed., *Technology 2001: The Future of Computing and Communications* (Cambridge : MIT Press, 1991).

[27]The most comprehensive data purporting to reflect this trend are contained in a series on the stock of foreign direct investment from 1960 to the mid-1980s; see US Department of Commerce, *International Direct Investment,* 1988 ed., (Washington, D.C., US Government Printing Office, 1988), 9. The report notes that the stock figures have been growing at rates exceeding the GNP growth rates of the countries concerned; but the statistics are poor, and the logic of the comparison feeble.

[28]Detailed data for this period are presented in J. W. Vaupel and J. P. Curhan, *The Making of Multinational Enterprises* (Boston: Harvard Business School, 1969).

[29]The original French edition was published in 1966. The English translation appeared as *The American Challenge* (New York: Athaneum, 1968).

[30]UN Centre on Transnational Corporations, *CTC Reporter* (30) (Autumn 1990): 38, 44.

[31]Ibid.

[32]For the United States, see US Department of Commerce, *U.S. Direct Investment Abroad: Preliminary 1988 Estimates* (Washington, D.C.: US Government Printing Office, 1990), Table 2.

[33]US Department of Commerce, *U.S. Direct Investment Abroad: Revised 1987 Estimates* (Washington, D.C.: US Government Printing Office, 1990), Table 57; and US Department of Commerce, *Foreign Direct Investment in the United States: 1987 Benchmark Survey, Preliminary Results,* (Washington, D.C.: US Government Printing Office, 1989), Table G–3.

[34]Richard E. Caves, *Multinational Enterprises and Economic Analysis* (New York: Cambridge University Press, 1982), 192–225.

[35]US Congress, Office of Technology Assessment, *Global Arms Trade,* 14–15.

[36]Irving B. Kravis and Robert E. Lipsey, "Technological Characteristics of Industries and the Competitiveness of the U.S. and Its Multinational Firms," National Bureau of Economic Research Working Paper, No. 2933 (Cambridge: National Bureau of Economic Research, April 1989), 3.

[37]Based on data in US Department of Commerce, *U.S. Direct Investment Abroad: 1966 Benchmark Survey Data* (Washington, D.C.: US Government Printing Office, 1969), 224, 229; and US Department of Commerce, *U.S. Direct Investment Abroad* (Washington, D.C.: US Government Printing Office, 1985), Table IIQ.1 and III.H2.

[38]National Science Foundation, *Highlights*, (Washington, D.C.: National Science Foundation, 9 March 1990), Table 2; also National Science Foundation *Free Report: Survey of Direct U.S. Private Capital Investment in Research and Development Facilities in Japan* (Washington, D.C.: National Science Foundation, 1991).

Andrew Moravcsik

Arms and Autarky in Modern European History

[handwritten annotation: Arms cost ↑ and budgets ↓ ⇒ arms producers must go elsewhere to get reasonable market to keep costs under control ⇒ too often commercial interests force the national security decision to export to potential enemies]

CONVENTIONAL WISDOM TELLS US THAT military planners faced with a choice between self-sufficiency and free trade will choose self-sufficiency. The experience of Europe since the Renaissance, however, sets this piece of conventional wisdom on its head. Throughout the last four centuries, military planners have often supported freer trade in arms, in the hope thereby of securing greater quantities of superior weaponry either through their own increased production or by purchase abroad. The military has often had good reason to be suspicious of autarky since nearly every state faces the *autarky-efficiency dilemma*—the inescapable fact that greater autonomy can be bought only at the price of reduced efficiency in armament production. There have been times when the military supported a policy of autarky; but more often that support has come from the domestic economic interests involved in the development and production of armaments.[1]

THE EARLY MERCANTILIST ERA

Early Arms Races

"War made the state, and the state made war," observes Charles Tilly of early modern Europe. From about 1500 to 1700, as modern states emerged in Europe, their development was marked by mercantilist economic policies and an expanding capacity to organize military force that historian Michael Roberts has termed

Andrew Moravcsik is Assistant Professor of Government at Harvard University and Research Associate at the Program on International Politics, Economics, and Security at the University of Chicago.

the "military revolution." The invention of gunpowder and corresponding improvements in fortifications led to a ten-fold increase in the size of armies and the cost of war. The need to administer and finance the expansion of military power led monarchs to strengthen the bureaucratic and financial powers of the European states.[2]

European rulers attempted to extend the military revolution to arms production as well. They hired military engineers and opened state cannon foundries and shipbuilding establishments. Of greater importance, they encouraged private manufacturers, who were "the chief beneficiaries of the rise of standing armies."[3] Despite the convergence of military politics and mercantilist economics, however, self-sufficiency in armaments production proved to be an elusive goal, even for great powers. Even where rulers commanded adequate peacetime supplies, crisis mobilization often required surreptitious purchases from abroad. Moreover, in those areas where independence from the imports of weapons was achieved, the price was often a dangerous level of dependence upon imported raw materials and other components, as well as a need to export to potential enemies.[4]

From the Renaissance through the end of the eighteenth century, the four essential categories of armaments were warships, artillery, ammunition, and small arms. The efficacy of policies aimed at national self-sufficiency varied according to the type of weapon; but in no case were they entirely successful. Nations came closest to achieving self-sufficiency in the production of ships and gunpowder. Yet the production of such items often required crucial imports from other countries, sometimes from enemies. All the great powers depended on uncertain supplies of Baltic timber for shipbuilding. And saltpeter, an essential ingredient in gunpowder, was scarce everywhere and widely traded. Until the mid-eighteenth century, the Spanish provided iron to the English navy, and the English supplied lead to the French army.[5]

In the production of artillery, efforts to achieve import autarky were even less successful. Neither imperial Spain nor Portugal developed indigenous arms industries of significant size. Both depended on large imports of foreign ordnance, including many from private manufacturers in Flanders and England, their perennial Protestant adversaries. Beginning in the sixteenth century, rulers sought the finest brass castings from private manufacturers in northern Italy, Flanders, Britain, and some of Germany's smaller principalities. Until destroyed by General Tilly in 1631, the largest gunmaking establishment in Europe was to be found at Suhl in Saxony, not in the territories of a great power. From there, cannon, pistols, and muskets were exported to France, Spain, and elsewhere. Saxony was soon supplanted by Sweden, which emerged in the mid-seventeenth century as the most self-sufficient of the great powers, having plentiful supplies of charcoal and high-quality iron and copper ores. By the 1650s, more than a thousand Swedish cannon annually were for sale in Amsterdam.[6] After tolerating heavy dependence on foreign sources in the seventeenth century, Russia, under Peter the Great, briefly succeeded in establishing self-sufficiency in the production of sophisticated cannon only to see the quality decline by the nineteenth century.[7]

Whatever limited success states may have achieved in stimulating domestic cannon production, they were unable to block exports to potential adversaries. Beginning in the fifteenth century, the monarchs of Spain, France, and England repeatedly attempted to increase domestic supplies and to block the diffusion of technology by restricting arms exports, but it proved impossible "to organize an adequate national supply and at the same time ensure that none of it would spill over abroad."[8] The fundamental problem was that productive capacity in major powers was often many times greater than domestic demand. In the seventeenth century, for example, England was a leader in the production of iron cannon. But orders from the English crown could barely sustain ten days of production a year, so English foundries sold most of their cast iron ordnance to domestic privateers or foreign governments. As a point of law, exports of such products required government approval; but if such approval was not forthcoming, the requirement was simply ignored. By the seventeenth century, the control of exports became so difficult that latecomers to the industry, including Holland and Sweden, did not even attempt it.[9]

The production and sale of small arms and ammunition remained almost entirely outside state control. Armies of the day were largely composed of mercenaries recruited by entrepreneurial captains, colonels, and princes, often from among defeated enemy troops. Recruiters or recruits were responsible for supplying their own small arms and ammunition, which they procured wherever convenient.[10] Producers outside the domains of strong monarchs remained the largest in Europe, successfully evading repeated attempts at subjugation. In the tiny bishopric of Liège:

> Military occupations, of which there were several, had the immediate effect of disrupting gun manufacture. Hence, if rulers wished to avail themselves of the products of Liège gunmakers' skills—which rapidly became the best and the cheapest in Europe and the world—they had to withdraw their soldiers and let the market again come freely into play.... Their very weakness allowed the Liègeois to set their own prices.[11]

As late as the mid-eighteenth century, the entire Kingdom of France produced twenty thousand muskets annually, while the artisans of Liège produced over *ten times* as many.

Mercantilism Revisited

The industrial policies of Jean-Baptiste Colbert, Louis XIV's chief minister in the 1670s and 1680s, illustrate the difficulties that governments experienced in early modern Europe and provide a telling example of the curious political coalitions that efforts at autarky called forth. Colbert, like other mercantilists of his day, believed that French power and prosperity depended on state policies of export promotion and import protection. To that end, he created state arsenals in the capital-intensive area of shipbuilding and favored large private enterprises for gunpowder, shot, tar, pistols, pikes, swords, cannon, and muskets. He procured examples of foreign goods, hired foreign technicians, and granted domestic firms royal monopolies and large orders.

Scholars commonly contend that a primary purpose of mercantilist policies, such as those of Colbert, was to create an economy self-sufficient in armaments—a *Kriegswirtschaft* or "war-economy."[12] Colbert's mercantilism, however, did not have a primarily military objective. Like other mercantilists of his day, he viewed domestic production and trade surpluses as the ultimate source of national power. He attacked "war expenditure and war undertakings because they undermined . . . the real source of power—economic activity" and hoped to replace traditional wars with trade wars.

Hence the most influential opponents of Colbert's protectionist measures proved to be those responsible for military policy, their objections resting on the attendant decline in the efficiency of arms procurement. The Marquis Le Tellier Louvois, a military officer and Colbert's successor as chief minister, considered Colbert's schemes for self-sufficiency to be bad military policy because they increased the price and reduced the quality of French arms. Indeed, while some of Colbert's projects were successful, most were disappointments. Domestic goods were often of mediocre quality and foreign imports continued. Even in shipbuilding, where Colbert's policies were most successful, France continued to import both raw materials and finished ships. After Colbert's death, Louvois opted for more efficiency and less autarky.[13]

Colbert's mercantilism, then, was a strategy for shaping trade, not for preventing it.[14] The leaders of the seventeenth century, unlike their nineteenth-century successors, pursued mercantilist policies primarily to accumulate a surplus of gold and silver bullion. As Colbert observed in his celebrated but often misunderstood paraphrase of Cicero, "trade is the source of finance and finance is the vital nerve of war." Finance assured adequate stockpiles of arms, paid for foreign mercenaries, and subsidized allies. Accordingly, Colbert rarely justified state aid to national armaments industries on the basis that they would assure a wartime supply of weapons or would permit France to develop more advanced weapons than its enemies. He treated arms industries more or less as he treated civilian industries. Indeed, under his rule, the expansion of civilian industry outstripped that of the military.[15] A century later, during the Seven Years' War, the foundations of naval power would still be defined in Colbert's terms. "The sinews of war," observed one eighteenth-century commentator, "depend more on gold than on steel."[16]

Why Autarky Failed

The failure of autarkic policies in the early modern period was partly a reflection of the limited administrative capacity of the absolutist state. Governments proved unable to administer export controls or to enforce blockades.[17] But there was a more fundamental reason as well: European governments had little reason to hope that by supporting their home industries and by withholding technology from others they could achieve military superiority over their prospective adversaries.

During the first few centuries of the modern period, governments
were not in a position to significantly shape technological developments in support of their military establishments. Cases in which
governments deliberately planned and achieved innovation were
rare. The naval gunnery of 1860 and the warships that carried them
"differed in no essential characteristic" from those of 1560.[18] If the
cannon cast in one foundry proved more brittle than the cannon cast
in another, this was simply one of nature's unexplained mysteries.
Existing technologies diffused far faster than new ones appeared.
Accordingly, where technological superiority was achieved, it generally could not be maintained.[19]

From a purely military perspective, moreover, there was little
reason to support the development of new technologies. Although
armies occasionally held a technological edge, the advantage was
rarely decisive in wars among the great powers. "Victory," notes one
military historian, "turned on the most skillful use of largely unchanging weapons and tactical rules known to everyone."[20] Eighteenth-century monarchs, like Frederick the Great, adhered to the
traditional view that superiority of personnel, leadership, tactics, and
finance determined military success. Although the British navy established military supremacy over those of France and Spain in the late
seventeenth century, the vanquished navies were considered technologically superior to the victor.[21]

By the eighteenth century, however, certain harbingers of change
began to appear. The professional soldier was supplanting the
mercenary. By mid-century, official prizes were being given for
specific scientific and technological innovations, a practice that
heralded greater state involvement in shaping the direction of technological progress. In France, Jean Baptiste de Gribeauval imposed
the standardization of arms and in the second half of the century
"reversed the trend and built up an important armaments industry."[22] In Britain, more effective policies were developed to limit
imports and to promote exports, to promote a merchant marine, and
to offer direct support to military-related industries, including iron,
copper, brass, gunpowder, masts, tar, and hemp. Blockades became
more efficacious.[23] Where arms production was concerned, the true

"military revolution" occurred only in the late eighteenth century; but its success was to be brief.

MERCANTILISM AFTER WATERLOO

The New Mercantilism

One of the issues that distinguished the nineteenth-century mercantilism espoused by Alexander Hamilton, Friedrich List, and other "national economists" from the mercantilist doctrines of the seventeenth century was its emphasis on the importance of self-sufficiency in armaments.[24] Hamilton believed the United States should be "independent of foreign nations for military and other essential supplies" in order to be "least dependent on the combinations, right and wrong, of foreign policy" of other states.[25]

The lessons drawn by Hamilton from the "extreme embarrassments" suffered by the United States, due to their "incapacity of supplying themselves" during the Revolutionary War, accorded with the lessons drawn by European powers from the embargoes imposed by the rival powers during the Napoleonic Wars.[26] Two decades of such warfare left European states with a strong urge to manufacture their own armaments, in some cases by creating a comprehensive system of state arsenals. Exports of arms remained relatively low until mid-century, as arsenals focused on domestic production. The trend toward large-scale capital-intensive industry also marked a decisive historical shift in favor of larger countries: the era in which a small country such as Sweden or the Netherlands could bid for great power status was over.

The Privatization of Arms Production

The system of state-regulated production and relatively low exports lasted barely three decades. By 1850 it was already breaking down under the pressures created by an acceleration in technological development. Liddell-Hart observes that "the forty years from 1830 to 1870 saw a greater change in the means of warfare, both on land and on sea, than during . . . all previous history." For the first time in history, new weapons, such as breech-loading rifles, repeating handguns, iron ships, submarines, and steel artillery, became obsolete before they wore out. Expenditures on armaments procurement became a much larger part of military budgets and secrecy became vital. Napoleon III, who wrote two treatises on artillery and established secret testing of new weapons systems, was not atypical of his age.[27]

Much of the technological progress resulted from the extraordinary dynamism of private enterprise, which developed technology surpassing that produced by state arsenals. Beginning in the 1840s, state-owned industries began to adopt mass-production techniques and to employ proprietary civilian technologies, particularly in areas like metalworking, chemicals, transportation, and internal combustion engines. Even where state production continued, private firms increasingly acted as subcontractors, providing many of the parts for complete weapons systems.[28] Despite these efforts, public arsenals fell behind private firms. Younger military officers began to urge direct procurement from the private sector. Relatively poor and lacking the means to support sophisticated arsenal production, Prussia was among the first to privatize arms production, turning to Krupp in 1859. Within five years, Krupp was nearly the sole supplier of artillery to Prussia.[29] In Britain, firms like Armstrong and Whitworth supported the development of sophisticated armaments, relying almost entirely on export markets, while the Royal Arsenal at Woolwich, having redesigned its ships a number of times to match private competitors, fell further behind.

By the close of the nineteenth century, the freedom of private firms to trade internationally during peacetime had become firmly established. British law, for example, provided that limits could not be imposed on arms exports except in wartime. Alfred Krupp spoke for several generations of European arms manufacturers when he declared that "a strict interpretation of patriotism [is] injurious to business." True to his word, Krupp sold to both sides of the Franco-Prussian War. In the years up to 1912, Krupp exported over 50 percent of its production to buyers in fifty-two countries. On the eve of World War I, the firm filled Russian orders for the latest artillery pieces and French orders for specially designed anti-Zeppelin guns while soliciting British orders for warships. In the 1880s, Hiram Maxim sold the "Maxim gun," the first modern machine gun, to his adopted homeland of Britain and to its future enemies, the Boers of South Africa and the German Reich.[30]

A liberal attitude also governed the exchange and sale of technology, which moved across borders essentially unchecked. The designers of improved bullets and time fuses sold their technology to all buyers. When World War I began in 1914, every major naval power in the world—Great Britain, France, Italy, Japan, Germany, and the United States—utilized "Kruppized" steel, the world's best, with the royalties being paid to Essen through an international trust. Property rights were honored, even among belligerents, with Krupp audaciously—but successfully—suing Vickers for royalties for wartime use of its patents.[31]

Governments tolerated such exports principally because of the imperatives of the autarky-efficiency dilemma. By expanding output, governments could bring down the costs of their own national requirements. High levels of production in peacetime also stimulated technological dynamism and laid the basis for adequate production capacity in wartime. In giving private producers their autonomy, however, European military establishments risked creating unregulated domestic monopolies, whose practices in the pricing of products and in the development of new technologies could damage the efficiency objectives of the military. To break the power of such monopolies, the armed services in Europe sometimes turned to foreign sources of supply—precipitating a major political row with the domestic interests involved. Efforts of the British admiralty in 1862 to acquire Krupp guns, for example, were blocked by Parliament in response to the complaints of Armstrong, Britain's leading gun producer. On the German side, the Prussian admiralty, also eager to reduce the monopoly power of Krupp, immediately began to explore the possibility of purchasing from Armstrong. Only Krupp's repeated interventions with Kaiser Wilhelm and Chancellor Bismarck blocked the military from considering the tenders of munitions manufactures in France and Great Britain.[32]

The Military-Industrial Complex

Even before the outbreak of World War I, however, there were signs that the privileged position of large-scale armaments producers was being undermined. With growing hostility in the international system and with the acceleration of technological progress, the military importance of small technological advantages increased. The export markets of arms manufacturers shrank, as smaller countries demanded turnkey factories, thereby restricting opportunities to export.[33] After World War I, endemic overcapacity often further increased the dependence of private firms on their home market. The period between the two great wars was one of high protectionism and diminished trade in Europe, including trade in armaments. World War I strengthened the resolve of statesmen to develop strong domestic industries with the "surge capacity" needed for a long war of attrition. Aircraft were supplanting artillery as the mainstay of modern armed forces, and small, relatively poor countries could produce aircraft simply by copying existing designs. Although dependent on foreign countries for the bulk of their procurement, Rumania, Yugoslavia, Poland, the Netherlands, and even Lithuania designed low-technology fighters during this period.

Yet exports of arms and military technology did not disappear. In the 1920s, France, a leading armaments producer, sold four hundred of its latest model tanks to Germany. The British government, short of funds and still convinced that free trade in armaments increased the wartime preparedness of its defense industries, allowed firms the freedom to trade. In 1934, British firms sold Hitler state-of-the-art airplane engines and sophisticated explosives. Purchases of military equipment in the 1930s permitted Japan and the Soviet Union to narrow the gap with the technological leaders. And France, Britain, and the United States enforced the comprehensive licensing of arms exports only with the rise of the Third Reich.[34]

THE POSTWAR ECONOMY

The Legacy of World War II

In the aftermath of World War II, Britain and Sweden were the only remaining major European manufacturers of a full range of high-technology weapons. Attempts to reestablish and to promote indigenous arms industries proved far more difficult than in the 1930s, not simply because of the destruction wrought by the war but because of rapidly rising fixed costs of armaments production.

World War II had been a period of intense technological development in armaments production. The Manhattan project symbolized the new era of governmental research and development programs, employing large numbers of scientists to develop key technologies and design sophisticated weapons. Even more important than the existence of governmental facilities was the ability of firms to invest immense amounts of capital. The fixed costs of new weapons, particularly of aircraft, had increased dramatically. Only with large markets in view could firms risk the resources required for the production of a new generation of weapons. The huge procurement budgets in the United States stimulated levels of technological innovation and industrial concentration that no single European state could match.[35] The decisive advantage of the United States did not lie in greater technological skills, an area in which it continued to lag behind Britain, but in the size of its domestic market and the level of its resources.

As part of the Cold War effort, the United States provided support to its principal allies: Britain received critical technology for its nuclear program; Germany participated in a number of high-technology cooperative programs; and the French aerospace industry received direct American aid totaling several billions of dollars. In the case of France, the US government launched the postwar rise of France's leading military aircraft company, Dassault, by buying the entire series of the company's first postwar model, 225 planes, and presenting them to the French air force.[36]

From the moment in the 1950s when independent defense industries reemerged in France, Germany, and Britain to the present day, European defense industrial policies can be seen as responses to the overriding challenge of generating adequate economies of scale. With exponentially rising fixed costs, greater complexity of production technology, and the emergence of significant learning economies, the management of the autarky-efficiency dilemma became the preeminent concern of European governments. In the aerospace industry three solutions were tried: concentration, exports, and collaboration.

Concentration

The dilemma was particularly acute in the production of military aircraft. One response by European governments was to consolidate their existing aircraft producers into a smaller number of firms.[37] The importance of concentration can be seen by contrasting France and Britain. Due to prewar nationalizations, the French aircraft industry began the postwar period more concentrated than that of Britain, giving it a decisive advantage in world markets. While Britain began the postwar period with superior technology and an identical global market share to that of the United States, it was unable to emulate

France rapidly enough, largely due to the resistance of domestic producers to proposals for consolidation. In the 1950s Britain surrendered its export markets to the United States and by the early 1960s, disappeared as an independent producer of classical fighters. Belatedly, the number of British main contractors was reduced to five in 1960 and to one in 1970; but it was too late.[38] By 1990, the process of concentration in the aerospace industry had reached its theoretical limit in Britain and Germany, with the formation of British Aerospace and Deutsche Aerospace, while France was dividing civil and military production respectively between Aérospatiale and Dassault.

Exports

Although concentration was a necessary condition for industrial survival in the postwar period, it was not sufficient; national markets were simply too small to support aircraft production. This led European governments to revive the prewar policy of stimulating exports. Here again the French led the way. The French strategy was to create a unique market niche by producing mid-performance, low-cost fighters and offering them, no strings attached, wherever the United States was unwilling or unwelcome to serve as a source. In the 1960s and 1970s, when much of US production was being funneled to Vietnam, France began exporting between 60 percent and 90 percent of the output of its major aeronautic systems, mainly to the Third World.

Indeed, the basic strategy of the French government with regard to the maintenance of a defense industry was predicated on privileged access to Third World markets. But the French strategy of targeting these markets for the promotion of its exports was not without costs. France's leading producers were obliged to focus their attention on designing and marketing to suit Third World needs. As a result, not only was the delivery of weapons systems to the French military slowed at times by the need to fill export orders, but their design was unacceptable, being inadequate for battles on the European central front. Today, in a striking affirmation of the French military's discontent, the French navy proclaims its preference for the McDonnell Douglas F-18 over the new French Rafale.[39] The final irony of the French government's policy of promoting exports in the Third World has been its inability to capture the long-term loyalty of the countries to which it has been directed. Such countries have been demanding production licenses and turnkey factories with insistence. And competitive offers from other sources have been on the increase, including offers of armaments produced by the collaboration of two or more countries. The French arms industry, it is widely agreed, is in crisis.

Collaboration

Cooperative armaments projects—"collaboration" or "codevelopment"—emerged in postwar Europe, especially in the aircraft field, as another means of addressing the autarky-efficiency dilemma. Through codevelopment, as in the multinational Concorde, Tornado, and Eurofighter projects, countries can amortize the enormous costs of development and the fixed capital required for high-technology weapons production. On the other hand, codevelopment projects require the participating countries to abandon some of the desired gains of autarky for an increase of efficiency.

The United States, with a lesser need for increasing the scale of production, has shied away from codevelopment programs in favor of "coproduction" programs, that is, programs in which foreigners license or buy the rights to produce American designs. But defense planners in European countries have not often had that option. Largely because of the proliferation of collaborative projects, no European nation remains self-sufficient in all weapons systems, and there has been a precipitous decline in the number of European nations self-sufficient in single classes of weapons. Even the French, while rhetorically asserting their independence, have participated in more collaborative projects than the United Kingdom. By the 1990s, 15 to 20 percent of French weapons were being codeveloped, as were all fighter aircraft being produced in Europe, except the French Rafale.[40]

Today it is becoming evident that even widespread collaboration is insufficient in ensuring European nations a supply of sophisticated weapons at reasonable prices. Collaboration can be relatively complex and expensive to negotiate. While collaborative projects have defied their critics by producing large weapons systems like tanks and aircraft as efficiently as single-nation projects, the expense of collaboration appears impractical for thousands of smaller high-tech weapons.[41] Moreover, some believe that the monopolies generated by concentration and collaboration are increasing costs by stifling competition, a complaint voiced most loudly by the British government.

These concerns have generated growing support for further measures to increase efficiency at the expense of autarky. Britain and France recently created a program to promote up to $200 million in annual bilateral trade of small defense purchases. In November 1988, the defense ministers of West European governments launched a plan for reinvigorating the Independent European Program Group (IEPG), a once moribund group created to increase coordination of West European procurement policies. The defense ministers proposed open bidding, public reporting of contracts, and more codevelopment projects. Their most innovative idea was to encourage the formation of competing multinational consortia in each weapons area, in the hope of combining the virtues of competition and collaboration.

These governmental initiatives have been accompanied by moves toward pan-European industrial rationalization and integration. In keeping with the spirit of Europe 1992, defense firms have moved to form multinational corporate alliances, tied together with exchanges of shareholdings.[42] The trend has been particularly pronounced in sectors such as electronics, where "dual-use" technology means that military rationalization is tied to ongoing civilian rationalization. Although the efforts in this direction are still only incipient, the creation of truly pan-European firms would mark an epochal change, possibly leading to an industrial structure that would render autarky not only impossible to achieve, but impossible to define.

National Security and Domestic Interests

Yet, despite these changes, purely national systems continue to account for over 70 percent of the production of major weapons systems in Great Britain and France, and roughly 45 percent in Germany. Waste due to redundant defense industrial capacity in Europe remains high, being estimated at 27 percent of total European defense spending in 1987. There are numerous explanations for the persistence of such waste, usually stressing political, bureaucratic, ideological, or military factors. But the most plausible explanation is that national economic interest groups have succeeded in imposing major barriers to increased trade and collaboration in the European armaments industry. Although it is sometimes difficult to distinguish military from economic motivations from the available evidence, a number of indications point in the direction of the latter.

First, the relatively low levels of collaboration among European nations are flatly inconsistent with the professed policies of the governments concerned. The UK government lists only three areas in which defense industrial autarky is indispensable, and none of these would be affected by the proposed collaborative projects that Britain appears to be resisting. Although France has not published a similar list of reserved areas, it hardly seems credible that defense planners would insist on a policy of autarky in fighter production as long as the AWACS command and control systems, without which the fighter planes cannot effectively operate, are American imports. Germany explicitly recognizes collaboration as an acceptable alternative for domestic production. The contradictions between stated policy and daily practice are consistent with the possibility that special interests are derailing government policy in individual cases.

A second hint that the pressures of economic interests may be the stumbling block in the procurement practices of European governments is that domestic sources dominate the supply of nonmilitary products far more than of military products with comparable technological requirements. According to my estimate, European governments have been procuring about 30 percent of their military products from foreign sources or sources in which foreigners collaborated. Yet such governments source only 3 percent of comparable civilian goods like telecommunications, transport, and power generating equipment from abroad.[43]

A third clue concerning the role of economic interests is the seeming lack of coherence in national security terms in the choices of weapons systems in which European governments are prepared to collaborate. France has obstructed collaboration on fighter aircraft, yet has promoted it on main battle tanks, helicopters, conventional missiles, and nuclear weapons. Germany has resolutely resisted collaboration on battle tanks, but has favored it on aircraft and conventional missiles, including antitank weapons. Britain refused to collaborate in developing battle tanks, reluctantly participated in cooperative ventures in civil aircraft and helicopters, and was a strong collaborator in fighter aircraft and nuclear missiles. Governments tend to oppose collaboration in those areas in which domestic firms have established a strong global export position, but welcome it in areas where they are weak.

Finally, the course of the negotiations over individual weapons systems points to the dominance of commercial interests. The projects discussed in the past two decades between France and Germany—including a main battle tank, a family of military helicopters, and a European fighter aircraft (the EFA)—provide instructive examples. Each of these weapons was an expensive, technologically significant system in which the potential for joint gains through collaboration was measured in hundreds of millions, sometimes billions, of dollars. In each case, the military and the political leadership initially reached compromises over the military specifications, only to see the negotiations stall over the industrial aspects of the collaboration, including the division of work shares, the design leadership, and the naming of subcontractors. The key factor contributing to success or failure in each case was the attitude of the most competitive firm—Dassault in airframes, Krauss-Maffei in tanks, Aérospatiale in helicopters.[44]

On the basis of evidence such as this, it is plausible to conclude that state officials in Europe today, including the military, tend to support increased trade and cooperation, while the interests of arms producers and those who work for them remain the primary source of continuing pressures for protection.

CONCLUSIONS

The appeal that autarkic policies have had for both scholars and statesmen is too obvious to require much elaboration; in the *Realpolitik* school, the advantages that such policies purport to provide for governments have been taken for granted. The evidence presented here, however, belies the view that the major motivation for defense industrial autarky is the concern of military planners for national security. The European experience turns a simple set of propositions about the advantages of autarky into a much more complex phenomenon.

The added complexity begins with the fact that in the European experience, states that have striven for autarky have had a number of different goals in mind. At times, states have simply sought to free themselves from the need to import weapons, hoping to rely on domestic weapons production alone.[45] At other times, countries have sought a second, more ambitious objective: to eliminate imports of crucial inputs used in the domestic production of weapons, including foreign raw materials, imported components, immigrant skilled labor, and crucial technologies. Finally, there has been a third autarkic objective, one commonly overlooked in a discussion of autarky. Some governments have tried to free themselves of the pressure—at times, the necessity—to export some of the output of their weapons producers. The pressure for such exports has often arisen out of the desire of defense planners to bring down costs and loosen budgetary restraints, but the consequence has sometimes been to place technology and weaponry in the hands of potential enemies.

When striving for any of these autarkic goals, European governments have usually been aware that they might have to pay a price for autarkic policies. Like any measures that limit international trade, autarkic policies in military procurement can deprive a national economy in the short run of the advantages that go with specializing in the production of a narrower range of products and in acquiring other needed armaments from abroad. This ineluctable fact creates among European states what I have termed the *autarky-efficiency dilemma*.

Governments have responded to the autarky-efficiency dilemma in different ways at different times. An explanation for these variations cannot easily be found by studying the differences in their political and military objectives. Instead, economic and technological factors, along with the political pressures applied by domestic producers of armaments, appear to provide the strongest clues.

Long-term technological changes have decisively altered the costs and benefits of autarky. For one thing, an acceleration in the rate of technological change has meant that European governments have had new opportunities for developing weaponry superior to that of their rivals; but to execute such plans, governments have felt the need to nurture and protect facilities in their jurisdictions capable of developing the new weaponry. Because innovations so generated have entailed high development costs, European governments have been under particularly heavy pressure to export some of their national output after they have satisfied their own needs. Rising costs also have meant that smaller, poorer countries have been in a weaker position to adopt autarkic policies than larger, richer ones, partly because of the size of their internal markets and partly because of the level of their available resources.

Changes in economic and technological factors also help explain why European countries have gone through three distinct phases in their responses to the autarky-efficiency dilemma.

In the early years of the modern era, from the Renaissance to about 1815, self-sufficiency in defense production was not always sought and almost never achieved since too many of the critical skills or indispensable materials of warfare lay outside the borders of each of the sovereign powers in Europe.

Between 1815 to 1945, there were some new shifts in the balance of advantage between autarky and open markets. During the early part of this era, technological change in weapons design continued to be slow. At the same time, mass-production techniques were being widely adopted. Meanwhile, state bureaucracies were developing new capacities for planning and administration. In combination, these trends increased the feasibility and desirability of national arms industries. The result was a widespread move among European nations toward autarkic military production, a move supported as much by industry sources as by the military. Even in this period, it should be noted, imports of essential raw materials and components continued at very substantial levels.

By the middle of the nineteenth century, however, the very forces that had briefly made autarky seem attractive were already undermining the policy. The relentless pressure of rising research, development, and production costs began to make autarky unaffordable, and the levels of output generated by the new mass-production techniques made access to foreign markets increasingly important. By the late nineteenth century, imports of technology and exports of arms between enemies were once again on the increase.

After 1945, the trend toward the globalization of markets and technologies gained force. At the same time, fixed costs placed autarky far beyond the means of any single country in Europe. The United States has remained the only country in the Western world that can maintain a defense establishment on the basis of its domestic industry without incurring prohibitive costs or a drastic decline in quality. Military establishments in most European countries continue to lean strongly toward liberalization, while succumbing from time to time to the pressures of arms manufacturers to protect their positions in domestic markets.

The European record may carry a lesson for the United States as well. US attitudes toward autarky in the procurement of military products have been shaped by attributes that could have described some European countries a century ago: its relative size, its technological and financial preeminence, and its capacity for political leadership. But these are perishable qualities. With the costs of armaments rising inexorably, Europe's present may yet be the future of the United States.

ACKNOWLEDGEMENTS

I would like to thank the Economics and National Security Program at Harvard University and the Program on International Politics, Economics, and Security (PIPES) at the University of Chicago for logistical and financial assistance. For comments on previous drafts, I am grateful to Anne-Marie Burley, Brian Downing, Ted Hopf, William Jarosz, Ethan Kapstein, Beth Kier, Timothy Naftali, Bruce Porter, Kamal Shehadi, Janice Thompson, Andrew Wallace, and Fareed Zakaria.

ENDNOTES

[1] State policy toward European defense industries await their first detailed scholarly treatments. An indispensable survey is found in William H. McNeill, *Pursuit of Power: Technology, Armed Force and Society since A.D. 1000* (Chicago: University of Chicago Press, 1982). Three particularly useful overviews are Carlo M. Cipolla, *Guns and Sails in the Early Phase of European Expansion 1400–1700* (London: Fontana, 1975); Michael Geyer, *Deutsche Rüstungspolitik 1890–1980* (Frankfurt: Suhrkamp Verlag, 1984); and Maurice Pearton, *The Knowledgeable State: Diplomacy, War and Technology since 1830* (London: Burnett Books, 1982).

[2] Michael Roberts, "The Military Revolution," in *Essays in Swedish History* (Minneapolis: University of Minnesota Press, 1967); Geoffrey Parker, "The Military Revolution 1550–1660—A Myth?" *Journal of Modern History* 46 (1976): 195–214; and Geoffrey Parker, *The Military Revolution: Military Innovation and the Rise of the West, 1500–1800* (Cambridge: Cambridge University Press, 1988).

[3] John Brewer, *The Sinews of Power: War, Money and the English State, 1688–1783* (New York: Alfred Knopf, 1989), xviii, 138. The best general sources on this period are Cipolla, and John Rigby Hale, *War and Society in Renaissance Europe, 1450–1620* (Baltimore: Johns Hopkins University Press, 1985), 46–51, 220–31.

42   *Andrew Moravcsik*

[4]See G. N. Clark, *War and Society in the Seventeenth Century* (Cambridge: Cambridge University Press, 1958), 61; he reports that "none of the states could supply itself within its own borders." See also Hale, 224–5.

[5]Fernand Braudel, *The Structures of Everyday Life: The Limits of the Possible* (New York: Harper and Row, 1981), 381; and Clark, 61–62. On Baltic timber, see Paul Bamford, *Forests and French Sea Power, 1660–1789* (Toronto: University of Toronto Press, 1956), 207.

[6]Swedish arms production was established and initially dominated by Dutch capital, although the Swedish monarchy eventually established self-sufficiency around 1620. Sweden also imported British and Dutch artillery until the early seventeenth century and Denmark even longer. But the dependence was subsequently reversed, with the Dutch, among others, purchasing Swedish ordnance. See Immanuel Wallerstein, *The Modern World System II: Mercantilism and the Consolidation of the European World-Economy, 1600–1750* (New York: Academic, 1980), 209–11; Hale, *War and Society*, 225; and Parker, *Military Revolution*, 24.

[7]On Russian policy, see Thomas Esper, "Military Self-Sufficiency and Weapons Technology in Muscovite Russia," *Slavic Review* 28 (2) (June 1969): 197, 207–8; and Richard Hellie, "Warfare, Changing Military Technology, and the Evolution of Muscovite Society," in John A. Lynn, ed., *Tools of War: Instruments, Ideas, and Institutions of Warfare, 1445–1971* (Urbana: University of Illinois Press, 1990), 90–97. For a contrasting view, see Gunther E. Rothenberg, *The Art of Warfare in the Age of Napoleon* (Bloomington: Indiana University Press, 1978), 202–4.

[8]Clark, 62. He is speaking of saltpeter, but the conclusion holds for most other military supplies as well.

[9]Cipolla, 24–50; Braudel, 395; Hale, 224–31; and Clark, 124–5.

[10]Geoffrey Parker, *The Thirty Years' War* (London: Routledge, 1984), 198; Hale, 219–20; and Parker, *Military Revolution*, 51, 64–65. On the recruitment of mercenaries, Thomas Ertman and Janice Thompson directed me to the classic work of Fritz Redlich, *The German Military Enterpriser and His Work Force: A Study in European Economic and Social History*, 2 vols. (Wiesbaden: Franz Steiner Verlag, 1964), esp. vol. 1, 321–2.

[11]The quotation and production statistics are from McNeill, *The Pursuit of Power*, 113. See also Hale, 223–4; Rothenberg, 122; and Lee Kennett, *The French Armies in the Seven Years' War* (Durham, N.C.: Duke University Press, 1967), 115.

[12]Edwin Meade Earle, "Adam Smith, Alexander Hamilton, Friedrich List: The Economic Foundations of Military Power," in Peter Paret, ed., *Makers of Modern Strategy: From Machiavelli to the Nuclear Age* (Princeton: Princeton University Press, 1986), 217, 219, 233. See also Jacob Viner, "Power vs. Plenty as Objectives of Foreign Policy in the Seventeenth and Eighteenth Centuries," *World Politics* 1 (October 1948): 10.

[13]Eli F. Heckscher, *Mercantilism*, 2d. ed., vol. 1 (London: George Allen and Unwin, 1955), 48, see also, 18–20. The views of Louvois were also consistent with his preference for defensive, land-based warfare. See Charles W. Cole, *French Mercantilism, 1683–1700* (New York: Columbia University Press, 1943), 107–8;

Charles W. Cole, *Colbert and a Century of French Mercantilism,* vol. 2 (New York: Columbia University Press, 1939), 333–49; McNeill, *The Pursuit of Power,* 63–116, esp. 89, 93, 98–99, 114; and Bamford, 206–11. On the general failure of Colbert's schemes, see Roger Mettams, *Power and Faction in Louis XIV's France* (New York: Blackwell, 1988), 189–92, 288–306.

[14]Robert Gilpin cuts to the heart of the issue, observing also that international trade increased faster than domestic trade throughout this period. See his "Economic Interdependence and National Security in Historical Perspective," in Klaus Knorr and Frank N. Trager, eds. *Economic Issues and National Security* (Lawrence, Kans.: Allen, 1977), 27–30.

[15]Cole, *Colbert,* vol. 1, 347–55; and John U. Nef, *War and Human Progress: An Essay on the Rise of Industrial Civilization* (Cambridge: Harvard University Press, 1950), 220–2. Eighteenth-century English writings on mercantilism display a "surprising lack of discussion on the role of manufacturing in the war effort." See David Hoogland Johns, *Eighteenth Century British Mercantilists and War: Their Viewpoint towards the Effect of War upon Trade and Navigation, Colonialization and Domestic Policy,* unpublished M. A. thesis, Committee on International Relations, University of Chicago, 1960, 71, 95.

[16]Cited in Johns, 78.

[17]Clark, 62–64; Hale, 227.

[18]Cipolla, 71.

[19]John Francis Guilmartin, *Gunpowder and Galleys: Changing Technology and Mediterranean Warfare at Sea in the Sixteenth Century* (Cambridge: Cambridge University Press, 1974), 158–75.

[20]Robert Osgood, "The Expansion of Force," in Robert Osgood and Robert Tucker, *Force, Order and Statecraft* (Baltimore: Johns Hopkins University Press, 1967), 51.

[21]Michael Lewis, "Armed Forces and the Art of War: Navies," in J. T. Bury, ed., *The Zenith of European Power, 1830–70* (Cambridge: Cambridge University Press, 1960), 274; Dennis Showalter, "Weapons and Ideas in the Prussian Army from Frederick the Great to Moltke the Elder," in Lynn, 189, 198; and Michael Howard, *War in European History* (Oxford: Oxford University Press, 1976), 100. For exceptions, see William H. McNeill, "Men, Machines, and War," in Ronald Haycock and Keith Neilson, ed., *Men, Machines, and War* (Waterloo, Ont.: Wilfred Laurier University Press, 1988).

[22]Cipolla, 71. See also Kolodziej, *Making and Marketing Arms: The French Experience and Its Implications for the International System* (Princeton: Princeton University Press, 1987), 9; Brewer, 29, 137, 167–8; and Heckscher, 193.

[23]See Redlich, vol. 2, 21–22, 95n, 80–81; David Chandler, *The Art of Warfare in the Age of Marlborough* (New York: Hippocrene, 1976), 75–79, 149–51; Rothenberg, 25–28; Michael Howard, *War in European History,* 54–74; and McNeill, *The Pursuit of Power,* 157–166, 177–8, 271.

[24]Earle conflates the two, imputing to mercantilism in general the ideas of Hamilton and List. See Earle, 217. See also Klaus Knorr, *The Power of Nations—The Political Economy of International Relations* (New York: Basic Books, 1975),

210. Heckscher contrasts the earlier "politics of provision" with the new mercantilist doctrine; see Heckscher, vol. 1, 98–101. For a more subtle treatment, see Gilpin, 27–30.

[25]Cited in Earle, 233.

[26]Ibid. On Europe, see Rothenberg, 120–4, 140–1, 180–1.

[27]The quotation is from B. H. Liddell Hart, "Armed Forces and the Art of War: Armies," in *The Zenith of European Power, 1830–1870,* vol. 10 of the *New Cambridge Modern History* (Cambridge: Cambridge University Press, 1957–1979), 302. See also Bernard and Fawn Brodie, *From Crossbow to H-Bomb,* rev. ed. (Bloomington: Indiana University Press, 1973), 137–71; Bernard Brodie, *Sea Power in the Machine Age* (Princeton: Princeton University Press, 1941), esp. 118–19; McNeill, *Pursuit of Power,* 223–61; and Kolodziej, 9–18.

[28]Robin Higham, "Complex Skills and Skeletons in the Military-Industrial Relationship in Great Britain," in Benjamin Franklin Cooling, ed., *War, Business, and World Military-Industrial Complexes* (Port Washington, N.Y.: Kenniket Press, 1981), 10; Volker Mollin, *Auf dem Wege zur "Materialschlacht": Vorgeschichte und Funktionieren des Artillerie-Industrie-Komplexes im Deutschen Kaiserreich* (Pfaffenweiler: Centaurus Verlag, 1986), 234ff; and Lewis, "Armed Forces and the Art of War: Navies," 288–94.

[29]Peter Batty, *The House of Krupp* (London: Secker and Warburg, 1966), 46–47, 50, 71; and William Manchester, *The Arms of Krupp 1587–1968* (Boston: Little, Brown, 1968), 89–93, 176–7. For debates over the role of state armories in Prussian production, see Geyer, 34.

[30]Batty, 76; Manchester, 98–100, 217–18, 275; Helms Engelbrecht and Frank Hanighen, *Merchants of Death: A Study of the International Armament Industry,* Reprint (New York: Garland, 1972), 47, 86–89, 103, 124–6, 133–4, 145, 151–3; and Basil Collier, *Arms and the Men: The Arms Trade and Governments* (London: Hamish Hamilton, 1980), 71–72.

[31]McNeill, *Pursuit of Power,* 231, 292; Clive Trebilcock, *The Vickers Brothers: Armaments and Enterprise 1854–1914* (London: Europa Publications Limited, 1977), 119, 133; Engelbrecht and Hanighen, 52–55, 81, 163–72; Manchester, 221, 224, 341; and Collier, 71–72.

[32]Manchester, 170–4, 212–17; Dennis E. Showalter, *Railroads and Rifles, Soldiers, Technology, and the Unification of Germany* (Hamden, Conn.: Archon Books, 1975), 163, 188; Dennis E. Showalter, "Prussia, Technology and War: Artillery from 1815 to 1914," in Haycock and Neilson, eds., *Men, Machines and War,* 144; and Batty, 70. Wilhelm's flagrant favoritism led many to suspect that he was in the pay of Krupp.

[33]Michael Howard, "The Armed Forces," in F. H. Hinsley, *Material Progress and World-Wide Progress, 1870–1898,* vol. 11 of *The New Cambridge Modern History* (Cambridge: Cambridge University Press, 1962), 206, 218; Dennis E. Showalter, "Prussia, Technology and War," 143; and Geyer, 57–60.

[34]Control of arms exports had been on the books in Britain since 1660 and was strengthened in response to scandals in the 1920s and 1930s, but had never been backed by effective bureaucratic enforcement. See John Staley and Maurice

Pearton, *The International Trade in Arms* (New York: Praeger, 1972), 24–30. On the 1930s, see Robert Harkavy, *The Arms Trade and International Systems* (Cambridge: Ballinger, 1975), 93, 146–8, 169–72, 188, 197.

[35]Keith Hayward, *The British Aircraft Industry* (Manchester: Manchester University Press, 1989), 128; and McNeill, *Pursuit of Power,* 355–60. On routes where they faced stiff competition, British airlines flew American civil aircraft.

[36]French manufacturers also licensed British designs. See Kolodziej, 40–49; Harkavy, 53–54; and Collier, 273–4.

[37]Hayward, 36, 40, 53, 56–61. In the mid-1950s, the break-even point for an airliner passed from fifty, a number that could be supported by a European domestic market to over one hundred.

[38]Harkavy, 64. In 1964 and 1965, the new Labour government cut all existing British classic fighter programs, led by the TSR-2, leaving only the vertical-lift Harrier, later codeveloped with the United States.

[39]Kolodziej, 102–6; and Andrew Moravcsik, "Armaments among Allies: Franco-German Armaments Collaboration, 1975–1985," in Robert Putnam, Peter Evans, and Harold Jacobson, eds., *Diplomacy and Domestic Politics* (Berkeley: University of California Press, 1992).

[40]Andrew Moravcsik, "The European Armaments Industry at the Crossroads," *Survival* (January-February, 1990), 65–86.

[41]Collaborative projects have an unjust reputation for inefficiency. See Moravcsik, "The European Armaments Industry," 73, 75, 83, from which the following section is drawn.

[42]Examples include the Siemens-GEC takeover of Plessey, the creation of Eurocopter (a subsidiary of Messerschmidt-Bölkow-Blohm and Aérospatiale), and links between Thomson and British Aerospace.

[43]See Moravcsik, "European Armaments Industry," 66; and EC Commission, Directorate-General for Economic and Financial Affairs, "The Economics of 1992: An Assessment of the Potential Economic Effects of Completing the Internal Market of the European Community," *European Economy* 35 (March 1988).

[44]Moravcsik, "Franco-German Armaments Collaboration."

[45]Trevor Taylor and Keith Hayward, *The U.K. Defence Industrial Base: Developments and Future Policy Options* (London: Brassey's, 1989), 102–3.

Coin is the sinews of war.

Rabelais

Trade causes perpetual strife both in time of war and in time of peace between all the nations.

Colbert

The natural effect of commerce is to bring about peace.

Montesquieu

Defense is of much more importance than opulence.

Adam Smith

Nothing depends as much on economic conditions as do the army and navy.

Friedrich Engels

Our defense is not in armaments, nor in science, nor in going underground. Our defense is in law and order.

Albert Einstein

Richard J. Samuels

Reinventing Security: Japan Since Meiji

S INCE THE MID-NINETEENTH CENTURY, Japanese security planners have had to navigate the Scylla of technological backwardness and the Charybdis of foreign dependence. From 1868 to
1945, the national response of the Japanese to their situation
included the use of military force. After 1945, Japan's security was
allowed to rest much more heavily on the nation's commercial and
technological achievements.

The Japanese saga however is far from closed. For as Japan has
reduced its condition of technological vulnerability and dependence,
other nations have begun to ask how Japan proposes to use its newly
achieved technological autonomy. Even among the Japanese there
have been signs of questioning on whether the nation's postwar
policies of maintaining low levels of defense-related production,
prohibiting the export of military goods, and living under the
protection of the US security umbrella still make sense in light of its
technological and economic performance. To gain a sense of how
that question is likely to be answered, one has to begin with history.

In the nineteenth century, Japan's policies toward its technological
backwardness were unambiguous, Japanese leaders exhorted the
nation to "revere the Emperor and expel the barbarian" (*sanno jōi*),
to "catch up and surpass the West" (*oitsuki oikose*), and to combine
"Western technology with Japanese spirit" (*wakon yōsai*)—in short,
to sacrifice for national security in a hostile world. The struggle for
technological independence has been a feature of Japanese strategy
ever since.

Japanese military and industrial strategies have been built on a
fusion of industrial, technology, and national security policies. This

---

Richard J. Samuels is Professor of Political Science at the Massachusetts Institute of Technology.

fusion, dubbed technonationalism, has persisted both in the prewar era, when Japan used military means to achieve its national objectives, and in the postwar period, when its policies were more completely commercial. Undergirding the policies in both eras has been a consistent and powerful belief that national security is enhanced as much by the ability to design and to produce as by the actual deployment of sophisticated equipment.

MILITARY TECHNONATIONALISM

Japanese arms production, particularly swords and armor, was an advanced art long before the establishment of the Tokugawa shogunate in 1600. Firearms were introduced in the mid-sixteenth century by European merchants blown off course to Tanegashima, on the island of Kyushu. The "Tanegashima gun," as it came to be known, promptly was back-engineered for domestic manufacture. The diffusion of Tanegashima gunsmithing technology (and indeed of guns themselves) was so complete that by the late sixteenth century, the Japanese reportedly fought their civil wars with more firearms than any European nation.[1]

The civil wars ended with the Pax Tokugawa, officially isolating Japan from the rest of the world for the next two and a half centuries. But the Japanese continued to monitor foreign developments. In the 1780s, Hayashi Shihei, a Sendai nobleman, attempted to build artillery, but could find only 150-year-old gunpowder. His "Treatise on the Affairs of an Insular Country" first articulated concerns about the backwardness of Japanese arms manufacture and the urgent need to protect Japan, and its manufactures, from foreign domination.

Almost simultaneously with the publication of the Hayashi treatise, one foreign power after another began to call upon Japan for trade and other concessions. The shogunate quickly heeded Hayashi's advice and resumed arms manufacturing. By the 1850s, each local domain (*han*) had begun manufacturing arms, though at widely disparate levels of technological sophistication. The best of the *han* arsenals, such as the Ishikawajima Shipyards and the Hyogo Iron Works, like the best of the shogun's own defense plants, such as the Nagasaki Works, are today among Japan's largest industrial enterprises and defense contractors.

Although arms manufacture was the most advanced manufacturing industry in pre-Meiji Japan—having been the first to introduce
modern tools and power systems—even the largest and most modern
arsenals in Japan were far short of world standards. In the years
before the Meiji restoration in 1868, the Krupp shipyards, Germany's
largest, produced ten times the number of steamships with more than
forty times the horsepower of those produced by the Nagasaki
shipyards, Japan's largest.[2]

To protect Japan from rapacious foreign powers and to stimulate
economic development, the Meiji government sought to standardize
and modernize the manufacture of munitions. Through acquisition
and direct management of existing arsenals, the government quickly
assumed the strategic heights of the economy. In the view of the
young Meiji oligarchy, modern transportation, communication, and
heavy industrial technologies were all necessary to secure the national
welfare. The slogan "rich nation, strong army" (*fukoku kyōhei*) was
the first official embrace of military technonationalism; it captured
well the ideological appeal of modernization.

Thus, arms manufacturing, the most modern industrial sector
before the Meiji restoration, led Japan's forced march to industrialization. By 1877, nearly two-thirds of the central government's
investments were directed toward the military, and throughout the
1880s the proportion remained above one-half.[3] Military demand
and technology were both key stimuli to the rest of the economy;[4]
military equipment dominated the exhibits at Japan's first international Industrial Promotion Fair in 1877.

If the institutional center of the early Meiji industrial strategy was
the rapidly expanding national arsenal system, the intellectual center
was technology borrowed from abroad and made Japanese. Foreign
tutelage for national strength was enshrined in the Charter Oath of
the Emperor Meiji in 1868: "Intellect and learning would be sought
throughout the world in order to establish the foundations of
Empire."[5] Japan developed its military-technological intelligence
system before completing its military-industrial infrastructure. Japanese engineers went abroad to identify and to acquire advanced
technology; foreign experts came to Japan to teach. Within two
decades young engineers had mastered a considerable body of foreign
design and manufacturing technology, much of it for the military at
the Imperial University. This practice served as a template for

technology monitoring and indigenization for the rest of the Meiji economy, and soon became standard commercial practice as well.

This indigenization strategy, however, was costly and took time to bear fruit. Although the army largely achieved independence in weapon production by the time of the Russo-Japanese War in 1905, the navy was dependent upon Western technology (British cruisers, for example) until nearly World War I. In a period of large trade deficits, imports of war materiel were nevertheless sustained.

In the evolving view of Meiji strategists, national power and industrial autonomy were interdependent. So, consequently, were military and civilian technologies: the first machine tools for mining were manufactured in 1869 in a government arsenal; the telegraph first was used to suppress the Satsuma Rebellion in 1877; in 1880 the Yokosuka armory produced most of Japan's motors for advanced looms, as well as helping to provide lighthouses, harbor facilities, and other critical infrastructure.

From the beginning, the manufacturing facilities dedicated to civilian production in Japan benefited in myriad ways from government investment in military production and technological leadership. In the 1880s, government armories and other government factories were transferred to private hands. Three successive war mobilizations—in 1905, 1914, and the 1930s—added greatly to the strength of the private sector. By the end of the 1930s, the military output of private factories would exceed that of government arsenals, even though private entrepreneurs were producing overwhelmingly for commercial markets. Most of this production nominally centered in the technologically sophisticated and highly integrated manufacturing and financial conglomerates (*zaibatsu*).

While the Japanese economy had been stimulated by demand for military production, it had not been captured by such production.[6] For instance, although by 1937 the *zaibatsu* accounted for more than half of Japan's total production of war materiel, arms manufacture comprised less than one-fifth of their total production.[7] Impatient with the caution of the *zaibatsu,* the military found it necessary to nurture "new entrepreneurs," such as Nakajima Aircraft and Nissan Motors, as well as other small firms.[8]

Although Japanese planners badly miscalculated the ultimate consequences of military technonationalism, their underlying strategy helped to guide the creation of domestic institutions in manufacturing and research that would persist and flourish in the second half of the twentieth century.[9]

COMMERCIAL TECHNONATIONALISM

The dominant characteristic of Japan's military production in the postwar period was how little there was of it. But contrary to much contemporary mythology, Japan did not achieve its technological position of the 1990s by ignoring the arms industry. Arms production attracted considerable attention by economic planners and businessmen in the early 1950s. US military procurement was an engine of Japan's early postwar reconstruction and continued as an important source of advanced technology into the 1990s.

Article Nine of the 1947 Japanese constitution prohibits Japan from maintaining a "war potential," and renounces Japan's "right of belligerency," but neither that article nor anything else in the constitution precludes the production or export of Japanese arms. In 1948, it is true, the United States reversed its Asian security policy and the intent of Article Nine, which it had authored, in order to establish Japan as a military-industrial bastion—what one Japanese prime minister much later dubbed its "unsinkable aircraft carrier" in the Far East. Procurement of Japanese goods by the US military and other forms of economic aid represented the price paid by the United States for Japanese bases and for Japanese participation in the United States's Cold War rearmament program.[10]

Nearly 70 percent of Japanese exports between 1950 and 1952 comprised US military "special procurement," (*tokujū*), which contributed significantly to the rehabilitation of the Japanese economy. Once the United States granted Japan the permission to resume arms and aircraft manufacture, Japanese industry wasted no time expanding capacity and shifting to munitions production. Weapons sales of 7 million yen in 1952 grew to 15 billion yen in 1954.[11] During the Korean War, 60 percent of the sales of Komatsu, which made Japan's first postwar artillery mortars, represented sales to the military.[12] In 1952 there were 160 separate firms manufacturing ammunition in Japan.[13]

Yet, despite new entrants, the industry was dominated again by former *zaibatsu* firms and their subsidiaries. The top four firms accounted for more than 70 percent of US orders. Few of them had anything like Komatsu's dependence on military markets. Besides, most large firms hedged their bets further by assigning about half the processing of their finished products to subcontractors, who thereby assumed much of the risk that the military boom might eventually fizzle.

This hedging reflected the intense ambivalence of Japanese industry and the Japanese public toward any overt dependence on military activities. The ambivalence could be seen in early postwar Japan in a split between industrial and finance capital. The former, representing the heavy industrial firms of the old *zaibatsu,* such as Mitsubishi, used former high-ranking military officers to generate ambitious rearmament plans and optimistic projections for the arms industry as the engine of postwar redevelopment. "Defense production"—a euphemism promoted by both industry and government—gained the Ministry of International Trade and Industry's support as a key element in Japan's technology strategy.[14] According to MITI aircraft and ordinance director Akazawa Shōichi, the industrial development of the Japanese arms industry was part of Japan's "technology lust."[15]

But in the early 1950s, the bankers and the Ministry of Finance (MOF) were not convinced of the wisdom of expanding the production of arms. They argued that arms production would divert scarce resources from sectors with greater (and more stable) prospects for growth. Former *zaibatsu* bankers, now assuming greater power in the postwar economic restructuring, refused financing to firms that were planning to commit more than 20 or 30 percent of their output to defense products.[16] Bureaucrats in the Ministry of Finance clearly recalled the pressures from militarists to which they had succumbed during the wartime. With fiscal stability having been only recently restored in accordance with the recommendations of a mission headed by a prominent US banker, Joseph M. Dodge, Japanese bankers and MOF officials feared a return to deficit budgeting.

The debate came to a head during the preparation of the 1954 fiscal budget. MOF firmly opposed MITI efforts to introduce fiscal support to the arms industry; MOF was quietly abetted by some MITI officials, who doubted the efficacy of support for the arms industry and instead wanted to secure support for the electric power industry, which they considered to be more strategic. MITI had to settle for limited regulatory power through the Arms Manufacturing

Law (*Buki nado Seizō Hō*) passed by the Diet in July 1953. Unlike other pieces of legislation of the period which granted special support to a number of key industries, this law signaled to the capital markets that arms production would *not* be targeted for special assistance. Defense contractors exited in large numbers, in some cases not to return for thirty or forty years.

The impact of this shakeout persists to the present day. In the early 1990s, the Japanese defense industry is very small; Japanese defense production amounts to barely one half of 1 percent of total Japanese industrial production. Barred from export markets since 1976 by a decision of the Japanese government, Japan's arms sales are equivalent to those of the nation's sushi shops. Despite the best efforts of defense industrialists and some bureaucrats, the Japanese defense industry, as defined by the production of weapons systems, has been the laggard in Japan's "economic miracle."

Nevertheless, despite Japan's limited production of weapons systems, its technological capabilities have positioned Japan as a formidable player in the global defense economy. Japanese firms have emerged as world leaders in the design and manufacture of materials, components, and essential subsystems. According to a foreign ministry report:

> Japanese manufacturers of fiber optics, avionics systems, and other leading edge technologies could build up substantial defense-related businesses without violating the weapons export embargo.[17]

Japan's technological capabilities and its strategy of commercial technonationalism have depended significantly upon its Cold War relationship with the United States. American firms have been the principal source of both military and commercial technology for Japan. Although the transfer of military technology has contributed less to Japan's postwar industrial development than has the transfer of commercial technology, military technology transfers have not been insubstantial.

To gain access to both US military and commercial technology, Japan followed the example of other US allies and ratified a Mutual Defense Assistance Agreement. First, however, Japan had to create a military to which technology could be transferred. In one of the most controversial moves in postwar Japanese politics, despite Article Nine of the constitution prohibiting the maintenance of "war potential," Japan in 1954 established the Japan Defense Agency (JDA) and the Japanese "Self-Defense Forces"(SDF). Although most of the US allies focused the resources they received under the assistance agreement on the development of their arms industry, Japan negotiated to maximize its freedom to diffuse the technology to civilian applications.[18]

As a result, although the mutual defense agreement with the United States was designed to transfer arms and military technology, the Japanese were granted "untied" mutual defense assistance for purposes of "economic development." Indulgent US Army engineers taught Japanese mechanical and civil engineers from Japan's construction engineering firms, such as Kumagai-Gumi, how to use and repair the heavy machinery employed in the construction of Japan's first postwar hydroelectric power plants.[19] Komatsu used military assistance funds to build bulldozers. Under license to provide Japan's first postwar military aircraft, the F-86 and T-33, the Japanese aircraft industry secured training and equipment that it applied for its first foray into commercial aerospace.

But one must not overstate the importance of the mutual defense program. Over the longer postwar period, American military transfers to Japan were dwarfed by the transfer of US commercial technology through the private sale of licenses and joint ventures. These were of far more consequence in nurturing both the military and the general industrial base in Japan, and hence Japanese national security. Between 1951 and 1984, according to one compilation, more than forty thousand separate contracts were signed by Japanese firms to acquire foreign technology; over that thirty-four-year period, Japan paid $17 billion in royalties—a small fraction of *annual* US R&D costs. With nylon from DuPont, nuclear power from General Electric and Westinghouse, the transistor from Bell Laboratories, and the television tube from Corning, US technology licenses were "the technological basis for nearly all of Japan's modern industries."[20] With US and European firms eager to sell their know-how and with US foreign policy aimed at maintaining a politically stable and economically viable ally in the Pacific, Japanese firms identified, acquired, and subsequently indigenized foreign know-how; yet, successive generations of Japanese products have routinely depended less than preceding ones on foreign technology.[21]

In general, therefore, Japan drew upon the US government's support for allies' military projects and the US public's appetite for commercial products to speed the transfer and indigenization of foreign technologies. By the 1990s, the country achieved the status of a technological superpower.[22]

CONSEQUENTIAL ENDOWMENTS

Japan's mid-century shift to commercial technonationalism from military technonationalism has proved to be especially supportive for Japanese industry for several different reasons.

Dual-Use Technologies

Japan's industrial growth was especially rapid in sectors closely linked to the materials and technologies that enhance the battlefield capabilities of modern weapons: data processing, telecommunications, optoelectronics, and lightweight materials. For example, by making integrated circuits in large volumes for consumer electronics and graphite fiber in large volumes for tennis rackets and golf clubs, Japanese manufacturers were able to accumulate knowledge and experience for military aerospace applications. By the late 1970s, Japanese suppliers had become an important source of technology for the US Department of Defense and were advertising their technical ability to provide "ruggedized" products to the military market at bargain prices.[23]

This ability to "spin-on" civilian technologies to military applications was the fruit—the unintended fruit—of a predominantly commercial strategy. Unlike in the United States where most research was funded by the government and where most government-funded research was undertaken for the Department of Defense and the weapons program of the Department of Energy, nearly four-fifths of Japanese R&D spending comprised corporate research funded by commercial firms overwhelmingly for civilian markets.

But the actual level of Japanese military R&D was surely higher than the official budget of the Defense Agency's Technical Research and Development Institute (TRDI). In the early 1990s, reported R&D expenditures were only 1 or 2 percent of Japan's defense budget. The TRDI was the only government agency officially engaged in defense research; but MITI, the Science and Technology

Agency, and the Japan Key Technology Center were all funding large scale R&D projects led by private firms in areas with significant dual-use applications, such as jet engines, microelectronics, and materials processing. These private firms, rather than the TRDI, were taking the responsibility for all prototype manufacturing and testing of defense systems. As a consequence, they informally subsidized defense R&D, and they routinely spread research costs across military and civilian projects.[24] Said one senior TRDI official:

> There is no black versus white, military versus civilian technology. All technology is gray. It becomes military or civilian in application. Today 81% of Japan's R&D efforts are focused on the commercial side. Our R&D base is like Mt. Fuji; the civilian R&D provides a bottom that is very broad.[25]

Japanese dual-use capabilities were first formally acknowledged by a study team of the US Defense Science Board in 1984, which concluded that Japanese technology was at or ahead of the most advanced US capabilities in sixteen different dual-use technologies. These technologies were widely acknowledged as the "key" or "base" technologies for advanced manufacturing in the next century, including gallium arsenide devices, microwave integrated circuits, fiber optic communications, image and speech recognition, flat displays, and ceramics.[26]

Industrial Structure

The Japanese system includes both a strategic commitment to the diffusion of innovation and the use of organizational and ideological infrastructures that facilitate such diffusion. As a consequence, technology travels readily between the military and civilian sectors of the economy.

Japan's leading defense contractors have also been Japan's most innovative commercial firms. As elsewhere, the top defense contractors have been among the largest firms in the economy. But unlike in the United States and much of Western Europe, these firms have been highly diversified and have depended little upon sales to the military.

In 1990 only two of the ten largest defense contractors in Japan were dependent upon defense procurement for more than 20 percent of their total sales; half had less than a 5 percent dependency (see Table 1).[27] Only the ammunition and aircraft manufacturing industry depended for more than 5 percent of its total sales upon the Defense Agency; of the remaining industries, only shipbuilding was dependent upon the military for more than 1 percent of total sales.

TABLE 1   Japanese Defense Firms 1990

Firm	Defense Sales (in billion yen)	Share of Defense Sales (percent)	Defense Sales as Percent of Total Firm Sales (percent)
Mitsubishi Heavy Industries	440	28.0	21.0
Kawasaki Heavy Industries	146	9.3	17.0
Mitsubishi Electric	100	6.4	4.1
Ishikawajima-Harima Heavy Industries	78	5.0	12.0
Toshiba Corporation	59	3.8	1.9
NEC Corporation	54	3.5	2.6
Japan Steel Works	34	2.2	28.0
Komatsu, Ltd.	22	1.4	3.5
Fuji Heavy Industries	21	1.4	3.1
Hitachi, Ltd.	20	1.3	0.5

Note: Figures from fiscal 1990

Source: Japan Defense Agency

By the 1980s, however, many Japanese firms, although primarily committed to serving civilian markets, began to realize that considerable potential for growth existed in defense production. In 1980, the four defense-related industry associations joined together with the Japan Electronic Machinery Association to create the Defense Technology Association of Japan (*Bōei Gijutsu Kyōkai*) in order "to strengthen, by public-private cooperation, the ability to independently conceive, research, and build the highest level of equipment." As if to underline Japan's dual-use competence and to punctuate these corporate shifts, Honda Shoichiro, founder of Honda Motors, was made Honorary Chairman, and Ibuka Masaru, founder of Sony, was made a special advisor.

In the years that followed, numerous firms that were well established in nondefense areas took tangible steps to reflect their interest in defense production. Hitachi, for example, established a Defense Technology Promotion Division in 1980. Fujitsu established a subsidiary devoted exclusively to defense systems development and set a corporate goal to bring its defense business up to 20 percent of total sales. Nissan revised its corporate charter to include "manufacture and sale of weapons."[28]

The firms involved in these policy shifts are especially well endowed to manufacture components for the global arms industry. Their activities in nondefense areas have ensured that components, already produced in volume, would be cost competitive and meet high-performance requirements. Their breadth also has endowed them with flexibility in the development and application of new technologies and products. Both scale and scope were enhanced by the *keiretsu* structure, in which a family of firms strengthened their capacity for strategic coordination through cross-holdings of equity, mutual directorships, and intragroup financing by a common bank. All but one of Japan's largest defense contractors are members of *keiretsu* networks, within which it is routine for firms to be guided (and technology to be diffused) as much by relationships as by price.[29] Moreover, Japanese firms have already demonstrated considerable expertise in the organization of production centered on small- and medium-lot batch manufacturing—a skill especially appropriate for producing the components, subassemblies, and subsystems that constitute a considerable portion of defense procurement needs.[30] Indeed, it is likely that the firms that have benefited most from the ambitions of Japan's *keiretsu* firms in the defense sector have been Japan's small- and medium-sized subcontractors. As in the 1950s, the larger firms depend upon their subcontractors for a considerable portion of the value-added in military systems.[31]

The Ability to Partner

Japanese firms that perform as the final assemblers in the defense industry have long enjoyed a set of stable relationships in markets in which they operate, notwithstanding that such markets are characterized by a small number of sellers. There have rarely been clear-cut winners and losers in Japanese defense procurement. Firms that fail to be designated as prime contractors often are assigned a significant subcontracting role, and are rewarded the next time around with a prime contract.[32] In the process, technology is more widely diffused to the benefit of the economy as a whole.

By the 1980s, the global defense industry outside Japan was undergoing changes in directions familiar to Japanese industry.

Whereas "winner-take-all" competitions for contracts among single firms had been typical in earlier years, competitions among "teams" of partner firms were becoming more common. These collaborations extended upstream to domestic research as well, as the United States and the European Community began experimenting with research consortia, such as Sematech and Esprit, to reduce costs and to diffuse innovation of precompetitive, generic technology.

This sort of cooperative R&D has been ubiquitous in Japan's leap from a position of technological backwardness to one of world leadership. Collaborative research has become the defining feature of Japanese research practice and the sine qua non for competitiveness in many technology-intensive sectors. Every major Japanese firm has participated in a large number of consortia, ranging from basic to applied research, and including manufacturing as well. Partnerships have included competitors in the same industry as well as suppliers and customers. In the 1980s, there was a startling acceleration in the creation of new institutions to generate knowledge in Japan, which uniformly involved competing firms. Reliance upon such collaboration, pioneered by the Japanese, seemed likely to transform the landscape of the technology process elsewhere as well.[33]

The Strategic Use of Foreign Partners

As we have seen, Japan's industrial development and national security have depended upon the capacity of the Japanese to identify, assess, acquire, and "indigenize" foreign technology. We are reminded, therefore, that from the Japanese viewpoint the licensing of production has never been an end in itself; it has been in the twentieth century, as it was in the nineteenth century, a means toward learning the processes that underlay the design and production of the products under license.

Foreign licensing has served to close gaps in Japanese manufacturing technology. It has made possible a "learning by doing" process that has enhanced domestic capabilities in military as well as in civilian areas. In the military areas, a pattern has emerged, as Japan has transformed itself from buyer to developer of weapons systems. First, foreign weapons were purchased with foreign funds. Soon, Japan paid for these weapons with its own funds. Within a very short time, Japan negotiated licenses to coproduce these systems. As if following some inexorable law of indigenization, the portion of foreign design and foreign components declined in each subsequent project at the same time that the portion of "dual-use" technology increased. Within a decade or so of having procured foreign licenses, domestic Japanese firms were usually in a position to produce the equipment on their own. By the 1980s, Japan was poised to build its own defense systems with its own technologies, largely generated in the civilian sector.

Yet Japan chose to pursue an intermediate strategy, largely for political reasons. It opted to codevelop these new weapons systems with the United States, its military ally and commercial competitor. Moreover, as Japanese firms moved upstream to R&D, virtually all their new initiatives in aerospace, materials science, and manufacturing technology made provisions for international collaboration in their research activities and invited foreign participation in their efforts.

Of course, there have been limits to the process of learning through the licensing of foreign technology. Since 1952, Japanese firms have coproduced nineteen different US airplanes and helicopters, yet Japan has not succeeded in developing a significant domestic aircraft industry. Although licensed production provides technological insight, equipment, and training from which a determined manufacturer can proceed, it does not routinely teach everything a firm needs to know in order to carry on production of its own. Here, the contrast between civilian and military applications is instructive. Both have depended upon "international cooperation." Both have sought indigenization as a goal. But after the 1950s, the transfers of key technologies for commercial applications was more uniformly successful than the transfers for military applications. It is ironic that this imbalance eventually enhanced Japan's potential to compete in the defense market, as the military use of commercial technologies increased.

Coherent Ideology and Strategic Commitment

Japanese planners have embraced and promulgated a vision of national security that elevates local control and national learning over the more conventional procurement criteria of cost, performance, and delivery dates. It was first articulated in the *Kaikoku Heidan* of Hayashi Shihei in the 1780s, and has been repeatedly invoked across several centuries of Japanese economic development and security planning. Nevertheless, although indigenization has been the unequivocal preference of some business and bureaucratic elites, it has not always been the formal policy of the Japanese government. In the postwar era, Japanese politicians have had to tread carefully around public opinion, which has remained suspicious of military industry, and the Japanese government has had to adapt to the changing designs of its security partner, the United States.

The experience of Nakasone Yasuhiro is instructive. In 1970 the new defense agency chief and future prime minister boldly sought to reduce dependence upon the United States and to introduce a more "autonomous defense" policy (*jishu bōei*). He proposed that indigenization be accepted as the formal centerpiece of JDA procurement policy. (Until then, the JDA would commit itself only to pursuing that policy "as appropriate.") His new "Basic Policy for the Development and Production of Defense Equipment" stated clearly that

> a nation's ability to equip itself for self-defense centers on its industrial capacity. The JDA will consider the nation's industrial capacity and promote the domestic development and production of equipment.[34]

Despite the strong support of the Defense Production Committee of Keidanren, Nakasone was rebuffed by his more cautious colleagues in the Liberal Democratic Party (LDP). Concerned that the public would not accept such a change and that the LDP could not survive further erosion of support, the cabinet opted instead to reaffirm its commitment to the US-Japan Mutual Security Treaty, to articulate a policy of "defensive defense," to tighten legal restrictions on arms exports, and to cap Japanese defense spending at 1 percent of Japan's GNP. To be sure, indigenization would be pursued more vigorously in practice than in law, and much more completely in commercial than in military markets. In the meantime, the official vision of "comprehensive security" would suffice to communicate to the world and to the Japanese people that national security was more a matter of economic advantage than of maintenance of a "war potential."

But a major question remained: how would Japan use its expanding capabilities for producing items desired by military establishments, including dual-use components and military end products?

WHITHER THE JAPANESE DEFENSE INDUSTRY?

Ishihara Shintaro, a member of the Japanese Diet, made headlines by arguing in 1989 that Japan could shift the balance of global power if it diverted shipments of microchips from the United States to the Soviet Union. Ishihara was of course engaging in hyperbole; but there was substance in his metaphor. Japan *had* achieved global power, and as its wealth grew, and as its investment in invention accelerated, Japan surely would have more of it.

In the short run, it seemed certain, Japan's alliance with the United States would continue to constrain Japanese defense spending and its military-industrial development. Even after the Persian Gulf crisis erupted in August 1990, Japan's defense industry was following the US and Soviet leads by scaling down its plans for growth. The 1990 Defense Agency White Paper, anticipating the 1991 visit by President Gorbachev and negotiations over the reversion of the northern territories to Japan, purged all reference to the Soviet Union as a threat to Japan.[35] Japan's new five-year defense program, announced in early 1991, called for a slower rate of growth in the military budget. Weapons R&D spending, however, would rise to 3 percent of total defense spending, two to three times the previous level.

Still, Japan was hedging its bets. While reducing the rate of increase in defense spending, Japan nonetheless was planning to increase defense spending in absolute terms. While firms abroad faced the need to reduce excess capacity and to convert defense plants to civilian production, Japanese firms were expanding their dual-use capabilities, as many firms made significant defense sales for the first time.

Moreover, with the Japan-US relationship under great strain since the 1980s, and with the original raison d'être of this alliance obliterated by the end of the Cold War, both nations were beginning to recalculate the costs and benefits of the relationship.[36] For many Japanese, it seemed high time to wean Japan from its dependence on the United States, and Japanese public opinion seemed ready finally to agree. Yet there was still no obvious replacement for the US consumers or for the US security guarantees on which Japan was heavily reliant, and there was no public support for rearmament—or, as the Gulf crisis demonstrated, for any bold departure from established constraints on force deployments.[37] For many Americans, there was no obvious replacement for Japanese capital or products, despite a growing conviction in the US public that Japan's success had come as a "free ride," unfairly and at the United States's expense.

In fact, in the months before Saddam Hussein's invasion of Kuwait and the Gulf war, Japan had replaced the Soviet Union in US public opinion as the greatest threat to the United States.[38] After the war, another dimension was added to US views of Japan. Japanese hesitations over a contribution to the anti-Iraq coalition and the unwillingness of some Japanese firms to supply the US military with key components during the war left an image of an economic giant which was but a political pygmy.[39] The effect among Americans was to accelerate a growing mistrust of Japanese intentions toward the United States.

These developments went hand-in-hand with new developments in US policy toward Japan. For one thing, the United States intensified its efforts to acquire Japanese military technology. In addition, as the FS-X controversy illustrated, more consideration was given to the possibility of restricting Japanese access to advanced US technology. Predictably, the threat of new restrictions has been seen as the beginning of a "technology blockade" in Japan. It has fueled a national backlash and emboldened advocates of autonomous defense. The respected *Asahi Jānaru* published an article in 1988, for instance, that claimed the United States was adopting a "Nazi-style" attitude toward technology transfer to Japan.[40]

The new emphasis in US policy also increased the desire of the Japanese to accelerate their defense research in order to protect themselves from unilateral US action. One way to contribute to this objective was to accelerate Japanese investments in the US-based defense industry, including firms engaged in R&D. Naturally, this created political difficulties. The Fujitsu acquisition of Fairchild in 1987 was aborted under significant political pressure. And in January 1991, the Bush administration was criticized for refusing to block the purchase by Japan's Fanuc Company of Moore Special Tool, the only US firm that manufactures precision machine tools meeting the Defense and Energy departments' specifications for nuclear weapons production.[41] As Japanese firms continued to seek advanced technological competencies in the United States, it seemed likely that sporadic US efforts to block such transactions would increase in frequency, and that development, in turn, would accelerate Japanese efforts at indigenous development.

In light of these developments, it is ironic that one of the factors contributing to the growth of Japan's defense industry has been US exhortations to "burden share." The Japanese public support for Article Nine of Japan's constitution has meant that any expansion of the country's weaponry must always be justified as "defensive" rather than "offensive" in character; the acquisition of items such as cameras for mounting on military aircraft, therefore, can generate raging debates in Japan. Such problems, however, have not prevented the JDA from responding to US pressures for more defense spending.[42] In the 1980s, Japan's defense budget grew faster than any other area of government spending except for foreign aid. And defense R&D was consistently the fastest growing line item within the defense budget. The predictable result is that today Japan's largely defensive "war potential" is among the largest and most technologically sophisticated in the world.

The rancorous dispute between the United States and Japan over the well-publicized FS-X in 1989 further abetted these developments. Under pressure from Congress and fearful that Japan would use transferred technology to compete in the commercial aerospace industry, the Bush administration decided to renegotiate a bilateral agreement to codevelop a new fighter aircraft for Japan.[43] Japanese defense industrialists used the opportunity to accelerate defense spending, particularly in R&D, and to look for ways of withholding Japanese advanced technologies from the United States.[44] Keidanren issued its first formal endorsement of arms production, and within three months, the Keidanren Defense Production Committee was made a standing committee, a move that for forty years had been judged too politically sensitive to merit Keidanren's support.

Other reactions occurred as well. For its part, the JDA announced several large-scale development programs, including programs to replace imported US missiles, jet engines, and helicopters with Japanese models. During the FS-X dispute, France offered Japan all the jet fighter technologies that the United States was withholding. In March 1990, Mitsubishi Heavy Industries stunned the industry by announcing an omnibus aerospace cooperative relationship with Daimler-Benz that will involve dual-use technologies, especially jet propulsion. Contracts to purchase European aircraft in late 1990, the first of such purchases by Japan, were linked to these European initiatives and to the "hangover" from the FS-X dispute.[45]

Japan will continue to fortify its defense technology base and to expand its alternatives in the global economy. But it is unlikely to take the initiative in greatly modifying or abandoning its alliance with the United States. Unless rejected by the United States, therefore, Japan can be expected to continue its restrained but increasingly flexible approach toward defense planning and military programs, while the Japanese industry remains poised to succeed by creating dependencies in a global market that requires its dual-use products and process technologies. Japanese technonationalism has guided the nation to reinvent security in war and in peace.

ACKNOWLEDGEMENTS

I am grateful for the financial support this project received from the MIT Japan Program and from the MIT Center for International Studies Japan Energy Endowment, the congenial facilities provided by the Science Policy Research Unit at the University of Sussex and the Faculty of Oriental Studies at the University of Cambridge, and comments from the participants in the planning conference for this volume, convened at the Harvard University Center for International Affairs. Conversations with Michael Chinworth, a former colleague at MIT, were also extremely helpful.

ENDNOTES

[1] Noel Perrin, *Giving Up the Gun: Japan's Reversion to the Sword—1543–1879* (Boston: David R. Godine, 1979), 4.

[2] Koyama, Kōken, *Nihon Gunji Kōgyō no Shiteki Bunseki* (A historical analysis of the Japanese defense industry) (Tokyo: Ochanomizu Shōbō, 1972), 56.

[3] Henry Rosovsky, *Capital Formation in Japan 1868–1940* (New York: Free Press, 1961), 25–26.

[4] Kozo Yamamura, "Success Illgotten? The Role of Meiji Militarism in Japan's Technological Progress," *The Journal of Economic History* 37 (1) (March 1977): 113–35.

[5] William Lockwood, *The Economic Development of Japan: Growth and Structural Change, 1868–1938* (London: Oxford University Press, 1955), 9.

[6] Elizabeth B. Schumpeter, ed., *The Industrialization of Japan and Manchukuo 1938–1940: Population, Raw Materials, and Industry* (New York: Macmillan, 1940), 15.

[7] Koyama, 228.

[8] Nakajima eventually became Fuji Heavy Industries, Japan's tenth largest defense contractor. Nissan, of course, is one of the world's leading automakers and one of Japan's top fifteen JDA contractors.

[9]It is in this sense that John Dower refers to World War II as "the useful war." See John Dower, "The Useful War," in *Daedalus* 119 (3) (Summer 1990): 49–70.

[10]Laura Hein, *Fueling Growth: The Energy Revolution and Economic Policy in Postwar Japan* (Cambridge: Harvard East Asian Monographs, 1990), 229.

[11]Hideo Otake, "Nihon no 'Gunsan Fukugōtai' to Zaisei Kiki," (Japan's military-industrial complex and the fiscal crisis), pt. 1, *Asahi Jānaru*, 18 July 1980, 12.

[12]*Ekonomisuto*, 11 March 1952; Hideo Otake "Nihon ni Okeru 'Gunsankan Fukugōtai' Keisei no Zasetsu" (The frustrated state of the 'military-industrial-bureaucratic complex' in Japan), in Hideo Otake, ed., *Nihon Seiji no Sōten* (The Japanese political debate) (Tokyo: San Ichi Shōbō, 1984), 21.

[13]Marie Soderberg, *Japan's Military Export Policy* (Stockholm: University of Stockholm, 1987), 51.

[14]Hideo Otake, "Nihon no 'Gunsan Fukugōtai' to Zaisei Kiki" (Japan's military-industrial complex and the fiscal crisis), pt. 3, *Asahi Jānaru*, 1 August 1980, 28.

[15]Quoted in Otake, "Nihon no 'Gunsan Fukugōtai' to Zaisei Kiki," pt. 1, 31.

[16]*Nihon Keizai Shimbun*, 2 August 1953; *Asahi Shimbun*, 18 June 1953.

[17]*JEI Report* #30A, 3 August 1990, 13.

[18]For the ultimate consequences of this and subsequent programs, see US Congress, Office of Technology Assessment, *Arming Our Allies* (Washington, D.C.: US Government Printing Office, 1990). For a blunt assessment of how one nation uses "offset" programs to enhance its commercial competitiveness, see Joo-way Kim, " 'Offset' as an Instrument of National Industrial Policy," S.M. thesis, Sloan School of Management, MIT, June 1991.

[19]This is the description of Senga Tetsuya, former executive director of the Defense Production Committee of Keidanren. He also notes the "kindness and courtesy" extended by US firms eager "to teach" (sell) technology to Japan in the early 1950s, and adds ironically that "it was a bit different than the situation today." See Kondo Kanichi and Osanai Hiroshi, eds., *Sengo Sangyōshi e no Shōgen* (Testimony related to postwar industrial history), vol. 3 (Tokyo: Mainichi Shimbunsha, 1978), 227–8.

[20]James C. Abegglen and George Stalk, Jr., *Kaisha: The Japanese Corporation* (New York: Basic Books, 1985), 126.

[21]Michael Green in "*Kokusanka*: FS-X and Japan's Search for Autonomous Defense Production," MIT Japan Program Working Paper, 90–09, 1990, discusses the difficulties some Japanese politicians had in formally embracing the doctrine of indigenization (*kokusanka*) and even the defense industry itself.

[22]Reinhard Drifte, *Arms Production in Japan: The Military Applications of Civilian Technology* (Boulder, Colo.: Westview Press, 1986), 11, cites without further reference an estimate that Japan received about $10 billion worth of advanced US technology between 1950 and 1983; Thomas R. H. Havens, *Fire across the Sea: The Vietnam War and Japan, 1965–1975* (Princeton: Princeton University Press, 1987) documents the extent to which U.S. military procurement stimulated the Japanese economy during the Vietnam War; and John H. Makin, "American Economic and Military Leadership in the Postwar Period," in J. Makin and D.

Hellman, eds., *Sharing World Leadership? A New Era for America and Japan* (Washington, D.C.: American Enterprise, 1989) estimates that had Japan spent as much of its GNP on defense as the United States, its growth between 1955–1986 would have been reduced by 1 percent annually.

23 Advertisement by Sekai Electronics in *Aviation Week and Space Technology,* 13 February 1984, and in *Air Force Magazine,* May, July, and September 1987.

24 Soderberg, 60. Michael Chinworth suggests that formal budgets mask "a massive corporate commitment" to the development of defense technology; see Michael W. Chinworth, "Economic Strategy and U.S.-Defense Collaboration," MIT Japan Program Working Paper, WP 90–07, 1990, 6.

25 Interview in *Defense News,* 19 February 1990.

26 Defense Science Board, ed., *Report of the Defense Science Board Task Force on Industry to Industry Armaments Cooperation, Phase II, Japan* (Washington, D.C.: Defense Science Board, 1984).

27 By contrast, only one of the top ten US defense contractors in the late 1980s was dependent upon defense for less than 10 percent of total sales. Two of the ten, in fact, relied on the military for more than 85 percent of sales. (Unpublished Keidanren memorandum, 30 November 1988).

28 The Nissan announcement reportedly "sent shock waves to the established defense industry." See "Military Power: Ultimate US-Japan Friction," *JPRS Report,* 2 July 1990, 17.

29 Ronald Dore, "Goodwill and the Spirit of Market Capitalism," in Ronald Dore, *Taking Japan Seriously* (Stanford: Stanford University Press, 1987), 169–92.

30 This argument is developed by John Alic, "Military and Civilian Technologies: Synergy or Conflict?", paper prepared for the Workshop on Computation and Information Technologies: Growth, Productivity, and Employment, Jerome Levy Economics Institute, Bard College, 13–17 June 1989.

31 For a general treatment of the importance of small- and medium-sized firms in the Japanese economy, see David Friedman, *The Misunderstood Miracle* (Ithaca, N.Y.: Cornell University Press, 1988). A detailed study of the relationship of large and small firms in the contemporary Japanese aerospace industry is in David Friedman and Richard Samuels, "How to Succeed Without Really Flying: The Japanese Aircraft Industry and Technology Ideology," paper presented for the National Bureau of Economic Research (April, 1992).

32 See Richard J. Samuels and Benjamin C. Whipple, "Defense Production and Industrial Development: The Case of the Japanese Aircraft Industry"; and "Defense Production and Industrial Development: The Case of Japanese Aircraft," in Chalmers Johnson, Laura Tyson, and John Zysman, eds., *Politics and Productivity* (Cambridge: Ballinger, 1989).

33 Jonah Levy and Richard J. Samuels, "Institutions and Innovation: Research Collaboration as Technology Strategy in Japan," in L. Mytelka, ed., *Strategic Partnerships: States, Firms, and International Competition* (London: Frances Pinter, 1991).

34 Cited by Green.

35 These negotiations failed utterly in April 1991.

[36]For examples of these reassessments, see Tsūsanshō, ed., *Nihon no Sentōk* (Japan's choices) (Tokyo: Tsūsanchō, April 1988); and Defense Science Board, ed., *Defense Industrial Cooperation with Pacific Rim Countries* (Washington, D.C.: Office of the Undersecretary of Defense for Acquisitions, 1989). Also see J. Pollack and J. Winnefeld, "U.S. Strategic Alternatives in a Changing Pacific," in a report prepared by RAND for the commander in chief of the US Pacific Command (Santa Monica, Calif.: RAND, June 1990).

[37]In April 1991, two months after hostilities ceased, the Japanese government dispatched minesweepers from the Maritime Self-Defense Forces. This was the first foreign deployment of Japanese troops since World War II and was the object of intense domestic debate.

[38]*Business Week,* 1 April 1990, 28.

[39]This metaphor is often credited to former minister of finance Miyazawa Kiichi, now Japan's prime minister. The Pentagon had difficulty acquiring key companies from Japanese electronics firms for military systems deployed in the Gulf War; *San Francisco Chronicle,* 30 April 1991.

[40]*Asahi Jānaru,* 1 July 1988.

[41]*New York Times,* 18 January 1991. In February Fanuc announced it would not buy Moore after all; see *New York Times,* 20 February 1991.

[42]For illustrations, see Soderberg, 42.

[43]See Clyde V. Prestowitz, Jr., *Trading Places* (New York: Basic Books, 1989). For accounts of the dispute see Gregory Noble, "Japan, America, and the FS-X Jet Fighter Planes: Structural Asymmetries in Bilateral Negotiations," paper presented to the annual meeting of the Association of Asian Studies, Chicago, April 1989.

[44]*Wing Newsletter* 22 (20) (24 May 1989).

[45]American Aerospace Industry, "Japan Market Today, Strong Competition from Europe," position paper issued in Tokyo, Japan, February 1991.

Aaron L. Friedberg

The End of Autonomy: The United States after Five Decades

O F ALL THE INDUSTRIALIZED NATIONS, defense planners in the United States have agonized most in recent years over how to deal with the globalization trend. For much of the half century after 1945, the United States was able to enjoy a position of virtual autonomy in defense production. The sheer size and relative technological sophistication of the US economy made it possible to efficiently produce almost everything necessary for defense. And this result, so reassuring from the point of view of military security, was achieved without extensive government efforts to plan and manage the nation's economy.

Since the 1980s, however, the trend toward globalization has confronted American decision makers with a choice between sustained autonomy and continued low levels of government intervention. This choice has arisen in four interrelated areas. First, increasing international competition has caused some hard-pressed domestic industries to appeal for protection on grounds that they are critical to defense production. Second, the eroding US edge has led to calls for much broader government policies to promote technological innovation. Third, expanding flows of capital into the United States have given rise to efforts to increase the federal government's powers to restrict foreign purchases of US firms in defense-related sectors. And, fourth, there have been parallel attempts to monitor and control the

Aaron L. Friedberg is Assistant Professor of Politics and International Affairs at Princeton University.

69

increasingly frequent instances of cooperation between US and foreign-based defense firms.

Despite the seeming challenge to its autonomy and security, however, the striking fact is that the United States has generally accepted the process and consequences of globalization, rather than attempting to resist them. As of the early 1990s, the federal government did not have any program to protect all the existing industries it thought relevant to national defense or to promote all the new industries that might be important in the future. Nor had it acted in any determined way to limit foreign direct investment or to restrict international industrial cooperation.

The simplest explanation for this pattern of response is ideological. For two hundred years the United States has developed under a set of liberal principles that distinguish it from most other countries. In accordance with these principles there has been a strong presumption (bolstered both by economic theory and evident American success) against state intervention in the economy. Resisting globalization, even for reasons of national security, would have required more tariffs, subsidies, and regulations. Rather than follow such a course, US leaders put their preference for efficiency and their belief in the market over their desire for autonomy.

But this way of accounting for the US response to globalization is incomplete. Liberal ideas, while dominant, have not gone unopposed. Their influence over policy has therefore had to do not only with their intrinsic appeal but with the power of the people who hold them. Since 1980 the most consistent support for noninterventionism has come from the executive office of the president, including at various times the president himself, the National Security Council, the Office of Management and Budget, and the Council of Economic Advisers.

It is not enough, however, simply to say that US policy has been liberal because the White House has wanted it that way. The United States is often described as having a "weak" political system, one incapable of formulating and executing a consistent and coherent policy in the face of special interest pressures. Yet, since the early 1980s the US response to globalization seems to have been both consistent and reasonably coherent. How has the White House been able to get what it wanted?

Part of the answer lies in the fact that as the proponents of traditional liberal principles, the president and his supporters have held the intellectual, political, and even moral high ground. The opposition, in addition to arguing against history and tradition, has been divided and dispersed. Within the executive branch, advocates of intervention could be found primarily in the Commerce and Defense departments, but these agencies have been able to form a united front only sporadically. Moreover, both departments have been subject to internal divisions. Inside the Department of Defense (DoD), for example, lower-ranking officials have often been overruled by high-level political appointees who, like their counterparts in other government agencies, were suspicious of interventionism and strongly inclined toward laissez-faire.

Outside the executive branch, some support for increased interventionism has come from industry and Congress. But here, too, there have been divisions. In the area of trade policy, for example, pleas for protection from domestically based industries have been frequently matched by appeals for openness from US-based multinational enterprises that rely on foreign trade to support a global strategy.[1]

Although congressional Democrats as a group have tilted toward intervention and Republicans toward laissez-faire, both parties have felt countervailing pressures. Republicans have been subject to interest group appeals for government help and to concerns about national security. Democrats have heard some pleas from constituents for nonintervention and they, too, have been wary of moving too far from laissez-faire.

Faced with pressures from opposing directions, Congress as a whole has not been willing nor able to force the executive to take any far-reaching interventionist measures and has fallen back instead on strategies of delegation and exhortation. In some areas, Congress has granted the president broad powers and then stood back from their actual application. On other issues, vocal congressional advocates of action have been content to settle for policies that were stronger in appearance than in substance, such as the imposition of reporting requirements on the executive branch. Both approaches have helped to alleviate interest group pressures and have left Congress free to criticize, but they also have given the White House broad leeway in pursuing its preferences.

Throughout the 1980s and into the 1990s, liberal economic beliefs have impelled the White House to resist calls for interventionist responses to the globalization trend. Ideological legitimacy, the weakness and dispersion of its opponents, and the fact that it has retained or has been granted a high degree of control over the actual implementation of policy has permitted the White House to succeed.

DEFENSE PROTECTIONISM

The idea that import restrictions might be useful to protect key defense-supporting industries is hardly a novel concept. But it emerged as a possible line of policy in the 1970s and 1980s as US military planners began to consider the prospect that the US and Soviet nuclear arsenals might soon neutralize each other, thereby increasing the possibility that war between the superpowers would take the form of a protracted conventional conflict. In such a struggle, as in World War II, the country's capacity to support sudden and sustained increases in military production could prove decisive.[2]

It was as they contemplated such scenarios that US strategists began to be seriously concerned with the expanded import penetration that had been building for over a decade. In the early 1980s, various studies found evidence of a dramatic growth in the importation of a range of products that might be critical to military mobilization.[3] If a foreign government chose to cut off exports in a political crisis, or if lines of communication were disrupted by hostile military action in actual warfare, the consequences could be grave.

Despite such concerns, US industries looking for protection from import competition in the 1980s got very little support from the Department of Defense. Many high-level DoD officials objected to import restrictions for reasons of principle. Their worries about preserving the domestic industrial base also conflicted with the desire to keep procurement costs down by using inexpensive imports and with the need to maintain good relations with important allied trading partners. Moreover, after a few bruising bureaucratic battles, the Defense Department learned that backing protectionism against the wishes of the White House was a losing proposition.

Nevertheless, in the early 1980s, industry spokesmen in pursuit of government protection against imports did try to make more frequent use of national security arguments. Two decades earlier, under the terms of Section 232 of the 1962 Trade Expansion Act, Congress had given the president the power to impose import restrictions in those cases where he believed that imports posed a threat to national security.[4] In the eighteen years from 1962 to 1980 there had been ten investigations under Section 232, only two of which (both involving oil) led to a positive finding. By contrast, in the first three years of the Reagan administration, the government had been asked to undertake five such studies, including, for the first time, one initiated at the request of the Department of Defense.[5]

The Reagan White House, already faced with a growing array of requests for import restriction on a variety of nondefense grounds, was fearful of opening yet another avenue of appeal for protection; accordingly, it moved quickly to tighten its control over the Section 232 process. Responsibility for overseeing all national security trade investigations was given to the National Security Council, and in 1982 elaborate new procedures were established which raised the hurdles that claimants had to clear.[6]

If the object of these steps was to allow the executive branch to "study a problem to death," as one former NSC official described it, the tactic seemed to work.[7] After an initial spurt, the flow of national security import cases slowed considerably. Of the six investigations of manufacturing industries conducted between 1981 and 1989, only one—involving machine tools—resulted in import restrictions.[8] However, even in that case, the administration was careful not to set a precedent. In 1986, after three years of what has been described as "one of the most bitter and divisive internal debates of the Reagan administration,"[9] the White House managed to avoid a formal finding under Section 232 by reaching an agreement with Japan and Taiwan under which they would restrict the export of certain types of machine tools to the United States.[10]

At the time, the disposition of the machine tool case was not universally interpreted as a triumph for liberal trade policy over protectionism, especially as it was accompanied by a similar agreement with Japan restricting the dumping of integrated circuits in the US market.[11] But machine tools and semiconductors have proven to be the exception rather than the rule. Even in these two cases the resistance of the White House to pressures for more overt measures of protection was remarkable. Both the machine tool and the semiconductor industries had launched unusually vigorous lobbying efforts. In both cases timing was also extremely important; with the congressional election of 1986 in the offing and protectionist sentiment apparently on the rise, the White House saw itself under great external pressure to help these two especially visible industries as a way of heading off demands for more sweeping action.[12]

Inside the executive branch, the appeals of the machine tool and semiconductor makers also enjoyed the support of a unified Commerce-Defense coalition. The Defense Department's support was lukewarm, reflecting internal divisions. In each instance the Commerce Department led the way, motivated more by somewhat vaguely defined fears about economic security than by concerns over national defense in the traditional military sense. In the case of machine tools the argument of the Commerce Department was that if foreign (and especially Japanese) firms were permitted to drive domestic producers out of business, the United States would find itself at a disadvantage in a range of other commercial manufacturing sectors. The machine tool industry was believed, therefore, to have an importance that far exceeded its direct contributions to military manufacturing.[13]

Economic security arguments and Commerce Department advocacy were even more crucial in determining the outcome of the semiconductor case. In this instance, the Commerce Department echoed the claims of industry representatives, asserting that semiconductors had a "leveraging impact" on an array of other civilian industries. If US-based semiconductor makers were allowed to go under, the impact on the domestic economy, it was claimed, would be devastating.

Despite these two deviations, the 1980s did not see a marked increase in defense protectionism. Instead, a decade that began with a flurry of anxiety over expanding dependency on foreign sources ended with a growing recognition that such a condition was not reversible at anything approaching a bearable cost. Acceptance of this fact was eased by the apparent dwindling of any possibility of protracted conventional war with the Soviet Union. Where government spokesmen had once emphasized the dangers of import dependence, they now described such a condition as inevitable "given the worldwide trend toward an interdependent global economy." In light of this central fact it was necessary that the country strike "a careful balance . . . between excessive reliance on foreign sources and undue

Government intervention in the marketplace."[14] Where exactly that balance might lie was unclear, but there could be little doubt that, at least as far as the executive branch was concerned, even a fairly high degree of reliance on foreign sources was preferable to any widespread use of import barriers intended to prevent it.

TECHNOLOGY PROMOTION

Along with occasional attempts to bolster selected industries by protective measures, the US government has also engaged in efforts to promote and support technological progress. As befits a country committed to liberal economic doctrines, however, these efforts have generally been designed to minimize intervention in the process of commercial innovation.

Since the end of World War II, the federal government has promoted technological progress in two ways: first, by supporting basic scientific research; and second, by spending considerable sums on applied research and development work, particularly when related to the nation's defense. For most of the postwar period, the government has consciously avoided involvement in promoting commercial innovation for its own sake. Government interference in this process would, it was widely assumed, lead only to waste and inefficiency.[15]

By the 1980s, however, the course of technological evolution and the position of the US economy had both changed in certain critical respects, calling into question the wisdom of a continued policy of benign neglect toward nonmilitary technology. First, within the United States and elsewhere in the world, spending on research in the commercial sector was increasing even faster than funding for military R&D. As a result, according to one expert, "military and space technology no longer [were] the dominant source of radical technological innovations, as they were before the late '60s."[16] Concurrently, the increasingly dynamic commercial sector was becoming a major source of innovations for weapons and other military systems. And, in a growing number of fields, foreign-based firms were drawing even with or actually pulling ahead of their competitors headquartered in the United States.

For both military and economic reasons, therefore, US planners began to reexamine existing assumptions about the proper role of the government in supporting "dual-use" technologies, that is, technologies with both civilian and military applications. By the 1990s, this reexamination had not yet produced a new consensus. As on the question of defense protectionism, the strongest resistance to proposals for an expanded government role in technology promotion has come from the White House. During the second half of the 1980s, advocates of change did succeed in getting the government to undertake some limited measures to promote dual-use technologies. But attempts to push policy one step further by providing substantial public support for commercial innovation were checked and beaten back.

The story of the opening rounds of the struggle over technology promotion policy can be told in terms of two proposed programs. The first, Sematech, involved the creation with partial government funding of an industry consortium dedicated to the perfection of new techniques for the manufacture of commercial semiconductors. The second program would have channeled substantial federal funds toward firms involved in the development of high definition television (HDTV). Why did Sematech succeed in gaining government support while HDTV failed?

From the start, the logical links between Sematech and US national security were reasonably clear. In 1987 the members of a Defense Science Board (DSB) task force on "defense semiconductor dependency" argued that, without a healthy commercial semiconductor industry, the United States would have difficulty in sustaining the superiority of its armed forces.[17] That superiority, the report reasoned, rested on technological supremacy and, in particular, on leadership in electronics. The ability to develop and to produce the most sophisticated semiconductors depended, in turn, on a capacity to make and sell large numbers of less-advanced products in the commercial marketplace. High-volume commercial production provided both the funds and the know-how needed to sustain an advantage at the leading edge of semiconductor technology. Thus, the DSB report concluded, although the Department of Defense had no inherent responsibility for the commercial viability of the US semiconductor industry, it was unlikely to be able to fulfill its requirements without a strong domestic semiconductor industry.

Once a domestic base for the production of semiconductors was acknowledged as being essential to national security, the next question was what the government could do to sustain it. Two decades earlier, DoD procurement had constituted a significant fraction of total worldwide demand, but by the 1980s such purchases were far from sufficient to support a thriving domestic industry. In order to keep US firms in business and available to satisfy the Defense Department's more specialized needs, those companies had to be kept in the mass-market game. Toward that end the Defense Science Board recommended the formation, with government encouragement and assistance, of an industry-wide consortium to develop techniques for manufacturing the next generation of commercial semiconductor devices.

While the national security argument for Sematech was hardly simple, the links by which proponents of governmental support connected HDTV with US defense were even more attenuated. The coming generation of high definition television receivers, it was said, would generate enormous revenues for those companies in a position to provide them. If US firms were not involved in manufacturing the new sets, billions of dollars would be added to the nation's trade deficit and substantial profits would be lost.[18] This, in turn, could prove critical for the future of the entire US domestic electronics industry. Finally, HDTV enthusiasts argued, the effort to perfect high resolution consumer products could help to drive the development of related commercial technologies that, almost coincidentally, would be useful to the military.[19] In a marked reversal from the typical arguments of previous decades, the federal government was being asked to support commercial technologies in the hope that they might some day produce defense "spin-ons."

The lukewarm reception accorded proposals for large-scale public funding of HDTV was due partly to the novel and somewhat dubious rationale that supported them and partly to the character and size of the government assistance that was suggested. Whereas Sematech aimed at perfecting generic production techniques, an HDTV project would have involved the government in the development of a specific commercial product. And, whereas Sematech cost the taxpayer $200 million a year in matching funds, some HDTV proposals called for over $1 billion in government grants, low cost loans, and loan guarantees.[20]

In part for these reasons, HDTV generated considerable disagreement among industry experts. Proposals for substantial federal support received the endorsement of the American Electronics Association, an organization of consumer electronics companies. But they also aroused objections from other observers who argued that the technologies embodied in existing HDTV programs were the wrong ones to support.[21]

Expert divisions of this kind helped to feed congressional controversy. By the close of the Reagan administration many Democrats had begun to argue openly for promoting industrial innovation for purely economic reasons. Congressional Republicans responded that government ought to stay out of the business of picking commercial technologies. Democrats hoped (and many Republicans feared) that HDTV would be the first step toward a new, post-Cold War technology policy. In contrast to Sematech, therefore, HDTV became an intensely symbolic and deeply partisan issue.

With Congress divided, the fate of HDTV was determined by the White House. With the arrival of a new administration, resistance to any major departures in technology policy was reaffirmed and even strengthened. Despite signs that the Secretary of Commerce and the head of the Defense Advanced Research Project Agency (DARPA) were sympathetic, the new Bush team made it clear that there would be no major HDTV initiative and even that programs already in place were in danger of being cut.[22] To drive home the point, the Secretary of Commerce was summoned to the White House, chastised for his enthusiasm for HDTV and warned against any more ventures into the world of commercial technology promotion;[23] some months later, the head of DARPA was removed from his position. For the time being, the traditional, anti-interventionist orientation continued to dominate government policy.[24]

CONTROLLING FOREIGN INVESTMENT

Although the White House occasionally saw the need for tactical retreats in protecting its liberal positions regarding import barriers and commercial technology promotion, it rarely showed any disposition for compromise over proposals to restrict the inflow of foreign direct investment. Proposals of this kind proliferated during the 1980s, as the share of US manufacturing assets owned by foreigners roughly doubled, from over 6 percent in the late 1970s to over 12 percent in the late 1980s. Many economists reacted to the accelerated pace at which foreigners were buying US companies or establishing new facilities on US soil by arguing that it was "part of a process by which the United States is becoming a 'normal' country in which multinational firms play about the same role as in other industrial countries."[25] This view was in accordance with the traditional US advocacy of openness to international capital movements. Until the 1980s, however, the magnitude of foreign investment in the United States had been relatively inconsequential. As the inward flow of investment increased, so, too, did domestic pressures for a reexamination of existing policy.

Inside the executive branch, the main concern had less to do with the increase in foreign direct investment as a whole than with a small but growing number of purchases of high-technology firms. According to one source, the annual number of foreign acquisitions of US high-technology companies more than quadrupled between 1981 and 1986, from about 30 to over 120. Whether or not the acquired companies were working for the government or for major US defense contractors at the time of their purchase, most were involved in developing new products with potential military applications.[26] Some in the Defense Department worried that even if these firms remained on US soil, their foreign owners might be unwilling or ineligible under US security regulations to help develop the latest weapons and communications systems. Commerce Department officials were also fearful that carefully targeted purchases could give foreign firms a competitive edge by permitting them early access to, or even control over, new critical technologies. There were also concerns that foreign owners might decide to strip these companies of their high-technology assets and close down key facilities in the United States.

The Defense and Commerce departments' concerns were heightened by the fact that as of the mid-1980s, there was no established mechanism for blocking foreign takeovers of US-owned companies. Although an interagency group had been established in the mid-1970s to review the possible national security implications of proposed foreign investments, it lacked the power to do more than make recommendations to the cabinet. Moreover, except in cases of national emergency or in those few instances already covered under existing laws, it was unclear if the president himself had the authority to interfere in commercial transactions between domestic owners and foreign buyers.

The foreign direct investment issue first gained widespread public attention at the end of 1986 when Fujitsu Ltd., a Japanese computer and semiconductor manufacturer, announced its intention to purchase the US-based Fairchild Semiconductor Corporation. Although the Defense Department eventually came to oppose the sale, newspaper accounts reported a split at first between officials who feared disrupting recently initiated efforts to promote the transfer of dual-use technology from Japan and those who worried about the reliability of Fairchild's new owners.[27] To the Commerce Department, Fujitsu's bid was the first move in a larger effort by Japanese companies to buy up their weakened American competitors, thereby gaining an advantage in leading-edge semiconductors and products built from them, especially supercomputers.[28]

Stymied in their efforts to get the White House to intervene, the opponents of the Fairchild sale succeeded in sabotaging the deal through press leaks and highly unusual public expressions of disapproval. Days after the Secretary of Commerce denounced the deal at a press conference, Fujitsu withdrew its bid.

The Fujitsu-Fairchild flap triggered an intense public debate over what to do about foreign direct investment. Fears of foreign penetration created an irresistible opportunity for populist posturing in Congress. In the aftermath of the Fairchild-Fujitsu affair, members of both the House and the Senate pressed for legislation that would have required the public registration of all major foreign investors and the screening of pending investments. Such intervention was justified on more than national security grounds, as proponents called for government action to protect "essential commerce" and "economic welfare."[29]

These proposals generated some support from organized labor, but they also stimulated strong opposition from an impressive coalition composed of US-based multinationals, foreign-owned corporations in the United States, and state governments eager to attract investors, regardless of nationality. Interventionist schemes were also vigorously opposed by the administration, which dispatched representatives of the Commerce and Defense departments to reassure Congress that the government already had sufficient legal powers to deal with any problems that might arise.[30]

Caught between a desire to do something and a fear of doing too much, and faced with a threatened veto of any broadly restrictive measures, Congress finally voted to include in the 1988 Omnibus Trade Bill a provision authorizing the executive branch to undertake investigations "to determine the effects on national security of mergers, acquisitions and takeovers proposed or pending" and granting the president power to "suspend or prohibit" any such transaction if it should "threaten to impair the national security."

These provisions handed the president an instrument that could have been sharpened into a powerful and potentially quite dangerous weapon. Instead, the White House set about to render it harmless by wrapping it in layers of protective procedure. Responsibility for conducting investigations was put in the hands of the Treasury Department, the federal agency least inclined to permit any disruption of foreign investment. Treasury officials proceeded to draft regulations that were intended to interfere as little as possible in the dealings of private parties while imposing strict limits on the government's ability to use its new powers.

In addition to these procedural constraints, the Bush administration also was careful not to set any precedents that might encourage a broad interpretation of the term "national security." At the direction of the White House, the interagency body charged with conducting investigations of foreign investment pointedly refused to define its responsibility as including the preservation of "long-term US commercial competitiveness." Instead, the interagency group focused its attention almost exclusively on determining the extent and nature of a target firm's direct involvement in defense-related work.[31]

To the great relief of those who had feared the potential chilling effect of the new procedures, all but 10 of the roughly 375 deals that the interagency group addressed during the first two years of its operations were set aside as not warranting a full-scale investigation. Of the ten acquisitions examined, only one was actually blocked, a case involving the attempted purchase by the Chinese government of a small Seattle-based aircraft parts firm.[32]

Instead of promoting governmental intrusions into the marketplace, the existence of a formal review process actually appeared to restrain ad hoc interventions of the sort the Commerce Department had initiated in 1987. In the early 1990s, some DoD officials are urging that the law be more broadly interpreted and that responsibility for its enforcement be placed in the hands of a more aggressive government agency. But as long as the Treasury Department and the White House continue to see eye to eye on foreign investment there is no reason to expect this to occur.

REGULATING TRANSNATIONAL INDUSTRIAL COOPERATION

From the beginning of the Cold War, the United States government encouraged cooperation between domestic defense firms and their counterparts in friendly nations. Over time these relationships have tended to move up what one recent study has termed the "collaborative scale." From simple sales of arms and equipment by US firms to foreign governments, these arrangements have moved to coproduction deals in which foreign firms built subsystems or were licensed to assemble American-designed products, and eventually to codevelopment projects in which the participants acted as equal partners in designing and building new weapons systems.[33]

Until the 1980s, the cooperation of US defense firms with partners overseas was relatively free of controversy, receiving widespread support from both Congress and the executive branch. As the forms of collaboration grew more complex, however, doubts began to arise over the benefits of such arrangements to the United States. Where coproduction has been involved, the question has been whether the US defense base has been weakened by the shifting of business overseas. With codevelopment projects, as in the FSX case, the debate has been over the longer run consequences to US competitiveness arising out of technology transfers.

As other countries built up their own defense industries the international arms business became ever more competitive. To avoid losing sales in foreign markets, major US weapons manufacturers found it necessary to provide increasingly significant "offsets" in the country concerned, usually in the form of coproduction agreements.[34] From the point of view of the US weapons manufacturers, a deal that required substantial portions of their weapons systems to be built overseas by foreign-owned firms was better than no deal at all. However, for the US companies that might otherwise have fabricated some of the parts, these offset arrangements have been seen as an absolute loss. The collapse of some of these supplying firms or their withdrawal from military contracting could shrink the US defense industrial base and reduce its capacity for emergency expansion.

For many years, the US government had refrained from interven-ing in these foreign offset agreements, leaving US weapons manufac-turers free to negotiate the deals they deemed necessary to win customers. Starting in the early 1980s, however, US defense subcon-tractors began to plead for protection from the harmful effects of offsets. Finding an effective response to their complaints, however, did not prove easy. Prohibiting the prime contractors from entering into offset agreements would have hurt them without helping the lower tiers of the defense industry. Suggestions that the federal government be empowered to make countervailing offset demands when negotiating with foreign suppliers were also strongly opposed by the prime contractors, as well as by the White House, on anti-interventionist grounds.[35]

In the face of these conflicting pressures, Congress demanded that the problem receive further study. Since 1984, the president has been required to prepare a report detailing the impact of offsets on "the defense preparedness, industrial competitiveness, employment and trade of the United States." Responsibility for this task has been kept within the White House, assigned to the impeccably anti-interven-tionist Office of Management and Budget (OMB). It is not surprising that the OMB reports have found no evidence that offsets cause any significant harm, even to the subcontractors who were supposedly most affected by them.[36] In keeping with these findings and in response to congressional demands for a formal declaration of policy, the executive branch simply has reiterated its long-standing position that the decision to engage in offsets, and the responsibility for negotiating and implementing offset arrangements, rests with the companies involved.

In the debate over the merits of collaborating with foreign produc-ers, codevelopment agreements have generated greater concerns among US defense planners than coproduction deals. Codevelop-ment, unlike coproduction, requires the participants to work together on problems as yet unsolved. The fear has been that prospective competitors might derive more out of the partnership in the transfer of leading edge technologies than US participants.

Such concerns figured strongly in the debate over FSX, a joint program to design and build a new fighter for the air force of Japan. Eager to augment its own national productive capabilities, the Japanese government had originally intended to procure an aircraft designed and built entirely at home. Pressed by the United States to buy an off-the-shelf US-made plane, the Japanese refused. Finally, they compromised by agreeing to have their own companies enter a joint development program with a US aerospace firm. As the details of this arrangement were being worked out, some on the US side began to wonder if a codevelopment deal was really such a good idea after all.

What was at stake in the FSX controversy was not simply the health of the US defense industrial base, but the much more amorphous concept of economic security. Critics of the proposed agreement claimed that by teaching the Japanese how to design a modern jet aircraft, the United States would be helping them to build up their own aerospace industry. Compared to what they gave up, the technology gained by the US participants in the FSX project would be of relatively little value. The net effect of cooperation, it was feared, would be to speed up the emergence of Japan as a competitor in the aerospace industry, one of the few high-technology areas in which US firms continued to dominate world markets.

In the end, however, the protests over FSX achieved very little. Armed with the legal authority to block a codevelopment agreement, Congress did have some capacity to influence its terms. The proposed FSX deal also aroused the concerns of the Commerce Department, a fact that did not escape the attention of its congressional critics. Toward the end of 1988, Congress specifically required that the Defense Department consult the Commerce Department on the broader economic consequences of all cooperative arrangements, something that had not been done during the FSX negotiations.[37] Early in 1989, in the face of mounting congressional pressure, the newly elected Bush administration ordered an interagency review, to be cochaired by the Defense and Commerce departments. This process resulted in a modest tightening of the original agreement intended to improve the balance of technology exchange between the United States and Japan.

Having made these concessions, the administration proceeded to push FSX through Congress, arguing that a rejection would humiliate Japan, damage alliance relations, and diminish the chances for future codevelopment projects that would be beneficial to the United States. These views were supported by representatives of the large aircraft manufacturers who claimed that, in any case, given the globalization of the aerospace industry, codevelopment arrangements were inevitable. The proper US goal, in the words of one industry spokesman, "must be to advance our technology more rapidly than our competitors, rather than vainly expecting to slow their progress."[38]

Congress responded to these arguments by approving the FSX agreement in principle while at the same time passing resolutions requiring a further tightening of its terms, but these resolutions failed by a narrow margin to survive a presidential veto. Aside from its impact on US-Japan relations, the only lasting effect of the FSX controversy was the creation, at the instigation of Congress, of an institutional mechanism for self-policing by the executive branch. The movement toward military codevelopment was therefore permitted to go forward.

CONCLUSION

Although warily at times, the US government has embraced the globalization trend rather than attempting to resist it. How stable is this response?

A radical departure in US policy from its present position of acquiescence seems improbable. If there is a change it is more likely to grow out of concerns about economic security than from worries over national defense. And it is more likely to come with a change in the outlook of the president than as a result of renewed pressures from other parts of the American political system.

Even in the late 1970s and early 1980s, in the presence of what was widely perceived to be a major military threat from the Soviet Union, the United States was not willing to pay the necessary price to preserve its self-sufficiency in defense production. In the absence of a clear external menace there is virtually no chance of a costly, concerted drive to restore military autonomy.

Nevertheless, national security concerns will give rise to continued efforts to control the international flow of technology. US officials can be expected to do what they can to ensure ready access by US arms makers to the new technologies that will lie at the heart of the next generation of weapons systems; without such access, the United States could lose its considerable qualitative advantages over potential military competitors. Many of the most important innovations, such as advances in materials, microelectronics, and computing, will come from the civilian sector and, if present trends continue, many will be developed first by foreign-based firms.[39] Ensuring prompt access will probably require some mix of international cooperation and policies designed to encourage the location of at least some of the sources of these technologies on American soil.

At the same time as they are seeking to ensure access to strategically significant technologies for their own country, US officials will attempt to deny it to others. In particular, they are likely to make renewed attempts to control the export to countries in the Third World of technologies associated with weapons of mass destruction. But efforts at restricting technological flows will have real limits.

If any attempt is made to shift government policy sharply toward increased interventionism, it will be based on concerns, however misguided, about national prosperity and competitiveness. Any such departure would require strong support from the top of the executive branch. The events of the 1980s demonstrated that the White House is capable of resisting pressures for intervention arising from industry, Congress, the media, and parts of the bureaucracy. On the other hand, national policy could shift with a change in the disposition of the White House. A president persuaded by appeals to economic security might use existing mechanisms to tighten controls on imports and foreign investment, promote the development of commercial technologies, and restrict the terms of some collaborative efforts between US and foreign firms.

The history, values, and institutions of the United States, however, are all pitched strongly against a marked move toward interventionism, regardless of its motivation. Such a shift would arouse objections both on ideological grounds and on the part of domestic interests hurt by restrictive measures. The presence of these equilibrating mechanisms means that changes at the margin are more likely than truly dramatic departures from the liberal policies of the past.

ENDNOTES

[1]On this phenomenon see Helen V. Milner, *Resisting Protectionism* (Princeton: Princeton University Press, 1988).

[2]See, for example, Paul Bracken, "Mobilization in the Nuclear Age," *International Security* 3 (Winter 1978/79): 74–93; Fred Charles Ikle, "Can We Mobilize

Industry?", *Wall Street Journal,* 26 December 1979; and Roderick L. Vawter, *Industrial Mobilization: The Relevant History* (Washington, D.C.: National Defense University Press, 1983).

[3]See Defense Industrial Panel of the House Armed Services Committee, *The Ailing Defense Industrial Base: Unready for Crisis,* report, 96th Cong., 2nd sess. (Washington, D.C.: US Government Printing Office, 1980). Also Defense Science Board, *Report of the Task Force on Industrial Responsiveness* (Washington, D.C.: Department of Defense, 1980).

[4]On the history of Section 232 see Edward E. Groves, "A Brief History of the 1988 National Security Amendments," *Law and Policy in International Business* 20 (3) (1989): 589–602.

[5]After this 1982 request, which led to an investigation of the metal fasteners industry, the Defense Department did not again take the initiative in a Section 232 case. For a record of cases and decisions, see US Department of Commerce, Bureau of Export Administration, Office of Industrial Resource Administration, *Section 232 Investigations: The Effects of Imports on the National Security* (Washington, D.C.: Department of Commerce, July 1989), 19–22.

[6]Richard Levine, "Trade vs. National Security: Section 232 Cases," *Comparative Strategy* 7 (2) (1988): 134–5. For a critique of the tightened procedures see the testimony of Clyde Prestowitz in US Congress, House, Readiness Subcommittee, Committee on Armed Services, *Issues Relating to the Plastic Injection Molding Industry,* 100th Cong., 2nd sess. (Washington, D.C.: US Government Printing Office, 1988), 83–4.

[7]Author interview, 13 April 1990.

[8]Two other investigations led to findings of potential harm but, in each case, the White House was able to work out compromises that did not involve import restrictions. In the case of ferroalloys, the administration decided to try to keep some firms alive by paying them to process and upgrade materials being held in federal stockpiles; see Levine, 137. See also US Department of Commerce, International Trade Administration, Office of Industrial Resource Administration, *The Effect of Imports of Chromium, Manganese and Silicon Ferroalloys and Related Materials on the National Security* (Washington, D.C.: US Department of Commerce, 1982). On the government's handling of the ball-bearing industry, see US Department of Commerce, International Trade Administration, Office of Industrial Resource Administration, *The Effect of Imports of Anti-Friction Bearings on National Security* (Washington, D.C.: Department of Commerce, July 1988); US Congress, Senate, Committee on Small Business, *Problems Confronting the Domestic Ball- and Roller-Bearing Industry,* hearing, 100th Cong., 2nd sess. (Washington, D.C.: US Government Printing Office, 1988); and "Presidential Decision: Anti-Friction Bearing Section 232 National Security Import Investigation," *Federal Register* 54 (11) (18 January 1989): 1975.

[9]Clyde Prestowitz, *Trading Places* (New York: Basic Books, 1988), 224.

[10]See "Statement on the Machine Tool Industry, May 20, 1986," in *Public Papers of Ronald Reagan: 1986,* bk. 1 (Washington, D.C.: US Government Printing Office, 1988), 632–3. And "Statement on the Revitalization of the Machine Tool

Industry, December 16, 1986," in *Public Papers of Ronald Reagan: 1986,* bk. 2 (Washington, D.C.: US Government Printing Office, 1989), 1632–3.

[11]See, for instance, William J. Long, "Expand the Military-Industrial Complex? No—It's Unnecessary and Inefficient," *Orbis* 33 (4) (Fall 1989): 549–59.

[12]On this period, see I. M. Destler, *American Trade Politics: System Under Stress* (Washington, D.C.: Institute for International Economics, 1986).

[13]Prestowitz carries an extensive account of the Commerce Department's view of these cases; see esp. 56, 217–45.

[14]See the testimony by the associate director of the Federal Emergency Management Agency in US Congress, House, Subcommittee on Economic Stabilization, Committee on Banking, Finance, and Urban Affairs, *Defense Production Act Amendments of 1989,* 100th Cong., 1st sess. (Washington, D.C.: US Government Printing Office, 1989), H.R. 486, 100.

[15]For general accounts see Jean-Claude Derian, *America's Struggle for Leadership in Technology* (Cambridge: MIT Press, 1990); David C. Mowery and Nathan Rosenberg, *Technology and the Pursuit of Economic Growth* (New York: Cambridge University Press, 1990), 123–68; Congressional Budget Office, *Using Federal R&D to Promote Commercial Innovation* (Washington, D.C.: US Government Printing Office, 1988); and Kenneth Flamm and Thomas L. Mc-Naugher, "Rationalizing Technology Investments," in John D. Steinbrunner, ed., *Restructuring American Foreign Policy* (Washington, D.C.: Brookings Institution, 1989), 119–57.

[16]See the testimony of Lewis Branscomb in US Congress, Senate, Subcommittee on Science, Technology, and Space, Committee on Commerce, Science, and Transportation, *National Science and Technology Policy,* 100th Cong., 1st sess. (Washington, D.C.: US Government Printing Office, 1989), 12. See also, US Congress, Office of Technology Assessment, *Holding the Edge: Maintaining the Defense Technology Base* (Washington, D.C.: US Government Printing Office, 1989), OTA-ISC-420, 33–38; and Department of Commerce, *Emerging Technologies: A Survey of Technical and Economic Opportunities* (Washington, D.C.: Department of Commerce, 1990), xiii.

[17]Report of the Defense Science Board Task Force, *Defense Semiconductor Dependency* (Washington, D.C.: Department of Defense, 1987), esp. 26–84.

[18]See the remarks of Congressman Edward Markey (D.-Massachusetts) in US Congress, House, Subcommittee on Telecommunications and Finance, Committee on Energy and Commerce, *High Definition Television,* hearings, 100th Cong. (Washington, D.C.: US Government Printing Office, 1989), 213. See also Robert B. Cohen and Kenneth Donow, *Telecommunications Policy, High Definition Television, and U.S. Competitiveness* (Washington, D.C.: Economic Policy Institute, 1989), 1.

[19]See, for example, Office of Technology Assessment, *Making Things Better: Competing in Manufacturing,* OTA-ITE-443 (Washington, D.C.: US Government Printing Office, 1990), 80–89; also Office of Technology Assessment, *The Big Picture: HDTV and High-Resolution Systems,* OTA-BP-CIT-64 (Washington, D.C.: US Government Printing Office, 1990), 61–77; and Jeffrey A. Hart and

Laura Tyson, "Responding to the Challenge of HDTV," *California Management Review* (Summer 1989): 132–45.

20On Sematech, see General Accounting Office, *Federal Research: The Sematech Consortium's Start-up Activities*, GAO/RCED-90-37 (Washington, D.C.: GAO, 1989). For a proposed HDTV program see testimony by the vice president of the American Electronics Association in US Congress, Senate, Committee on Commerce, Science, and Transportation, *Commercialization of New Technologies*, hearing, 100th Cong., 1st sess. (Washington, D.C.: US Government Printing Office, 1990), 56–64.

21See "Turn off HDTV Subsidies," *Washington Times*, 14 June 1990. Parts of the case against HDTV are presented in Office of Technology Assessment, *The Big Picture*, 10–12.

22See statement of Craig Fields in US Congress, Senate, Committee on Armed Services, *Department of Defense Authorization for Appropriations for Fiscal Years 1990 and 1991*, hearings, 101st Cong., 1st sess. (Washington, D.C.: US Government Printing Office, 1989), 198–205; and the testimony of Secretary of Commerce Robert Mosbacher in *High Definition Television*, 101st Cong., 1st sess. (Washington, D.C.: US Government Printing Office, 1990), 12–16.

23See Hobart Rowen, "The Verdict's Still Out on High-Tech Help," *Washington Post*, 24 September 1989; Andrew Pollack, "The Setback for Advanced TV," *The New York Times*, 30 September 1989; John Markoff, "Pentagon's Technology Chief Out," *The New York Times*, 21 April 1990; John Burgess and Stuart Auerbach, "Official's Transfer Prompts Hill Inquiry," *Washington Post*, 25 April 1990; and Evelyn Richards, "Uncle Sam as Venture Capitalist," *Washington Post*, 29 April 1990.

24See "A Talk With John Sununu: 'We Ought to Make Changes That Help the Whole System,'" *Business Week*, 5 February 1990, 59. Also Peter Riddell, "Contesting the Cost of Rebuilding America," *Financial Times*, 14 June 1990.

25Edward M. Graham and Paul R. Krugman, *Foreign Direct Investment in the United States* (Washington, D.C.: Institute for International Economics, 1989), 44.

26See Defense Science Board, *The Defense Industrial and Technology Base* (Washington, D.C.: Defense Science Board, Office of the Undersecretary of Defense for Acquisition, 1988), 37.

27Art Pine, "U.S. Considers Challenging the Merger of Schlumberger and Fujitsu Chip Units," *Wall Street Journal*, 31 October 1986; Mike Tharp, "Uncertainty on Fairchild-Fujitsu Plan Grows as Justice Agency Begins Review," *Wall Street Journal*, 17 November 1986; Andrew Pollack, "Fujitsu Chip Deal Draws More Flak," *The New York Times*, 12 January 1987; William Safire, "Goodbye, Mr. Chips," *The New York Times*, 26 January 1987; and Brenton B. Schlender, "Plans to Acquire U.S. Chip Maker," *Wall Street Journal*, 17 March 1987.

28See Peter T. Kilborn, "Two in Cabinet Fight Sale to Japanese," *The New York Times*, 12 March 1987; also David E. Sanger, "Japanese Purchase of Chip Maker Canceled After Objections in U.S.," *The New York Times*, 17 March 1987.

29See the discussion in US Congress, Senate, Committee on Commerce, Science and Transportation, *Acquisitions by Foreign Companies*, hearing, 100th Cong., 1st sess. (Washington, D.C.: US Government Printing Office, 1987), 1–20.

[30]For the Commerce Department position see US Congress, House, Subcommittee on Commerce, Consumer Protection, and Competitiveness, Committee on Energy and Commerce, *Foreign Takeovers and National Security,* 100th Cong., 1st sess. (Washington, D.C.: US Government Printing Office, 1988), 15–24. For the views of the Defense Department see hearing before the Subcommittee on Economic Stabilization of the House Committee on Banking, Finance and Urban Affairs, *Mergers and Acquisitions-Foreign Investments,* US Congress, 100th Cong., 1st sess. (Washington, D.C.: US Government Printing Office, 1988), 9–21 and 42–49.

[31]General Accounting Office, *Foreign Investment: Analyzing National Security Concerns,* GAO/NSIAD-90-94 (Washington, D.C.: GAO, 1990), 18, 24–5.

[32]See General Accounting Office, *Foreign Investment,* 9.

[33]US Congress, Office of Technology Assessment, *Arming Our Allies: Cooperation and Competition in Defense Technology* (Washington, D.C.: US Government Printing Office, 1990), 41.

[34]For general overviews, see Judith K. Cole, "Evaluating Offset Agreements: A Balance of Advantages," *Law and Policy in International Business* 19 (4) (1987): 765–809. Also, US Congress, House, Subcommittee on Economic Stabilization, Committee on Banking, Finance, and Urban Affairs, *The Impact of Countertrade and Offset Agreements on the U.S. Economy,* hearing, 98th Cong., 2nd sess. (Washington, D.C.: US Government Printing Office, 1984); and Office of Management and Budget, *Offsets in Military Exports* (Washington, D.C.: OMB, 1990), 16–24.

[35]For the DoD position on offsets, see testimony in US Congress, House, Subcommittee on International Economic Policy and Trade, Committee on Foreign Affairs, *Countertrade and Offsets in International Trade,* hearings, 100th Cong., 1st sess. (Washington, D.C.: US Government Printing Office, 1988), 185–95.

[36]For the early controversy over these findings see US Congress, House, Subcommittee on Economic Stabilization, Committee on Banking, Finance, and Urban Affairs, *Offset Agreements,* hearing, 99th Cong., 2nd sess. (Washington, D.C.: US Government Printing Office, 1986).

[37]See General Accounting Office, *U.S.-Japan Co-development: Review of the FS-X Program,* GAO/NSIAD-90–77BR (Washington, D.C.: GAO, February 1990).

[38]See testimony of Edward C. Bursk, chairman of the International Council, *Aerospace Industries Association in Implications of the FS-X Aircraft Agreement,* 84.

[39]For a list of the technologies most important for designing future weapons, see Department of Defense, *Critical Technologies Plan* (Washington, D.C.: DoD, 1990). For a projection of likely national leadership in many of these areas, see US Department of Commerce, *Emerging Technologies.*

Michael Mastanduno

The United States Defiant: Export Controls in the Postwar Era

A STRIKING PARADOX OF US FOREIGN POLICY has been the country's pervasive use of export controls as instruments to prevent the buildup of other countries' military strength, weaken their economic capabilities, influence their domestic or foreign policies, and signal approval or disapproval of their behavior.

At first glance, the widespread use of export controls as a weapon of national security and foreign policy seems to have involved the negation or suppression of some basic values in the national political culture. It has involved systematic interference with the operation of market forces, has overridden the pressures of the US business community, and has bestowed powers of arbitrary choice upon the federal bureaucracy.

Moreover, the globalization trend of markets, technology, and industrial structure has exacerbated the contradictions between the country's export control policies and its larger policy orientations. For example, the United States's growing reliance on foreign markets to maintain domestic economic growth and prosperity has increased the direct and indirect costs of employing export controls. At the same time, a number of other factors have reduced the effectiveness and added to the costs of such controls: the diffusion of technology beyond US borders and the creation of alternate sources of supply; the proliferation of multinational enterprises; and the increasing dependence of the military on technologies shared with commercial markets.

Michael Mastanduno is Assistant Professor of Government at Dartmouth College.

A SEARCH FOR CAUSES

In export control policy, the United States has acted in defiance of globalization.[1] Other essays in this volume suggest that the propensity of the United States to employ export controls for foreign policy purposes has been much stronger than that of most other industrialized countries. What accounts for the distinctiveness of US policy?

The giant size and relative insensitivity of the US economy to the effects of international trade may provide a partial answer. But those characteristics can hardly explain why the United States has resorted to controls with greater regularity even as its economy has become more sensitive to, and dependent upon, international trade.

The content of US foreign policy could also suggest an explanation, but it is one that at best seems incomplete. True, the extensive foreign policy agenda of the United States has generated more occasions for action than would be the case for governments with less extensive foreign policy interests. The country's determination to project its internal values, such as anticommunism and the promotion of human rights, and its interest in restricting the proliferation of nuclear weapons has produced numerous occasions for considering the use of pressure on foreign countries. Yet, given the mounting economic costs and the declining efficacy of export controls, their persistent use by US officials still calls for explanation.

Part of that explanation lies in history. In a classic study of the embargo policies of World War II, W. M. Medlicott emphasizes the distinctive US "style" of economic warfare, highlighting such features as the aggressive use of US economic power to ensure the compliance of other governments.[2] His analysis suggests that US officials tended to exaggerate the wartime accomplishments of export control policy, and thus heightened their expectations of its efficacy in the Cold War.

Of greater importance, the early phases of the Cold War prompted the United States to build on wartime experiences with an extraordinary set of laws, institutional arrangements, and political relationships for continuing to pressure other governments. Notwithstanding the general commitment of the United States to promote a liberal international economic order, the country's export control system in the early Cold War period maintained the wartime shift in the burden of proof from those in government seeking to control advanced technology to those in industry seeking to export it. At that stage, the US private sector had not yet developed a stake in the export of technology to the communist bloc; and where matters of security were concerned, it had carried over from wartime an attitude of deference and acquiescence to government officials. By the late 1980s, despite drastic changes in the global economic environment and in the requirements of US security, the attitudes, relationships, and institutions formed in the early Cold War period had not greatly altered.

Although US policymakers have been slow to react, they have not been oblivious to the globalization trend. Indeed, since the 1960s, export controls have proven to be one of the most contentious issues in US foreign policy, at times pitting government against industry, the executive branch against Congress, and various agencies within the executive against each other. In the context of these debates, major proposals for the reform of the export control system have emerged, roughly once a decade[3]; however, attempts to cut back on the application of export controls have typically been watered down or reversed. Persistent pressures from various quarters—some from within the bureaucracy, some from outside—have usually won out.

The dramatic events of 1989–1990 in Central Europe have called into question not only the operation but also the very necessity of the postwar export control system; however the end of the Cold War is not likely to lead to the demise of the routine use of export controls. As long as the United States remains an economic power and pursues an active foreign policy, the temptation to rely heavily on export controls in support of that policy will be very strong. Such controls will be seen as having a substantial role to play, for example, in preventing a return of the Cold War with the Soviet Union and in keeping lethal technologies from ambitious dictators in the developing world. Indeed, in the aftermath of the Gulf War, the Bush administration appeared poised for a major, possibly unilateral expansion of controls, with a shift from the East-West to the North-South arena. Moreover, if the United States adopts the position that economic rivalry will serve in the post-Cold War era as a substitute for great power military competition, the temptation to apply export controls will be stronger still. In short, a system that has proven extraordinarily resilient is likely to find ways to justify its continued existence.

BASIC CHARACTERISTICS

By 1947 the Truman administration was prepared to conduct comprehensive economic warfare with the explicit purpose, according to National Security Council records, of inflicting "the greatest economic injury to the USSR and its satellites."[4] To carry out that policy the administration stretched its wartime powers to control all items that were deemed to be in short supply in the domestic economy. In 1949, at the height of Cold War tensions, Congress finally provided the executive with peacetime authority to interfere systematically with US trade for reasons of national security.

The Export Control Act of 1949 was an extraordinary piece of legislation. Writing almost two decades after its passage, legal scholars Harold Berman and John Garson concluded that "no single piece of legislation gives more power to the President to control American commerce."[5] The act provided that export controls should be used to protect national security, promote the foreign policy of the United States, or prevent domestic economic shortages. As subsequent application of the law demonstrated, it was virtually impossible to conceive of an instance in which export controls could *not* be justified according to at least one of these purposes. Moreover, the act authorized the executive to "prohibit or curtail" *all* exports, commercial or military, including technical data and other intangibles. And, although ostensibly directed at the Soviet Union and its communist allies, the act enabled the executive to restrict US trade regardless of destination. For American firms, what traditionally had been a right to export suddenly became a privilege, even in peacetime, to be granted by the government.

The system that emerged in the context of the 1949 Export Control Act had several enduring features that combined to create a presumption of the dominance of political and security objectives over economic objectives. Executive officials formulated lists of items they believed could contribute significantly to the military potential of communist states. The shipment of such items was thereupon subject to control to all destinations, and the controls were to be implemented through a tedious process of case-by-case review. If a noncommunist country was the intended destination, the central question was whether an item would be diverted or transshipped to communist countries.

The process obviously left considerable discretion in the hands of executive officials. Discretionary authority was enhanced by the fact that such officials made licensing decisions in secret, and were under no obligation to provide exporters with a justification for denial. Until the 1970s, there were no time limits on executive deliberations. Firms were advised not to pressure the government for more timely responses; the result of such demands would simply be license denials.[6] Since export control authority was exempt from judicial review, aggrieved exporters could not challenge decisions in federal court.[7]

The case-by-case approach also provided incentives to executive officials to place items of questionable strategic utility under control. "Better safe than sorry" was the ruling principle. During the 1950s, most applications were expeditiously denied and very few proposed shipments to the East survived the screening process. When internal and external pressures pushed the executive to a more discriminating approach in the 1960s and 1970s, the principal effect was simply to make the review process more complex and prolonged.[8]

Another enduring feature of export control policies involved the sharing of responsibility for formulation and implementation across various executive agencies. After World War II, the lead responsibility for the administration of controls was lodged within the Commerce Department, with the expectation that it would work closely with other interested agencies. The State Department was granted the lead role in multilateral coordination, again with a presumption of close interagency coordination. Other agencies, including the Defense Department, the Central Intelligence Agency, and the Treasury, were expected to participate according to the desire and the need for their institutional expertise. Conflicts were to be resolved in a network of interagency committees and, ultimately, by the president.

This decision-making process typically generated a considerable amount of interagency conflict. By the 1970s the State, Commerce, and Defense departments were increasingly at odds regarding the purpose and extent of controls. A single agency had the power to stall the liberalization of controls in both the list review process and the determination of individual license applications. As the Defense Department gradually increased its formal and informal authority during the 1970s and 1980s, it assured the maintenance of a conservative bias in the system, even in the face of changes in global markets and the structure of international economic relations.

Still another characteristic of the US export control program has been the minimum involvement of business in the formulation of policy. In West European states and Japan, government agencies and business organizations have collaborated closely on the construction of control lists and the administration of controls, with a shared commitment to minimize economic burdens. In the United States, no such partnership has existed. US firms have been consistently frustrated by the Byzantine nature of the control system and their inability to decisively influence the substance of policy. Yet their protests on the whole have been restrained and episodic.

The tradition of business deference established in the early years of the Cold War continued into the 1950s. American firms, unlike their West European counterparts, made no effort to build a stake in the markets of communist countries. US corporate managers also tended to be chary of commerce with state-trading nations, being unfamiliar with problems of barter trade and inconvertible currencies. Moreover, US public opinion served as an inhibiting factor, exposing firms that expressed even a passing interest in this trade to charges of "trading with the enemy."[9]

It was not until the mid-1960s that some US firms began to make efforts to reduce the obstacles posed by export controls. Such efforts have continued ever since, but with only modest success. To be sure, successive amendments to the Export Control Act have been consistent in directing the executive to mitigate the burden of controls on US industry. Nevertheless, the liberalization of national security controls promised by the Export Administration Act of 1969 never fully materialized. During the 1970s, the US government increasingly resorted to controls that were not directly aimed at holding down the communist bloc's war making potential.

Provisions of the 1979 Export Act sought to circumscribe the ability of the executive to use export controls as a broad foreign policy tool. But almost immediately after its passage, the US administration imposed sanctions against the Soviet Union in reaction to its invasion of Afghanistan and against Poland in reaction to its imposition of martial law. Soon after, the US government imposed sanctions against firms based in Western Europe that were participating in the Siberian gas pipeline project. US firms lobbied successfully for the removal of pipeline sanctions, but shortly thereafter the administration embarked on a more far-reaching effort to strengthen its powers over shipments to noncommunist destinations.

The pipeline affair illustrates another characteristic of US export controls, namely, a persistent tendency of US authorities to attempt to extend the system beyond US borders. Early in the postwar era, US officials recognized that export controls would have little effect unless they were coordinated internationally. After experimenting briefly with a series of bilateral arrangements, in 1949 the United States encouraged its West European allies to participate in a multilateral control regime that has come to be known as CoCom. CoCom membership eventually came to include all NATO countries except Iceland, plus Japan and Australia. CoCom has operated on the principle of consensus. The sentiment of the great majority of its member countries has been that export controls should be narrowly focused on items of direct military utility and should interfere to the minimum extent possible with international trade.

Despite that majority sentiment, US participation in CoCom has done little to limit US efforts in the application of export controls. Upon the creation of CoCom in 1949, US officials explicitly reserved the right to maintain national security controls in excess of agreed CoCom levels. Such a position was not unrealistic at the time since the United States possessed a near monopoly in the development and production of items deemed to have national security significance. The position became less realistic as the dominant technological position of the US economy eroded. Nevertheless, the national control list of the United States has consistently been more comprehensive than the multilateral CoCom list; the United States has taken longer than other members to process license applications; and, notwithstanding the protests of other members, the United States routinely has asserted the authority to control the reexport of products and technologies originating in the United States, on the grounds that such items retain their nationality even after crossing several national borders and after having been transformed in the process of production.

In some ways, the norms of CoCom have actually *encouraged* the United States to act in defiance of the trend toward globalization of markets. As principal guardian of the regime's effectiveness, the United States has traditionally assumed responsibility for imposing CoCom controls on non-CoCom suppliers. During the 1950s this was a relatively manageable task, involving US officials in confidential, bilateral arrangements with Sweden and Switzerland, reinforced by the threat of US economic sanctions. By the 1970s and 1980s, however, the global diffusion of technology greatly complicated the effort. US officials found themselves routinely interfering in US trade with noncommunist nations in an effort to extend the effects of CoCom controls.

US efforts to make CoCom controls more effective have been directed at CoCom members as well. Although CoCom's control lists are determined by consensus, member governments are responsible for the administration and enforcement of controls. It is not surprising that there have been significant differences in the extent to which countries have enforced their controls. Beginning in 1980, the United States and its CoCom partners sought to harmonize their national systems. US frustration with the slow pace of negotiations and the seeming foot-dragging of some members, including notably West Germany and Japan, led US officials to apply US export controls directly to those countries as a source of leverage.

RESISTING REFORM

America's export control system was fashioned in the crisis circumstances of the initial Cold War era, when threats to national security were judged to be particularly severe, and before the trends associated with globalization began to exert a decisive influence on either international economic relations or the US economy. Both the 1960s and the 1970s presented the executive branch with substantial opportunities to adjust export control policy to the globalization trend. In both periods, however, reform efforts ultimately had the opposite effect, leading export control policy to become even less responsive to changes in the international environment.

The impetus for reform during the 1960s came from the palpable failure of the United States to maintain the support of its CoCom partners for a comprehensive embargo on trade with the East. During the Korean War, the United States had managed to convince its allies of the merits of that strategy, but by the war's end pressure mounted in CoCom for the relaxation of broad controls. Multilateral controls were adjusted downward in 1954, 1957, and 1958, while US controls continued largely unchanged at the levels developed during the Korean War.[10] By the late 1950s, the demand from Eastern Europe for technology and capital goods increased significantly, and firms in Western Europe and Japan rushed to satisfy it.

When the Kennedy administration took over in the early 1960s, the US position seemed scarcely tenable. To many, maintaining a differential between US and CoCom controls seemed economically irrational; it was denying US firms the benefits of trade while doing little to affect the economic or military potential of the Soviet bloc. An alternative possibility was for the United States to adjust its national controls downward to the CoCom consensus and to simplify its licensing procedures, thereby enabling US firms to compete on a more equal footing. Such a move would have diplomatic benefits as well, relieving US officials of the persistent need to twist the arms of other Western states in an effort to replicate US controls. Another option was for the United States to try to use its controls as a bargaining counter to extract political concessions from the Soviet Union and other communist states; under that option, trade liberalization would take place primarily as an instrument of politics, relegating economic objectives to second place.

The struggle to adjust US policy persisted throughout the 1960s. A majority in Congress seemed to prefer the status quo, despite its seeming irrationality and despite its defiance of the liberal tradition. Interested US firms, still limited in number and influence, supported the idea of placing US controls on a more equal footing with others. However, the executive branch, primarily through officials in the White House and the State Department, expressed a preference for using controls as a bargaining chip.

Until the end of the decade, the congressional view prevailed. The Export Control Act was revised in 1962, making it more difficult for the executive to liberalize national security controls. Subsequent legislation prevented executive officials from granting most-favored-nation status or export credits as a means of building bridges to the East.[11]

With the winding down of the Vietnam War and the onset of US-USSR detente, however, economic considerations gained weight. The payments position of the United States was rapidly eroding and the competitive position of US business was declining. The Export Administration Act of 1969 reflected these concerns, finding that

> the unwarranted restriction of exports from the U.S. has a serious adverse effect on our balance of payments. The uncertainty of policy toward certain categories of exports has curtailed the efforts of American business in these categories to the detriment of the overall attempt to improve the trade balance of the United States.[12]

The act called for the downward revision of the US control list and closer cooperation with the US business community.

The partnership between government and business envisioned in the act never emerged. The reason was evident: although both the business community and the executive supported trade liberalization, they did so for very different reasons. US firms were interested in economic benefits, while the executive was more interested in the manipulation of trade to achieve foreign policy objectives. Henry Kissinger, then national security advisor, summarized the Nixon administration's attitude, noting that "expanding trade without a political *quid pro quo* was a gift; there was little the Soviets could do for us economically."[13] Samuel Huntington, later serving on the National Security Council in the Carter administration, made a similar point in calling for "conditioned flexibility" in export control policy and suggesting that the United States must be prepared to "open and close the economic door" as foreign policy interests warranted.[14]

Such differences explain why the Nixon administration made no serious move to reduce export controls until 1973, after it had extracted various political concessions from the Soviets. Subsequently, the Carter administration added items to the list with the explicit intention of maximizing potential foreign policy leverage.[15] As of 1979, the US control list was still significantly more comprehensive than that observed by other CoCom members. And the US government still took substantially longer than other governments to render decisions on any given license request.[16] By that time, the Commerce Department had become more responsive to industry concerns, but the Defense Department was still assessing license requests according to the Cold War criteria of the 1950s and 1960s.[17]

During this period, another development underlined the relative weakness of those who were troubled by the economic implications of using export controls for political ends. By the late 1970s, the US government was using export controls for foreign policy purposes that extended well beyond relations with the Soviet Union. What has been called the "sanctions habit" became institutionalized, and the interruption or manipulation of trade became a standard US response to a wide range of foreign policy problems.[18] During the 1970s, the target list included Cuba, North Korea, North Vietnam, Kampuchea, Uganda, Ethiopia, Libya, South Africa, Namibia, Chile, Argentina, Nicaragua, Iran, and Pakistan; objectionable behavior included the violation of human rights, support for international terrorism, participation in regional conflicts, and efforts to acquire nuclear capabilities.[19]

The gradual expansion in the targets and purposes of export controls understandably created alarm and frustration in the US business community. US firms had begun their lobbying efforts for the relaxation of national security controls on trade with the East during the 1960s. By the late 1970s they continued to face significant disadvantages in that area. By that time, however, they also were confronting export controls aimed at securing foreign policy objectives only remotely related to security. The latter were in some ways a more significant obstacle since they could occur at any time, against any target, for myriad reasons. Moreover, when the United States employed these new controls, it tended to do so unilaterally; accordingly, such restraining effects as CoCom might have had on US behavior in the security field were not even present in these cases.

Another major opportunity to adjust export control policy to the imperatives of globalization emerged in the mid-1970s. In an effort to check the pressures for trade liberalization that had been generated by detente, the Defense Department directed its Defense Science Board to conduct a comprehensive investigation of the United States's technology control policies, an investigation chaired by J. Fred Bucy, then executive vice president of Texas Instruments. The resulting study—completed in 1976 and commonly known as the Bucy report—proved extremely influential, and its logic and arguments set the framework for policy debate over national security export controls in both the Carter and Reagan administrations.[20]

The report was unequivocal on one major issue of interest to the business community, namely, whether export controls should be applied to transactions with friendly Western countries. While advocating the strengthening of CoCom, the Bucy report simultaneously called for a more vigilant US approach, recommending that "for the most critical technologies, the US should not release know-how beyond its borders, and then depend on CoCom for absolute control." It recommended sanctions against CoCom members that the United States believed inadequately protected critical technology, including the denial of such technologies. With regard to countries that were not members of CoCom, the report called for even more stringent restrictions: "The U.S. should release to neutral countries only the technology we would be willing to transfer directly to Communist countries."

The Bucy report's central recommendations, however, were directed at another issue, namely, the type of transactions to be placed under control. According to the report, the existing system overemphasized the control of products and underemphasized that of technology; the result was said to be a control list that was far too long and a licensing system that was far too cumbersome. The key to military superiority, according to the Bucy report, was the mastery and control of design and manufacturing know-how; all other considerations were secondary. Thus, export controls needed to be reoriented to focus on the small subset of "critical technologies" and "keystone equipment," the export of which would result in "revolutionary advances" in the military capabilities of potential adversaries; that emphasis, it was thought, would produce a shorter and more manageable list.

The impact of the Bucy report's recommendation to concentrate on critical technologies, however, depended on how such technologies were defined. On this score, the report carried a telling observation, obviously at variance with the idea of a narrow list of controlled technologies; it suggested that the widespread use of Western computers, even in commercial applications, would enhance the "cultural preparedness" of the Soviet Union and Eastern Europe to exploit advanced technology, which could be detrimental to Western security.

Nevertheless, when the Carter administration addressed the recommendations in the Bucy report, its reactions seemed reassuring to the business community. The administration decided explicitly not to extend technology controls to Western destinations on the grounds that the resulting economic and diplomatic costs would outweigh the potential national security benefits.[21] The possibility that the range of transactions covered by the controls might be more narrowly focused, however, swiftly melted away. In 1978, Bucy himself was asked to advise the administration on a highly significant case involving a $144 million export license request from Dresser Industries for the export of technologies for deep well drilling and drill bit manufacture. Bucy confirmed the fears of US exporters by concluding that these were critical technologies that should be restricted by the US government.[22]

The propensity of federal agencies to define critical technologies very broadly was reaffirmed in other developments. In 1977, responding to the Bucy recommendation, the Carter administration directed the relevant agencies to develop a list of such technologies. When completed four years later, the list made a mockery of the notion that a focus on technology would result in a more streamlined export control system. According to RAND analyst Thane Gufstafson, the initial list contained

> a virtual roll-call of contemporary techniques, including videodisk recording, polymeric materials, and many dozens of others equally broad. If this collection had automatically become the basis for the official Commodity Control List, the entire Department of Commerce would not have been large enough to administer the export control program.[23]

The process by which the list was constructed helps to explain its all-encompassing content. The Defense Department's Office of Defense Research and Engineering received nominations from numerous agencies, including the military services, NASA, Defense Intelligence, the CIA, the National Security Agency, and the State and Commerce departments. Each agency contributed what it deemed to be militarily critical technologies with little regard for the question of whether effective control of the technology was a realistic possibility. In the end, the list seemed intended to simply add extensive new controls over technology to the existing controls over products.

In the end, neither the bureaucracy nor the affected industries quite had their way. Industry representatives spent the better part of the 1980s seeking to block the Defense Department and its congressional supporters from substituting the new list for the existing and already burdensome Commodity Control List. Although the substitution did not occur, US representatives in CoCom nevertheless made frequent use of the new list to guide their initiatives in that body.[24]

RESTRICTIONS WITHOUT RESTRAINT

Ronald Reagan took office in 1981 with a commitment to advance the interests of US business. Yet, far from responding to business complaints and changes in the US economic position, the Reagan administration in the 1980s made greater use of the far-reaching authority to control exports that had been granted to the executive at the beginning of the Cold War. During the 1970s the Soviets had stepped up their efforts to acquire significant technologies of military importance from the West, and their new programs seemed to be paying off.[25] Since the administration was proposing to invest heavily in a wide array of advanced technologies for military purposes, it was anxious to plug existing leaks. At the same time, administration officials saw an opportunity to exacerbate the Soviet industrial slowdown, forcing the regime to confront a series of difficult trade-offs among consumption, investment, defense spending, and foreign commitments.

The Reagan administration's increased emphasis on export controls as a strategic instrument coincided with an increase in the power of the Department of Defense in the policy process. One of several key players during the 1970s, the DoD emerged by the early 1980s as an even more dominant influence in export control decision making. Defense officials expanded their influence by drawing upon an amendment to the Export Administration Act in 1974, which granted the DoD a formal role (and informal veto) in the review of license applications for Eastern destinations. The Bucy report, which had recommended a lead role for the DoD in the process of formulating lists of regulated items, also contributed to DoD's growing influence. Of greater importance, key Defense officials such as Secretary Caspar Weinberger and Assistant Secretary Richard Perle placed a higher priority than their counterparts in other agencies on exercising control over US policy in this area and were willing to devote significant departmental resources to the task. The DoD, for instance, funded a major enforcement program of the Customs Service, partly in order to assist Customs in wresting control over enforcement from DoD's main institutional rival, the Commerce Department.[26] By 1985, the Defense Department had outmaneuvered the Commerce Department to gain a formal role in licensing decisions related to shipments outside the communist bloc and had rolled over the State Department to increase its influence in CoCom negotiations.[27]

The ascendancy of the Defense Department had an especially severe impact on policies affecting trade with noncommunist countries. Until the Reagan era, most administrations had made some attempt to minimize the impact of East-West trade controls on US economic relations with noncommunist states. In 1954 the Eisenhower administration drew back from attempting to extend US controls to West European destinations, accepting instead a CoCom compromise. In 1978 the Carter administration rejected the recommendation of the Bucy report to expand restrictions on trade with noncommunist countries. Indeed, until 1982, the Commerce Department routinely validated applications for export to the noncommunist world with little or no review.

The Reagan administration's departure from earlier policies on export controls produced a new wave of clashes with allies. The most dramatic example, of course, involved the US effort to terminate Western participation in the Siberian gas pipeline deal by asserting US jurisdiction over the sales of US-owned subsidiaries located in Western Europe. While the assertion of extraterritoriality was not new, the manner in which the United States exercised that contentious authority was unprecedented. The administration drew upon a 1977 amendment to the Export Administration Act empowering the executive, even in the absence of war or national emergency, to regulate the exports of US-owned subsidiaries in foreign countries. It sought to apply its contested authority not only to such subsidiaries but also to the licensees of US-owned enterprises in Western Europe. Finally, the US administration proposed to apply its newly assumed powers retroactively, to transactions previously consummated.

It is not surprising that governments in Western Europe resisted, formally protesting that the retroactive exercise of already questionable authority was "contrary to international law" and constituted "unacceptable interference in the commercial policy of the European Community."[28] The US government was not deterred and subsequently applied punitive sanctions against firms based in Western Europe that were participating in the pipeline project.

The pipeline sanctions episode was not an isolated event in the Reagan administration's efforts to restrict technology transfer among noncommunist countries. Its principal instrument was an assertion of control not only over US exports but also over reexports from other countries. Firms in Britain, West Germany, Spain, Sweden, and other Western countries faced licensing delays and the threat of being barred from access to US technology and components, particularly in the computer and electronics areas.

The administration's efforts reached even further. In the early 1980s, administration officials denied some foreign nationals who had been invited to meetings in the United States the right to attend such meetings or to have access to scientific papers and computer programs.[29] According to officials of Britain's International Computers Ltd., the US government demanded that the firm obtain export licenses for the know-how carried in the minds of US engineers they had hired.[30] In addition, the administration cracked down on the issuance of licenses authorizing multiple shipments of controlled items to approved end users in noncommunist states. Several prominent US firms, including Digital Equipment, had such license privileges restricted when some of their equipment was found to have been transshipped to the Soviet Union.[31]

The efforts of the Reagan administration bore some fruit. CoCom controls were strengthened, and some countries outside of CoCom, including Sweden, Austria, South Korea, Spain, and Australia, were persuaded to tighten up their restrictions as well; indeed, the latter two eventually joined CoCom. Nevertheless, the administration appeared to be waging an uphill battle. As US officials concluded negotiations with one set of suppliers, using access to US technology as the principal source of leverage, other suppliers appeared. In 1989, US negotiators were engaged in discussions with Indonesia, Malaysia, Taiwan, Pakistan, and Brazil, among others.

The benefits to national security from these efforts at restriction were achieved at considerable cost not only in diplomatic but also in economic terms. During the 1970s, US manufacturing firms had acquired a reputation as being unreliable suppliers in the East. During the 1980s, many acquired that same reputation in noncommunist markets. By the middle of the decade, there was considerable evidence that foreign firms were moving away from US sources of supply in sectors most affected by export controls.[32]

The efforts of US industry to reverse the DoD-inspired policy bore little fruit until 1987, when concern over the record-breaking trade deficits of the United States led the White House to launch a program designed to improve the position of US firms in world trade. At the same time, the link between declining US competitiveness and the expansion of export controls was dramatically publicized in a study of the National Academy of Sciences mentioned earlier. Finally, the relaxation of tensions between the United States and the Soviet Union induced US officials to reconsider the balance between economic and national security objectives in their export control policy.

Even with the support of the White House, however, proponents of trade liberalization were not home free. Although significant progress was made during 1987 and 1988 in scaling back controls applied to noncommunist destinations, the Defense Department did not abandon its opposition and managed to delay, water down, or turn back several liberalizing initiatives.[33] By the first year of the Bush administration, US firms and allies continued to struggle against what they regarded as an overly comprehensive control list, as well as a burdensome, case-by-case licensing process.

FACING THE FUTURE

The ongoing debate over US export control policy was overtaken by the dramatic events of 1989–1990: the end of the Cold War, the disintegration of Soviet power in Eastern Europe, and the political and economic reforms inside the Soviet Union. These developments called into question the necessity of the national and multilateral export control regimes that had been created as an instrument of the Cold War.

A reappraisal took place in 1990, driven primarily by the Bush administration's fear that cooperation in CoCom would collapse altogether in the absence of drastic US initiatives in the direction of trade liberalization. At a historic high-level CoCom meeting in June 1990, the United States agreed to fundamental changes in the multilateral control system. Among other things, US negotiators endorsed a scheme whereby East European states could eventually be removed from the list of CoCom targets, provided that they developed satisfactory measures to prevent the transshipment of controlled technology to the Soviet Union. Of greater importance, US representatives agreed to scrap the existing CoCom list of dual-use technologies and to create from scratch a highly selective "core list." After sometimes contentious negotiations, such a list—which the Bucy report seemed to have envisioned fourteen years earlier—was adopted by CoCom members in May 1991.[34]

The US experience in the postwar era suggests that those who wish to use export controls as an instrument of national power will prove adept at resisting change and at adapting control policies to new purposes and targets. A number of possibilities exist with regard to the future direction of export control policy.

One possibility is that US officials will abandon the core list and return to more restrictive controls on trade with the former republics of the Soviet Union, in particular, Russia. Such an initiative would most likely be prompted by a decisive shift to the right in Russian politics, accompanied by corresponding changes in Russian domestic and foreign policy. Indeed, following the Soviet crackdown in Lithuania early in 1991, the Bush administration delayed CoCom negotiations, placing efforts to create a short core list in jeopardy. While the administration did eventually agree to the core list, it accepted the advice of the Department of Defense and the National Security Agency to resist liberalization in two critical areas in which competition to sell to the East had been particularly intense— computers and telecommunications.[35] US officials justified these continued restrictions—and indeed the maintenance of the CoCom regime—on the grounds that the Soviet Union remained a formidable military power, and that CoCom controls provided an insurance policy in the event of a return to political conflict with the Soviet Union or its successor.

A stronger possibility is that export control policy will continue to shift from an emphasis on the former Soviet Union and Eastern Europe to the control of nuclear, chemical, biological, and ballistic missile technologies to all destinations. In that case, the principal targets will be the countries of the developing world, in particular the Middle East and North Africa. By the end of the 1980s, interested members of Congress were floating the idea of reorienting US controls and the CoCom agreements in that direction.[36]

A key issue, as usual, has been the need for multilateral coordination. As was the case for East-West controls, US officials have proved willing to proceed unilaterally in pursuit of national security objectives, even if this has meant placing US firms at a competitive disadvantage. For example, during the 1980s, despite its failure to convince other suppliers to cooperate, the United States adopted extensive measures aimed at blocking nuclear proliferation, including controls on commercial technologies that could be put to nuclear use. Early in 1991, under the impetus of the Gulf War, the Bush administration launched an Enhanced Proliferation Control Initiative, designed to bring under control a broad array of technologies and products that could be useful in the development of biological and chemical weapons, as well as of ballistic missiles. US industry braced for a new round of conflict with the US government, aware that other governments might resist imposing similar controls. The new program contemplated license requirements not only for such widely available items as desktop computers and chemical manufacturing plants, but even for items such as pocket calculators and slide rules.[37] Yet as one US official commented, the concerns of US industry were not likely to carry great weight because neither politicians nor industry officials would want to be accused of being "soft" on proliferation—any more than they wanted to be viewed as soft on communism during the Cold War.[38]

A final possibility is that US export control policy could shift in a more radical direction—to a pursuit for competitive economic advantage in relations with Japan and Europe. Although such an approach seems unlikely in light of the dominant US ideology, it does appear to strike a responsive chord in at least some segments of US government and industry. In the context of the Toshiba incident in 1987, when the United States had imposed sanctions on Toshiba, ostensibly for violating agreed CoCom export controls, it was difficult to determine whether the US Congress sought to punish the Japanese firm for diverting critical technology to the East or for its economic success in the US market. The FSX episode of 1989, involving the reconsideration of a defense agreement on the grounds that it might provide commercial advantages to Japan, raised the issue of competitive economic advantage among Western states even more explicitly. By 1990 it was apparent that the US defense and intelligence communities might be mobilizing to assist US firms in global economic competition.[39]

In short, the prospects for export control policy in the 1990s remain uncertain. The collapse of the Cold War and the continued march of globalization cannot be counted on to weaken the attachment of the US government to export controls as an instrument of statecraft.

ENDNOTES

[1]For a general treatment, see Kenneth Oye, "International System Structure and American Foreign Policy," in Kenneth Oye, ed., *Eagle Defiant* (Boston: Little, Brown, 1983), 3–32.

[2]See W. M. Medlicott, *The Economic Blockade*, vol. 2 (London: H.M.S.O., 1952 and 1959), 411–15, 659–61.

[3]See, for example, J. Irwin Miller, et. al., *Report to the President of the Special Committee on U.S. Trade Relations with East European Countries and the Soviet Union* (Washington, D.C.: The White House, 29 April 1965); Defense Science Board Task Force, *An Analysis of Export Control of Advanced Technology: A DoD Perspective* (Washington, D.C.: Office of Defense Research and Engineering, 4 February 1976); and National Academy of Sciences, *Balancing the National Interest: U.S. National Security Export Controls and Global Economic Competition* (Washington, D.C.: National Academy Press, 1987).

[4]Report by the National Security Council, "Control of Exports to the U.S.S.R. and Eastern Europe," cited in William Long, *U.S. Export Control Policy: Executive Autonomy vs. Congressional Reform* (New York: Columbia University Press, 1990), 15.

[5]Harold J. Berman and John R. Garson, "United States Export Controls—Past, Present, and Future," *Columbia Law Review* 67 (5) (May 1967): 791–890, at 792.

[6]Long, 21; and US Congress, Office of Technology Assessment, *Technology and East-West Trade* (Washington, D.C.: US Government Printing Office, 1979).

[7]Franklin D. Cordell and John L. Ellicott, "Judicial Review under the Export Administration Act of 1979: Is It Time to Open the Courthouse Doors to U.S. Exporters?," in National Academy of Sciences, *Finding Common Ground: US Export Controls in a Changed Global Environment* (Washington, D.C.: National Academy Press, 1991), app. H, 321–35.

[8]See Office of Technology Assessment; and US General Accounting Office, *Administration of U.S. Export Licensing Should Be Consolidated to Be More Responsive to Industry* (Washington, D.C.: US Government Printing Office, 31 October 1978).

9See, for example, Nathaniel McKitterick, *East-West Trade: The Background of U.S. Policy* (New York: Twentieth Century Fund, 1966), 44–47.

10Gunnar Adler-Karlsson, *Western Economic Warfare, 1947–1967* (Stockholm: Almquist and Wiksell, 1968).

11See Thomas A. Wolf, *U.S. East-West Trade Policy: Economic Warfare vs. Economic Welfare* (Lexington, Mass.: Lexington Books, 1973).

12Export Administration Act of 1969 (Public Law 91–182), sec. 2.

13Henry Kissinger, *White House Years* (Boston: Little, Brown, 1979), 152.

14Samuel Huntington, "Trade, Technology and Leverage: Economic Diplomacy," *Foreign Policy* 32 (Fall 1978): 63–80.

15See US Congress, Senate, Committee on Banking, Housing, and Urban Affairs, *Use of Export Controls and Export Credits for Foreign Policy Purposes*, hearings, 95th Cong., 2nd sess., October 1978.

16See US General Accounting Office, *Administration of U.S. Export Licensing*; and US General Accounting Office, *Export Controls: Need to Clarify Policy and Simplify Administration* (Washington, D.C.: US Government Printing Office, 1 March 1979).

17Robert Klitgaard, "Limiting Exports on National Security Grounds," in *Commission on the Organization of the Government for the Conduct of Foreign Policy*, vol. 4 (Washington, D.C.: US Government Printing Office, 1976), pt. 7, 443–75.

18See Kenneth Abbott, "Linking Trade to Political Goals: Foreign Policy Export Controls in the 1970s and 1980s," *Minnesota Law Review* 65 (5) (1981): 739–889.

19A detailed list can be found in Gary Clyde Hufbauer and Jeffrey J. Schott, with the assistance of Kimberly Elliott, *Economic Sanctions Reconsidered* (Washington, D.C.: Institute for International Economics, 1985).

20US Office of Defense Research and Engineering, *An Analysis of Export Control of Advanced Technology: A DoD Perspective* (hereafter Bucy report), (Washington, D.C.: Office of Defense Research and Engineering, 4 February 1976). The various quotations are from iii, 1–3, 25, 29.

21Report of the President to the Congress, prepared for US Congress, House, Subcommittee on International Security and Scientific Affairs, Committee on International Relations, *International Transfer of Technology*, 95th Cong., 2nd sess., December 1978.

22See the statement of J. Fred Bucy in US Congress, Senate, Permanent Subcommittee on Investigations, Transfer of Technology, and the Dresser Industries Export Licensing Actions, Committee on Governmental Affairs, hearings, 95th Cong., 2nd sess., 3 October 1978, 6–10. See also Machinery and Allied Products Institute, *U.S. Technology and Export Controls* (Washington, D.C.: MAPI, April 1978).

23Thane Gufstafson, *Selling the Russians the Rope? Soviet Technology Policy and U.S. Export Controls* (Santa Monica, Calif.: RAND, 1981), 4.

24See National Academy of Sciences, *Finding Common Ground*, 95–96.

25See US Central Intelligence Agency, *Soviet Acquisition of Western Technology* (Washington, D.C.: Central Intelligence Agency, April 1982); and US Department of Defense, *Soviet Acquisition of Militarily Significant Western Technology: An Update* (Washington, D.C.: Department of Defense, September 1985).

26See Linda Melvern et. al., *Technobandits: How the Soviets are Stealing America's High-Tech Future* (Boston: Houghton Mifflin, 1984), chap. 6.

27See US General Accounting Office, *Export Licensing: Commerce-Defense Review of Applications to Certain Free World Nations* (Washington, D.C.: US Government Printing Office, September 1986); and William Root, "State's Unwelcome Role," *Foreign Service Journal* (May 1984): 26–29.

28European Community, "Notes and Comments on the Amendments of 22 June 1982 to the Export Administration Act," reprinted in A. V. Lowe, *Extraterritorial Jurisdiction* (Cambridge, U.K.: Grotius, 1983), 197–211.

29See Joel Greenberg, "Science's New Cold War," *Science News,* 2 April 1983, 218–22; and National Academy of Sciences, *Scientific Communication and National Security* (Washington, D.C.: National Academy Press, 1982).

30Kevin Cahill, *Trade Wars: The High Technology Scandal of the 1980s* (London: W. H. Allen, 1986), 82–84.

31Janet Lunine, "High Technology Warfare: The EAAA of 1985 and the Problem of Foreign Re-export," *NYU Journal of International Law and Politics* 18 (Winter 1986): 663–702, at 680–6.

32National Academy of Sciences, *Balancing the National Interest,* 247.

33See "The Pentagon Won't Budge on High Tech Trade," *Business Week,* 7 December 1987, 114–15.

34See *Export Control News* 4 (6) (30 June 1990); and *Export Control News* 5 (5) (30 May 1991): 2–6.

35Steven Greenhouse, "U.S. and Allies Move to Ease Cold War Limits on Exports," *New York Times,* 25 May 1991, A1.

36John J. Fialka and Eduardo Lachica, "Easing of Technology Export Controls May Boost Smuggling in the Middle East," *The Wall Street Journal,* 19 June 1990, A22.

37John Markoff, "U.S. Wants Technology Curb," *New York Times,* 21 January 1991, D1; and Jay Beckoff, "Industry Comments Point to Flows in Proliferation Controls," *Export Control News,* 5 (4) (29 April 1991): 7–8. US firms were concerned in particular that new controls might disrupt existing contracts in targeted countries, and thus give them reputations as unreliable suppliers in the developing world.

38*Export Control News* 5 (5) (30 May 1991): 15.

39See Michael Wines, "Security Agency Debates New Role: Economic Spying," *New York Times,* 18 June 1990, A1.

Christopher Mark Davis

The Exceptional Soviet Case: Defense in an Autarkic System

THE CASE OF THE SOVIET UNION PROVIDES a unique opportunity to explore the merits of closed and open borders in developing a national defense capability. In the years from the beginning of the Stalinist era to the entry of the Gorbachev regime, the Soviet state attached an exceptionally high priority to programs designed to enhance the capabilities of the defense industry and the armed forces. It created and generously supported a massive military-industrial complex and adopted a strategy to promote its national security that had particular features by world standards. Among these was the attempt to minimize the integration of defense-related industries in a global economic system dominated by its capitalist adversaries. In the end, the Soviet leadership's traditional policies failed to achieve its security objectives. The Gorbachev regime's reforms in the defense field from 1985 to 1991 attempted to correct perceived problems while maintaining the essential features of the old system. By the summer of 1991, however, conservative members of the elite in the national security area decided that the actual and impending changes in the political and economic spheres threatened the survival of the communist state; ironically, the failure of their inept coup in August hastened its destruction. The anticommunist revolution and the breakup of the Soviet Union make it critical both to understand the reasons for the failure of previous security policies, including that of autarky, and the prospects for radical changes in the defense industries of the Soviet Union's successor states.

Christopher Mark Davis is Lecturer in Russian and East European Political Economy at Oxford University and a Fellow of Wolfson College.

113

TRADITIONAL SOVIET POLICIES: 1928–1985

Soviet views regarding the development of a national defense industry and the use of foreign economic linkages in national security
strategy were established during the Stalinist period from 1928 to
1953, shaped by Marxist-Leninist ideology and realist politics.[1]
Within the Soviet Union, the Stalinist elite perceived enemies everywhere, justifying a dictatorial regime to safeguard the existing
communist system. In the external sphere, the leadership viewed
relations with capitalist countries as inherently conflictual, possibly
involving a world war. State survival therefore required a national
security strategy based on a self-sufficient economy—"socialism in
one country," which demanded a massive effort on various fronts,
including not only the building up of military capabilities but also the
vigorous pursuit of propaganda, diplomacy, espionage, and even
arms control agreements.

The elite of the Stalinist era recognized that they had a markedly
backward economy to support their ambitious goal, and they insti-
tuted a set of policies they thought to be responsive to that fact.
Industry was nationalized and agriculture collectivized. The production and consumption goals of the central planning system were set in
terms of quantities, and prices were used only as an adjunct for
achievement of physical targets. National plans favored investment in
heavy industry and the production of materials for defense. The
result was an economy with characteristics and responses that were
considerably different from those of a demand-driven capitalist
market economy.[2]

The leadership believed that its plans for the development of
military power required a large, sophisticated defense industry and
recognized that some features of a command economy could place
those plans in jeopardy.[3] While tolerating weaknesses in the civilian
sector, such as poor quality of output and technological backwardness, the leadership established various mechanisms to protect the
defense industry from similar problems. A supraministerial management body was charged with the execution of defense production
plans, and special departments within the Communist party and
government agencies were made responsible for supervising the
development of the defense sector. Premium wages and extra benefits, such as better housing and health care, were made available to

employees in the defense industry, and many of the consumer goods supplied to those associated with military programs were produced within the defense sector and were counted as part of its outputs. Apparent inefficiencies in the defense industry, such as excess production capacity and the profligate use of materials, were readily tolerated.[4] And, when producers in the industry encountered production problems, they received prompt responses from the central authorities, including the easing of budgetary restraints.

The main goal of the Stalinist state in doing business with the rest of the world economy was to enhance its national security.[5] To this purpose it used the trade system to import crucial industrial products, subject to the constraints imposed by its own limited foreign exchange earnings, its ability to obtain trade credits, and the restraints imposed on such trade by Western governments. Throughout the Stalinist period, in order to prevent leaks of information and to avoid dependence on potential enemies, enterprises in the defense industry and in their related research and development institutes were insulated from direct contact with Western economies. At the same time, the defense industry benefited from the massive acquisitions of German scientific personnel and production facilities as a result of the Soviet victory in World War II. Thereafter, the industry had preferential access to hard currency, which it used to buy or steal Western technology.

On the whole, this combination of policies enabled the defense sector to achieve many of its objectives during the Stalinist era. The aggregate growth of the Soviet economy by some measures exceeded that of Western economies. Soviet defense industries increased their output of military goods and upgraded the technological standards of deployed weapons systems, including nuclear weapons, tanks, and jet aircraft. But the Stalinist economic system attained these goals by ignoring efficiency criteria and foregoing most of the benefits that could be gained from trade. That choice was reflected in the low productivity and shoddy quality of civilian output and, hence, in the poor living standards of most of the population.

After Stalin's death in 1953, Soviet leaders made important alterations to official ideology, foreign policy, and national security strategy. Placing somewhat greater emphasis on civilian welfare, they modified their policy of autarky to allow an expansion of foreign trade.[6] In the 1950s, there was a substantial increase in trade with communist countries in the Council of Mutual Economic Assistance (CMEA) in both military and civilian goods. Even more significant was the growth of imports of critical technologies from the West. This opening did not directly affect the defense industry, which remained isolated from the capitalist world, but it did raise the technical standards of a number of civilian sectors, providing crucial inputs to the defense effort.

Despite the various adjustments of policies, the remedial efforts of the Soviet government were undermined by a continuing belief in the efficacy of state ownership, central planning, and autarkic foreign economic policies, as well as by the political resistance of conservative groups in the Soviet power structure. By the mid-1960s the Soviet Union was finding it increasingly difficult to keep up with the West in terms of technological progress, even in the high-priority defense industry.

During the regimes of Brezhnev, Andropov, and Chernenko, covering the period from 1964 to 1985, the Soviet Communist party continued to cling to its traditional ideological tenets, including the inescapable character of the conflict between the interests of capitalist and communist countries, as well as the desirability of national self-sufficiency. The competition between the systems, it was supposed, might be resolved peacefully, but then again it might lead to world war. In any event, socialism would triumph in the end.

Still, Soviet leaders were well aware that the country's economy suffered from major weaknesses. Accordingly, during the 1960s and 1970s, they adopted numerous reforms aimed at accelerating technological innovation, raising living standards, and shifting the emphasis in economic development from a mere growth in numbers to an improvement in the efficiency of production and the quality of consumption.[7] But in the end, these policies neither improved economic performance nor produced significant organizational change. Instead, Soviet leaders maintained, and even fortified, all the institutions and processes of central planning, while reaffirming the favored position of the defense sector.

As a result, the fundamental problems of the Soviet economy remained, reflected in declining growth rates that increasingly fell below those of other major nations.[8] According to the US Central Intelligence Agency, the ratio of Soviet GNP to US GNP (both expressed in US dollars) rose from 50 percent in 1965 to a peak of 58 percent in the mid-1970s, but then dropped back to 53 percent in 1985. Over the same period, the Soviet Union's share of world GNP declined from 15.3 percent to 13.8 percent.

During this time, the technical progress of the military sector in the West continued unabated, greatly helped by the diffusion of technology from dynamic civilian firms operating in a competitive market environment.[9] In contrast, the defense industry of the Soviet Union continued to confront formidable obstacles that prevented it from assimilating technological advances from the outside world and to be hampered by the lack of innovation in its own civilian economy. The technological gap between Soviet industrial products and those of the rest of the world continually widened, especially in the crucial area of electronics.

With resistance to significant change so strong during the Brezhnev-Andropov-Chernenko eras, the Soviet Union's traditional institutions and mechanisms for conducting its foreign trade remained largely unaltered. Responsibility for foreign trade continued to rest in monopoly organizations separated from production units inside the Soviet Union. Despite that unchanging structure, however, the country managed to expand its foreign trade considerably, partly as a result of a considerable increase in its exports of a few key raw materials such as oil and gas. From 1965 to 1985 the value of Soviet foreign trade turnover grew by a factor of ten, from 14.6 to 142.1 billion rubles. Socialist countries accounted for about two-thirds of the country's trade in this period and market economies for one-third. Still, the foreign trade of the Soviet Union remained disproportionately small by Western standards, and its small share of hard currency markets for industrial goods actually fell because of the uncompetitiveness of its products.

Meanwhile, the Soviet elite's support for programs to enhance national security was unremitting. Heavy emphasis was placed on the development of the armed forces and the achievement and maintenance of nuclear parity, coupled with the prudent use of military power in low-intensity conflicts. According to CIA estimates, the Soviet Union's defense spending, when measured in real terms, nearly doubled during these two decades. The country's activities in areas such as diplomacy, propaganda, and espionage continued to receive substantial support.

In this period, the Soviet Union accorded a high priority to programs supporting the national defense industry. The industry's leaders were especially well placed to press their demands, having close links to the leaders of the Communist party in the Politburo and to key high-level institutions, including the Central Committee Secretariat and the Military-Industrial Commission.[10] Using their influence, they secured generous budgets and privileged access to domestic supplies and to imports.

These advantages helped the defense industry to obtain significant volumes of electronics, chemicals, and noncritical military supplies from countries in the Warsaw Pact, which could produce goods with standards that were above the average for the Soviet economy.[11] They also received large quantities of Western technology, covertly acquired through *spetsinformatsiya,* or special information programs.[12] Sources such as these kept the Soviet establishment abreast of recent developments in the West and provided means of improving their research projects and technical standards of production. To be sure, the unpredictable, erratic nature of these supplies and the lack of opportunity for detailed communication with the foreign originators of the technology limited the value of covert acquisitions. Nevertheless, these foreign resources helped the defense industry to increase the output of most major weapons systems, to improve the technical capabilities and quality of its products, and even to expand the shipment of arms to friendly foreign countries and allies.[13]

Yet, despite these achievements, by the early 1980s it became clear that the gap was widening between the demands of the Soviet military for technological innovation and the supply capabilities of the defense industry and its related research institutes. In fact, serious problems with the reliability and effectiveness of defense industry products were growing. A number of factors were responsible for this deteriorating situation.

For one thing, enterprises in the defense industry operated in sellers' markets for the goods and services they produced.[14] Although the quality of their output was usually better than average for the Soviet economy, the difference was due mainly to superior manpower and materials and to expensive quality control programs, rather than to exceptional factory management. Given an environment in which shortages were chronic and pervasive, customers (even military ones) were grateful for the products they received and were prepared without much complaint to accept the late deliveries and arrogant attitudes of producers. Firms in the defense industries, for their part, placed the greatest emphasis on raising the volume of their output, rather than on improving quality or timeliness of delivery. The lack of competition between suppliers, the minimal importance of consumer feedback, and the bureaucratic politics of the defense industry made managers risk-averse and complacent about the technical standards of their products.[15]

The behavior of the defense industry could be explained in part as characteristic reactions of enterprises in a shortage economy: the emphasis on volume of output, the hunger for investment, the insatiable demands for materials and labor, and the strong tendency to build up reserve productive capacity. Because of the high priority given to the defense industry, including its power to make peremptory demands on the civilian economy for needed supplies, the industry did not suffer nearly as much from the problems created by chronic shortages as did the Soviet economy at large.

However, by the late 1970s, the growing complexity of weapons production was making the defense industry increasingly reliant on branches of the malfunctioning civilian economy. The slackening of political control over the society and the adoption of a confusing array of conflicting priorities in the 1980s made it more difficult to protect defense institutions. The contributions of the civilian sector proved deficient in quality and quantity, adding to the troubles of the defense establishment. The margin of superiority that had distinguished the performance of the defense sector from that of the rest of the Soviet economy began to disappear.

The response of the Soviet leadership was to place even a larger share of the country's resources in the defense sector. In Western Europe, defense expenditures were running at about 2 to 5 percent of GNP, and in the United States such outlays were in the 6 to 7 percent range. But, according to the CIA, the Soviet defense burden rose from a range of 12 to 14 percent of GNP in 1965 to a range of 15 to 17 percent in 1985. During that twenty-year period, there were of course variations in the level of Soviet defense expenditure, as Soviet leaders periodically reassessed the gravity of the external threat. But, by and large, the heavy military burden on the economy lowered its overall capacity to perform, preventing the Soviet Union from keeping up with the rest of the world. In the end, the very emphasis on defense ironically had adverse effects on the country's defense capabilities and led to its decline as a great power.[16]

The Early Gorbachev Years

By 1985 Soviet leaders had recognized the widening discrepancy between the nation's military commitments and its economic capabilities, as well as the dire long-term consequences of remaining in the Cold War arms race and maintaining autarkic economic policies. In subsequent years, radical reforms were introduced in the political system in hope of improving the situation. Security strategy and military doctrine were revised in accordance with the *novoe myshlenie,* or new thinking.[17] Programs of disarmament and conversion, changes in enterprise laws, and the relaxation of barriers to contacts with Western firms gradually altered the defense industry's operating environment. At the same time, however, various forces inside the Soviet Union resisted the officially inspired strivings toward democracy, a market economy, and an opening up of borders. These forces were especially strong within the defense industry, a privileged bastion of the system. By the early 1990s, it became clear that the reform policies of the Gorbachev regime had not improved the performance of defense enterprises or enhanced the standing of the Soviet Union as a world power.

In 1985, in the earliest version of the Gorbachev economic reform strategy, the regime adopted the ambitious goals of accelerating economic growth and technological progress and raising the quality of industrial goods up to world standards. To achieve these objectives, however, Gorbachev proposed a relatively conservative set of policies consistent with those adopted earlier by his predecessor, Yuri Andropov, during the years from 1982 to 1984. That approach, reflected in the Twelfth Five Year Plan, covering the years 1986 to 1990, proposed to achieve reforms without fundamentally altering the system of central planning and controlled markets.[18]

During these early years of the Gorbachev regime, therefore, the Soviet leadership maintained the traditional economic system, with its built-in emphasis on autarky, even as it was debating the relative benefits of self-sufficiency and interdependence. It was indicative of official thinking of the time, and ironic in hindsight, that one of the government's first initiatives, taken in December 1985, was to try to strengthen the Soviet Union's ties to Eastern Europe. An extraordinary session of the Council of the CMEA convened to adopt a new and ambitious socialist integration program. Two months later, at the 27th Party Congress of the USSR, Prime Minister Ryzhkov said:

> The headlong pursuit of imported machinery and technology which obsesses many leaders has a demoralizing effect on collectives of researchers. Seeing how easily equipment can be acquired from abroad, they basically lose enthusiasm, their work becomes less intense, and they give up in the face of difficulties. We are far from unwilling to use the results of the international division of labor and the exchange of scientific and technical knowledge, but we must rely primarily on our own vast scientific potential.[19]

The policies of the Gorbachev regime governing the development of the defense sector from 1985 to 1988 were particularly slow to change. Defense economic policy was governed by the relatively conservative Twelfth Plan, which called for high and increasing levels of military spending.[20] According to Western sources, allocation of resources to defense grew in real terms by about 2 or 3 percent per annum. To be sure, some surface changes appeared, including the adoption of a new military doctrine of "reasonable sufficiency." Remedial personnel policies were stressed, such as the avoidance of alcohol and the strengthening of incentives. And new control mechanisms governing the operations of defense institutions were introduced.

The defense industry, however, retained its privileged status and traditional organization. Its enterprises continued to obtain preferential access to material inputs from civilian sectors and CMEA partners, as well as from the legal and covert channels to the West. Moreover, military orders from the Soviet armed forces, Warsaw Pact allies, and Third World customers remained robust, so the output of most categories of weapons systems remained high.[21] The industry's labor force grew, as some enterprises that had been subordinate to a number of civilian machine-building ministries were placed under the control of the defense sector in the hope of stepping up their efficiency. In the process, some of the industry's top officials were transferred into important jobs in the civilian sphere, but on the whole, not much changed at the enterprise level.

During 1987 and 1988, there was substantial internal debate among the Soviet elite over perestroika and national security strategy. The reformist faction proved victorious. As a result, in December 1988, in a speech before the United Nations General Assembly, Gorbachev was able to outline some new security concepts and steps toward demilitarization. Subsequently, further measures were introduced to accelerate disarmament and to cut defense spending, some of them in accordance with multilateral agreements and others to be undertaken unilaterally.[22]

Toward the Brink: 1989–1991

At first, the Soviet economy appeared to respond well to the plans and reform policies of the Gorbachev regime. But by 1989 the economy was faltering badly. During the next two years, the long-standing deficiencies of the Soviet economy were compounded by new problems, such as the center's loss of control over the country's enterprises and the proliferation of nationality-related political disruptions.[23] Plan targets in crucial industries, including fuels, metal production, and machine building, were chronically underfulfilled,

TABLE 1   The Soviet Defense Burden under Gorbachev

Year	GNP (in billions of 1982 rubles)[a]	GNP Change (percent)[b]	Defense Expenditures (in billions of 1982 rubles)[c]	Defense Expenditures (as percent of GNP)
1985	682.6	0.7	111.0	16.2
1986	710.3	4.1	115.3	16.2
1987	719.5	1.3	120.5	16.7
1988	735.2	2.2	124.0	16.8
1989	745.8	1.4	116.6	15.6
1990	708.5	−5.0	109.6	15.5
1991	588.1	−17.0	98.6	16.8

(a) For 1985–1989, CIA/DIA, *The Soviet Economy Stumbles Badly in 1989*, report presented to the US Congress (Washington, D.C.: Joint Economic Committee, April 20, 1990), Table C-1; 1990 is calculated at 5 percent below 1989; 1991 is calculated at 17 percent below 1990.

(b) For 1985, CIA, *Handbook of Economic Statistics, 1986*, CPAS 86-10002 (Washington, D.C.: US Government Printing Office, 1986); 1986–1989, CIA/DIA, Table C-4; 1990 *The Soviet Economy Stumbles*, CIA/DIA, *Beyond Perestroyka: The Soviet Economy in Crisis*, report presented to the US Congress (Washington, D.C.: Joint Economic Committee, May 1991); 1991 is the negative growth rate reported in "Ekonomika stranchlenov sodruzhestva nezavisimykh gosudarstv v 1991 godu," *Ekonomicheskaya Gazeta*, 6 (February 1992).

(c) For 1985–1988, see Dmitri Steinberg "Trends in Soviet Military Expenditure" *Soviet Studies*, (42) (4) (October 1990): 687; 1989 and 1990 down 6 percent from previous years according to CIA/DIA, *Beyond Perestrokya*; 1991 is an estimated cut of 10 percent from 1990 level.

due in part to falling labor discipline and clashes among nationalities. Output targets for consumer goods and agricultural production were not achieved. Indicators of technological progress, efficiency, and productivity all deteriorated.

Furthermore, the growth of wages was allowed to exceed that of labor productivity, strengthening inflationary pressures in the economy and raising the deficits in the state budget to about 10 percent of GNP by 1990. This combination of factors intensified excess demand in retail markets, producing pervasive shortages, queuing, forced substitution, and forced saving.[24]

The national economic reform became more radical in 1990 and 1991. Included in the new measures were the self-financing in industry, leasing of land in agriculture, reduction of the scope of the production orders emanating from the state, expansion of wholesale trade, price reform, encouragement of cooperatives, and an increase in the private ownership of property.[25] The process of reforming foreign trade practices that had commenced in September 1986 had accelerated over subsequent years. But the collapse of the CMEA forced a scrapping of ideas about socialist integration. There also was a critical rethinking of Soviet policies toward economic aid, and Third World allies were notified that assistance would be scaled back in the future. In the end, the various reforms designed to affect economic relations with the rest of the world did not actually open up the Soviet economy or improve foreign trade performance.

Total exports in current prices were lower in 1990 than in 1985, and imports were at about the same level. In 1990, the Soviet Union had trade deficits with both socialist and market economies, and its debt in hard currencies was almost twice the 1985 level. Moreover, plans to bring in foreign enterprises on a large scale foundered. Although there were over fifteen hundred joint ventures with foreigners registered in the Soviet Union by 1991, fewer than half of them were actually functioning. Many of these were in service activities, such as business consultancy and trade, and most involved trivial amounts of capital investment. Besides, as domestic economic conditions deteriorated, the number of registrations of new joint ventures fell off.

By 1991 it was clear that the Soviet economy had not become more integrated in the global system and was, in fact, breaking up internally. Prime Minister Pavlov noted:

> A disruption of economic ties has started, a striving towards autarky and attempts at overcoming the crisis on one's own have become stronger. There has been colorful proliferation of barter and limits on the movement of goods between regions are being set up.[26]

The problem of economic disintegration became so acute that a presidential decree was issued in April 1991 aimed at nullifying any bans by individual Soviet republics or regions on exports of goods to other areas of the Soviet Union.

The deteriorating economic situation affected the character and pace of reforms in the defense industry. After December 1988, the defense industry was directed to move further into the production of civilian commodities and to accelerate the transfer of advanced technology to the civilian sphere. [27] According to the new conversion program, the defense industry's output of arms and military equipment would fall by nearly 20 percent between 1988 and 1991, and the civilian goods' share of defense output would rise from 40 percent in 1988 to a projected 60 percent by 1995.[28] Military orders declined rapidly as the central authorities cut procurement for the Soviet armed forces. The heavy flow of weapons to Warsaw Pact allies and the Third World fell off precipitately, a trend accelerated by growing Soviet concern over unpaid debts of 86 billion rubles and by the UN embargo of Iraq.[29]

By the early 1990s, production conditions within defense firms were deteriorating, due to shortages and irregular deliveries of inputs. The reorientation of the economic system toward the use of markets and decentralized decision making undermined the value of central support, reducing the ability of the bureaucracy to guarantee the availability of supplies. Unfortunately for defense firms, this weakening of priority protection occurred in a time of intensified shortages and growing supply disruptions throughout the economy. With uncertainties on all sides, managers of defense industry enterprises remained risk-averse and were reluctant to embark on major new projects. The cuts in military R&D budgets also contributed to the sluggishness of technical progress. Moreover, the budgets of defense enterprises were hardening relative to the slack conditions of the past, a change brought about by the government's policies of encouraging self-financing, removing subsidies, and tightening bank credit.

Labor problems appeared in the defense industry as well. Work discipline slackened throughout the Soviet economy. Firms located in republics affected by national unrest experienced high rates of absenteeism and low productivity. Additional labor complications in the defense industry were generated by the growth of cooperatives, the relaxation of price controls, and the profit opportunities offered by civilian enterprises. Although the average working conditions, wages, bonuses, and benefits of staff in defense enterprises did not deteriorate much before 1989, the more successful civilian firms could outbid them for skilled labor.

Defense firms also experienced difficulties in securing needed supplies from foreign countries. Lacking direct experience in international markets, they had difficulty in adjusting to their new freedoms, including their expanded opportunities to trade with the West. Imports of commodities and technology from Eastern Europe declined due to the abolition of the CMEA Military-Industrial Commission and the Warsaw Pact technical committees that had governed such exchanges, as well as the shift to hard-currency trade in exchanges with Eastern Europe. By 1991, in an effort to overcome such difficulties, over one hundred defense firms were negotiating or setting up partnerships with Western firms. But these arrangements produced little in the way of technology or capital by 1991.

As a consequence of the adverse developments that the Soviet defense industry was obliged to confront, it became difficult for it to produce products of superior quality, and the differential in the performance of defense enterprises relative to that of firms in the civilian sector narrowed. According to an official in the defense industry:

> Unfortunately, despite its better technical equipment, higher qualifications of workers, and significant scientific potential, the productivity of labor, capital-output ratio [*fondootdacha*], energy intensity and other integral indicators of the defense complex on average correspond to those of the national economy in general and lag behind equivalent indicators of developed industrial countries.[30]

Yet, despite these developments, the defense industry was able to cling to many of its traditional policies and practices. Defense firms continued to operate in sellers' markets for military goods because of the maintenance of domestic monopoly arrangements and the absence of any competition from foreign firms. Although the military was increasingly vociferous in its criticism of the restraints imposed

by existing supply arrangements, no significant changes were introduced in the current rigid system of procurement.[31] The conversion
effort achieved only minor successes, in part because defense industrialists repeatedly took advantage of the conflict and confusion
among the central authorities to avoid fulfilling requests for greater
civilian production. Moreover, there is some evidence that they made
use of their market power to overprice the goods they supplied to the
civilian sector. It also was the case that budgets of defense firms
remained soft by Western standards. Unprofitable defense establishments were not forced into bankruptcy and managers continued to
expect a bailout by the bureaucracy whenever they encountered
financial difficulties.

Another continuing source of strength for the defense industry in
this period was the *spetsinformatsiya* system. According to one
source:

> Gorbachev regarded covert acquisition of Western technology as an
> important part of economic perestroika . . . all the evidence suggests
> that the scale of Soviet S&T [scientific and technological espionage] has
> tended to increase rather than to decrease. . . . The main expansion of
> Line X [of the KGB] work at the start of the 1990s, however, appeared
> to be taking place in Japan and South Korea.[32]

Offsetting the possible expansion of the Soviet effort (and perhaps
explaining it) was the loss of the services of the highly productive East
European intelligence agencies, especially those of Eastern Germany.

Furthermore, even by the middle of 1991, the central management
structures of the industry were still intact. A military-industrial
commission continued to function as did special military departments
in the key planning bodies and ministries. Only in the structure of the
Communist party did one see significant change. In an attempt to
reduce party interference with the operations of enterprises, the
special department of the Central Committee devoted to the defense
industry, headed by Oleg Baklanov, was abolished. But a commission
on military policy, also under Mr. Baklanov, continued to provide
some party oversight.

DEFENSE INDUSTRIES IN THE POST-SOVIET SUCCESSOR STATES

Until the spring of 1991, conservative officials within the Communist
party and the state organizations probably believed that they con-

trolled the vital political processes in the Soviet Union and could force the Gorbachev government to do their bidding. This assessment must have been reevaluated after the surprise meeting in April between Gorbachev and republican leaders to sign a union treaty that promised substantial devolution of powers. The conservatives' unease over this prospect may have been due in part to the proposals of the Yeltsin government in Russia for a radical reform of the defense sector. These proposals included the transfer of defense industry establishments to the republics' control, abolition of all union bodies, privatization, divestiture of civilian components from defense firms, cuts in military orders, and the creation of competitive markets for weapons.[33]

During the summer, the leaders of the KGB, police, Communist party, armed forces, and defense industry developed contingency plans to prevent the breakup of the Soviet Union and the destruction of the Communist system. Their efforts were reflected in the coup launched August 19.[34] However, the high-ranking members of this conservative group did not appreciate the irrevocable nature of political change at the lower levels of society or the force of nationalism. Even in elite military units and defense industry enterprises, many people from all generations resisted the Emergency Committee's orders. As a consequence, the coup was a catastrophic failure for the conservative forces.

One immediate consequence was that the Communist party was eradicated as a political force. Central government leaders and organizations were further discredited, and their powers were undermined. The republics were spurred to declare their independence and take steps to achieve this status. Throughout the early autumn President Gorbachev attempted to create a union of equals on the basis of a new treaty, but his efforts were rejected by republic leaders. Instead, in early December, they agreed to form a Commonwealth of Independent States (CIS). By the end of 1991, President Gorbachev had resigned, and the Soviet Union ceased to exist as a nation.

The Soviet economy had disintegrated at an accelerated pace throughout 1991. Compared with 1990 levels, the grain harvest fell 27 percent, industrial output decreased 8 percent, foreign trade dropped 39 percent, and the gross national product declined 17 percent. Imbalances and shortages in the economy intensified because of the breakdown of central control over fiscal and monetary policy.[35]

The new republic governments did not immediately introduce comprehensive measures to correct the growing economic crisis. It was not until early January 1992 that Russia and the other republics finally embarked on the transition from command to market economies by introducing programs that called for price liberalization, rapid privatization, severe cuts in the state budget expenditure, tax reform, stimulation of competition, reform of the banking system and monetary policy, and the opening of foreign trade.[36] By the end of the first quarter, some goals had been achieved such as reductions in the monetary overhang, but serious structural problems remained unresolved.[37]

The army emerged somewhat credible from the August crisis because of the resistance by key officers and military units to orders from the Emergency Committee. The new minister of defense, Yevgenii Shaposhnikov, devised a program for accelerated reform in the armed forces and a phased reduction in its size. But these policies were based on the assumption that a union treaty would be signed, and the government under President Gorbachev would retain power in the security field; however, the formation of the CIS threw these plans into disarray. The original commonwealth agreement provided only vague promises concerning the future development of the central armed forces. While follow-up negotiations were in progress, several member states, notably Ukraine, asserted their rights to form independent armies and seize control of military assets in their territories. This sparked heated arguments between Russia and Ukraine and provoked military officers to strongly criticize their political leaders. By April 1992, the decomposition of the unified Soviet military into independent armies of the new commonwealth states appeared to be inevitable.

The defense industry was reorganized in a revolutionary manner in the autumn of 1991. The various republics seized control of production and research facilities in their territories and developed new management structures to direct their work. By the end of the year, there appeared to be no surviving central coordination of the defense industry in the CIS. The commonwealth states introduced their own conversion programs to guide and assist defense firms during the transition to the market system and a shift to civilian production.[38]

At the plant level, defense establishments were profoundly affected by the reduction of military orders for weapons and equipment, deteriorating supply conditions, and their loss of high priority status.

Major uncertainties beclouded any forecast of future developments in the survival of the CIS as a political and economic alliance: the reaction of the hybrid economies in the commonwealth to market forces; the sustainability of the democratization process; and the possibility of armed conflicts developing between major ethnic groups within the former republics and between the new states. At least three scenarios concerning prospects for disarmament in the CIS can be elaborated: the successful transition to market economies and the survival of the commonwealth; a peaceful breakup of the commonwealth leading to more severe economic difficulties; and an acrimonious breakup resulting in economic tensions and wars between the commonwealth states.[39] Only the first, most optimistic one, is outlined below.

In this scenario it is assumed that the arms control treaties with the United States—the CFE and START treaties—are implemented; but they become largely irrelevant documents because domestic pressures generate a radical disarmament. The size of the armed forces on CIS territory falls from three million in 1991 to one million in 1995. The conditions and pay of the regular officers and volunteer soldiers are improved and an attempt is made to raise the quality of their equipment to world levels. Nuclear weapons are kept under central control and inventories are drastically reduced. Most commonwealth states develop their own armed forces, primarily national guards without offensive missions. As defense budgets are cut, the commonwealth defense burden falls from 17 percent in 1991 to 8 percent in 1995.

The defense industries in the commonwealth states continue to supply weapons and equipment to their central and national armed forces, but at reduced levels. The CIS governments introduce conversion programs, but over time the scale of state intervention is reduced as market forces dictate the pace and nature of demilitarization. The average size of defense enterprises falls as units producing civilian goods split off and high-tech teams form small private or cooperative firms. The surviving weapons producers operate on an independent, self-financing basis in competitive markets.

In foreign economic relations, energetic efforts are made to export arms abroad to earn hard currency.[40] There is a dramatic opening of the defense sector, and the number of defense-related joint ventures rise rapidly. Some of the new governments grant permission for western firms to invest directly in weapons-producing subsidiaries. Western governments liberalize CoCom and national controls governing exports to the East, and the scale of the Russian *spetsinformatsiya* system is reduced. By 1995 defense enterprises in the current territory of the Soviet Union are closely integrated with the world economy.

CONCLUSIONS

In the Soviet Union, the drive for self-sufficiency and the development of a national industrial base encouraged the creation of a command economy, with special elements of protection and support for the defense sector. For a considerable period of time, the Soviet strategy enabled the nation to build a formidable military machine. But the Soviet Union had to pay a high economic price for its autarkic policies. The isolation of scientific institutes and production enterprises from the world economy, coupled with the increasing sophistication of military hardware, repeatedly produced technological lags. By 1985, the heavy defense burden was undermining the economic power of the USSR while not contributing to greater national security.

Although the Gorbachev regime adopted a different national security strategy and opened the Soviet economy, it was difficult to change the behavior of economic institutions. To effect such changes, the Soviet Union would have been obligated to alter its basic political and economic systems. From 1989 to 1991 its economy was a hybrid, guided neither by central commands nor market signals. The consequence of this confused situation was that the country's economic performance deteriorated in all sectors, including defense.

The nations emerging from the old Soviet Union appear to recognize that a strategy based on an excessive commitment to defense and autarky is not effective in achieving national security goals in the modern world. In the future, it is possible that these new countries will sustain their programs of economic transition and radical arms reductions. Success in this effort should produce a gradual convergence of the defense industries in the post-Communist nations with those in the west. History suggests, however, that the transition from centralized systems to market systems in large countries is a long uncertain process. There is no certainty that all the commonwealth states will evolve into nations that are fully integrated into western political, economic, and security institutions.

ACKNOWLEDGEMENTS

Research for this paper was supported by grants from the Ford Foundation through the projects on "The Economics of the Soviet Defense Sector" and "Soviet Defense and Conventional Arms Control Policies: 1985–2000," and from the British Economic and Social Research Council through the project on "Central Control, Disequilibrium and Private Activity in Socialist Economies." I thank Roy Allison and Philip Hanson for their helpful early discussions of relevant research issues, Peter Almquist and Julian Cooper for their insights and suggestions concerning the Soviet defense industry, and Edwin Bacon for his research assistance.

ENDNOTES

[1] The basic features of realism and mercantilism are discussed in Stephen Gill and David Law, *The Global Political Economy* (London: Wheatsheaf, 1988).

[2] For empirical and theoretical analyses of the socialist shortage economy, see Janos Kornai, *Overcentralisation of Economic Administration* (London: Oxford University Press, 1959), and his *Economics of Shortage* (Amsterdam: North-Holland, 1980).

[3] Soviet thinking on the relationship between military and economic power is discussed in A. I. Pozharov, *Ekonomicheskie Osnovy Oboronnogo Mogushchestva Sotsialisticheskogo Gosudarstva* (Moscow: Voennoe Izdatel'stvo, 1981); Y. E. Vlas'evich, A. S. Sukhoguzov, and V. A. Zubkov, *Osnovy Voenno-Ekonomicheskikh Znanii* (Moscow: Voennoe Izdatel'stvo, 1989); and Christopher Davis, "Marxist and Soviet Defense Economics, 1848–1927," *History of Political Economy*, Special Issue on "Economies and National Security: A History of Their Interaction," 23 (1991).

[4] The mechanisms and policies used to protect the institutions of the defense sector in the Soviet Union are discussed in Christopher Davis, "The High Priority Military Sector in a Shortage Economy," in Henry S. Rowen and Charles Wolf Jr., eds., *The Impoverished Superpower: Perestroika and the Burden of Soviet Military Spending* (San Francisco: Institute for Contemporary Studies, 1990).

[5] On this theme, see Franklyn D. Holzman, "Foreign Trade," in Abram Bergson and Simon Kuznets, eds., *Economic Trends in the Soviet Union* (Cambridge: Harvard University Press, 1963), 301–2.

[6]According to Franklyn Holzman, the share of exports in Soviet national income was 0.5 percent in 1937 (which probably was typical for the Stalinist years) but had risen to 2.3–2.6 percent by 1959; see Holzman, 290.

[7]See Paul Dibb, *The Soviet Union: The Incomplete Superpower,* 2nd ed. (London: International Institute for Strategic Studies, 1988), 70.

[8]The importance of relative economic performance in the world power balance is discussed in Paul Kennedy, *The Rise and Fall of the Great Powers: Economic Change and Military Conflict from 1500 to 2000* (New York: Random House, 1987), 430–1, also the introduction and epilogue. Many analysts think that the estimated Soviet growth rates and GNP magnitudes are too high; see Christopher Davis, "Economic Influences on the Decline of the Soviet Union as a Great Power: Continuity Despite Change," *Diplomacy and Statecraft* 1 (3) (1990).

[9]See Matthew Evangelista, *Innovation and the Arms Race* (Ithaca: Cornell University Press, 1988). Similar arguments are made in Thane Gufstafson, "The Response to Technological Challenge," in Timothy J. Colton and Thane Gufstafson, eds., *Soldiers and the Soviet State: Civil-Military Relations from Brezhnev to Gorbachev* (Princeton: Princeton University Press, 1990).

[10]The organization of the Soviet defense industry during the Brezhnev era is thoroughly discussed in Peter Almquist, *Red Forge: Soviet Military Industry since 1965* (New York: Columbia University Press, 1990).

[11]A thorough analysis of Soviet links with East European countries in the defense area is presented in Michael Checinski, "CEMA/WTO Military-Economic Trends," *Problems of Communism* 36 (2) (1987).

[12]The *spetsinformatsiya* is described in Philip Hanson, *Soviet Industrial Espionage: Some New Information* (London: Chatham House Discussion Papers, 1987); and Jacques Sapir, *The Soviet Military System* (Oxford: Polity, 1991), chap. 8.

[13]See Mark N. Kramer, "Soviet Arms Transfers to the Third World," *Problems of Communism* 36 (5) (1987): 55.

[14]This novel argument was first made in the 1987 Ph.D. dissertation by Peter Almquist, which was published as *Red Forge: Soviet Military Industry since 1965* (see endnote 10). Updated empirical support for the proposition that a seller's market exists is provided in Peter Almquist, "Soviet Military Acquisition: From a Sellers' Market to a Buyers'?", in Susan Clark, ed., *Soviet Military Power in a Changing World* (Boulder, Colo.: Westview, 1991). Theoretical discussions of the behavior of socialist firms in a sellers' market can be found in Christopher Davis and Wojciech Charemza, eds., *Models of Disequilibrium and Shortage in Centrally Planned Economies* (London: Chapman and Hall, 1989).

[15]Almquist, *Red Forge*; and Andrew Cockburn, *The Threat: Inside the Soviet Military Machine* (New York: Vintage, 1984).

[16]Evidence in support of the argument that the Brezhnev regime failed to achieve its security objectives is presented in Kennedy, esp. 512; and Davis, "Economic Influences." In Christopher Andrew and Oleg Gordievsky, *KGB: The Inside Story of Its Foreign Operations from Lenin to Gorbachev* (London: Hodder and Stoughton, 1990), it is argued that the Soviet leadership perceived the nation as

being in severe danger in the early 1980s and initiated Operation RYAN to detect signs of the expected preemptive nuclear attack by the US.

[17]Reforms in the national security strategy and defense sector are evaluated in Dale R. Herspring, *The Soviet High Command, 1967–1989* (Princeton: Princeton University Press, 1990); Bruce Parrott, ed., *The Dynamics of Soviet Defense Policy* (Washington, D.C.: The Wilson Center Press, 1990); Colton and Gustafson; and Michael MacGwire, *Perestroika and Soviet National Security* (Washington, D.C.: The Brookings Institution, 1991); Roy Allison, ed., *Radical Reform in Soviet Defense Policy* (London: Macmillan, 1992).

[18]Ed A. Hewett, *Reforming the Soviet Economy: Equality versus Efficiency* (Washington D.C.: The Brookings Institution, 1988).

[19]Nikolai I. Ryzhkov, "Ryzhkov's Report on Basic Guidelines at the 27th Party Congress," *Summary of World Broadcasts*, SU/8200/C (1986): 13.

[20]In Nikolai I. Ryzhkov, "Sluzhit interesam naroda," *Ekonomicheskaya Gazeta* 5 (51) (1989), it is stated that the Twelfth Five Year Plan incorporated "growth of expenditures on defense at a tempo higher than the growth of national income."

[21]US Department of Defense, *Soviet Military Power 1990* (Washington, D.C.: US Government Printing Office, 1990), 38.

[22]Roy Allison, "Gorbachev's Arms Control Offensive: Unilateral, Bilateral and Multilateral Initiatives," in C. G. Jacobson, ed., *Soviet Foreign Policy at the Cross-Roads* (New York: St. Martin's, 1990); Edwin Bacon, "The Internal Debate on the Reform of the Soviet Armed Forces," M.Soc.Sci. diss., University of Birmingham, U.K., 1990; and MacGwire.

[23]E. Gaidar, "Trudnyy vybor: ekonomicheskoe obozrenie po itogam 1989 goda," *Kommunist* (2) (1990); K. Kagalovskii, "Ekonomicheskii krizis. Gde iskat' vykhod?," *Kommunist* (4) (1990); and "Ekonomika SSSR v 1990 godu," *Ekonomika i Zhizn* (5) (1991).

[24]Anders Aslund, *Gorbachev's Struggle for Economic Reform* (London: Pinter, 1991); CIA/DIA, *The Soviet Economy Stumbles Badly in 1989*, report presented to the US Congress (Washington, D.C.: Joint Economic Committee, 20 April 1990); and CIA/DIA, *Beyond Perestroyka: The Soviet Economy in Crisis*, report presented to the US Congress (Washington, D.C.: Joint Economic Committee, 16 May 1991); and Anders Aslund, "Gorbachev, Perestroyka, and Economic Crisis," *Problems of Communism*, 40 (1-2) (1991).

[25]Nikolai I. Ryzhkov, "Effektivnost, konsolidatsiya, reforma—put k zdorovoi ekonomike," *Ekonomicheskaya Gazeta* (51) (1990); Mikhail S. Gorbachev, "Osnovnye napravleniya po stabilizatsii narodnogo khozyaistva i perekhodu k rynochnoi ekonomike," *Pravda*, 18 October 1990; and Valentin Pavlov, "The Report by U.S.S.R. Premier Valentin Pavlov at a Session of the U.S.S.R. Supreme Soviet on 22nd April," *Summary of World Broadcasts*, SU/1054 C1/1–10 (24 April 1991).

[26]Pavlov, 4.

[27]Ethan B. Kapstein, "From Guns to Butter in the U.S.S.R.," *Challenge* (September-October 1989); W. H. Kincade and T. K. Thomson, "Economic Conversion in the U.S.S.R.: Its Role in Perestroika," *Problems of Communism* 39 (1) (1990); Peter Almquist and Kevin O'Prey, "Beating Swords into Agro-industrial Com-

plexes," *Arms Control Today* (December 1990); and Julian Cooper, "The Soviet Defense Industry, Military Cuts, and Conversion," *Soviet Economy* 7(2) (1991).

28I. S. Belousov, "Konversiya. Chto eto znachit" (Interview with A. Pokrovskii), *Pravda*, 28 August 1989. An updated statement on the "State Program of Conversion of the Defense Industry" that was approved by the Soviet government on 15 December 1990 can be found in an article by the head of the Gosplan military department, V. Smyslov, "Gosudarstvennaya programma konversii oboronnoi promyshlennosti," *Voprosy Ekonomiki* (2) (1991). See also Julian Cooper, *The Soviet Defense Industry: Conversion and Reform* (London: Royal Institute for International Affairs/Francis Pinter, 1991).

29I. S. Belousov, "Voennyy eksport v svete glasnosti," *Pravitel'stvennyy Vestnik* (2) (1991): 12.

30A. Isaev, "Reforma i oboronnye otrasli," *Kommunist* (5) (1989).

31The military's complaints are reviewed in Peter Almquist, "Creating a Military-Industrial Complex: The Dark Side of Conversion," (Birmingham: Discussion Paper, 1991). Almquist cites criticisms by the then commander in chief of the Air Forces, Y. I. Shaposhnikov, of the monopoly position of the defense industry. General Shaposhnikov was appointed Minister of Defense following the August 1991 coup.

32Andrew and Gordievsky, 521–3.

33This assessment is based on conversations in November 1990 in Moscow by the author and Deputy Prime Minister RSFSR Gennadii I. Filshin and his defense industry managers and with Mr. Oleg Baklanov, chairman of the Commission on Military Policy, at Central Committee headquarters.

34One of the key signatures on the martial law decree was that of the defense industrialist and first deputy chairman of the Defense Council USSR, Oleg Baklanov, who also went to the Crimea to deliver the ultimatum to Gorbachev to resign.

35"Ekonomika stranchlenov sodruzhestva nezavisimykh gosudarstv v 1991 godu," *Ekonomicheskaya Gazeta (Ekonomika i Zhizn)*, 6 (February 1992).

36Russia's transition program was outlined in Boris Yeltsin, "My perekhodim nakonets k novomu ekonomicheskomu kursu," *Ekonomika i Zhizn*, 45 (November 1991).

37"Memorandum ob ekonomicheskoi politike Rossiiskoi Federatsii," *Ekonomicheskaya Gazeta (Ekonomika i Zhizn)*, 10 (March 1992).

38 Aleksandr Rutskoi, "Problemy konversii predpriyatii i organizatsii oboronnogo kompleksa Rossii budet resheny," *Ekonomika i Zhizn*, 52 (December 1991).

39In these three scenarios, the prospects for disarmament in the CIS are evaluated in Christopher Davis, "The Defense Sector in the Soviet Economy During *Perestroika*: From Expansion to Disarmament to Disintegration" in F. Gerard Adams, ed., *The Macroeconomic Dimensions of Arms Reductions* (Boulder, Colo.: Westview Press, forthcoming).

40Vyacheslav Shchepotkin, "Oboronnyy kompleks mozhet ne razoryat 'a kormit,'" *Izvestiya*, March 31, 1992.

Theodore H. Moran and David C. Mowery

Aerospace

S INCE THE EARLIEST YEARS OF THE AEROSPACE industry, national governments have protected and promoted their domestic aerospace firms for reasons associated with national welfare and national security. In recent decades, however, the need to capture the economies of large-scale production and a growing need to gain access to foreign technologies and markets have propelled the principal US and European aerospace manufacturing firms beyond their national borders.

This trend has intensified a familiar debate in countries aspiring to a major role in the aerospace industry: how to manage the movement across their borders of the goods, services, capital, and technology that the industry requires in order to promote their national interests. As usual, the debate has revealed two camps: one that draws on the standard liberal prescriptions of easy access and freedom of choice as a means of bringing efficiency and dynamism to the industry; and a second that draws on so-called neomercantilist recommendations, entailing use of the state to strengthen national firms and keep control over the industry.

NATIONAL POLICIES IN RETROSPECT

Europe led the United States in many of the technological and commercial aspects of the aerospace industry prior to World War II. Because the US industry has had such a dominant position in world

Theodore H. Moran is Karl F. Landegger Professor and Director of the Program in International Business Diplomacy in the School of Foreign Service at Georgetown University.

David C. Mowery is Associate Professor of Business and Public Policy in the Walter A. Haas School of Business at the University of California, Berkeley.

markets in recent times, however, it is useful to first look at the influence of US policies on the global structure of the industry.

US Policies

As early as 1915, the aircraft industry in the United States was distinguished by the US government from other US manufacturing industries by the existence of a federally funded program for research in generic civil and military technologies. Directed by the National Advisory Committee on Aeronautics (NACA), the program made important contributions to civilian and military aircraft design and technologies during the interwar period. NACA research, for instance, aided the US aircraft industry in some notable successes before World War II, such as the launching of the DC-3.

When measured by its technological and commercial achievements during this period, however, the US commercial aircraft industry was far from dominant in world markets. The early development of the turbojet engine and the swept wing was undertaken by European scientists and engineers. Indeed, one scholar has suggested that the United States lagged so badly in theoretical aerodynamics before World War II that US aerospace technicians and engineers were incapable of recognizing the potential of the jet engine.[1]

During and after the war, however, the technological sophistication of the US aircraft industry greatly improved. In 1958, the newly organized National Aeronautics and Space Administration (NASA) took over responsibility for the research program. The NASA research budget was dwarfed during the postwar period by an enormous military investment in aerospace research and development that took place through other channels. Yet, the NASA program played an important ancillary role throughout the period.

In addition, US industry benefited by technology transfers from wartime allies, along with the emigration of skilled scientific personnel from Europe. The buildup of military R&D programs in the early 1950s was particularly impressive; measured in 1990 dollars, military R&D expanded from roughly $4 billion in 1950 to more than $14 billion in 1952,[2] generating important benefits for the US commercial aircraft industry. A large share of the technology developed for the engines and airframes of the long-range military bombers and tankers of the early 1950s had important commercial applications, helping to lay the foundation for the Boeing 707.

During the postwar years, the perceived importance of the aerospace industry for US national security also led the US government to intervene directly in order to rescue military aerospace contractors threatened with bankruptcy. When Douglas Aircraft ran into trouble in the mid-1960s as a result of its problems in the commercial aircraft market, federal loan guarantees and favorable antitrust reviews supported the shotgun marriage of Douglas to McDonnell, creating McDonnell Douglas. In 1971, the Lockheed Corporation, faced with bankruptcy as a result of cost overruns in the development of its wide-bodied L-1011, was rescued by a federal loan guarantee of $250 million. As one analyst concluded in his study of the civil and military aerospace industry, "the [federal] government simply will not allow a major defense contractor to fail completely, whatever its commercial sins."[3]

One of the most important forms of public support for the postwar development of the civil aerospace industry in the United States was unplanned and indirect. Until 1978, federal regulation by the Civil Aeronautics Board restricted competition among interstate airlines, limiting new entries and price discounting. During the regulated era, competition was based primarily on service and quality, spurring the major airlines to vie with one another to place orders for new generations of commercial transports. This competition induced the rapid adoption of new aircraft technologies. In the process, US producers of airframes and engines exploited their proximity to the largest civilian market in the world to build a dominant position. Thereafter, they used their technological and financial dominance as a kind of springboard for exports, a strategy commonly used by Japanese producers in other export sectors.

However, the internal sources of stimulus and support for the American aerospace industry eventually began to decline. Deregulation of domestic airlines in 1978 strained the financial capacities of competing lines and removed one of the incentives for early adoption of new aircraft. The aggregate expenditures of NASA and the Department of Defense on aeronautics research, when measured in real terms, leveled off and even declined slightly after 1975.[4] With the exception of a few technologies such as avionics, technological spill-overs from military to civilian sectors became less important. Cases began to appear that indicated a reversal of the previous relationship between military and civilian technological development; the KC-10 military tanker, for instance, owed much of its technology to the commercial DC-10. It was evident that the US aerospace industry had entered a new era.

Europe and Japan

As we observed earlier, other industrial democracies also invested considerable public resources in the sustenance or revival of their postwar national aerospace industries. During the 1950s and 1960s, governments in Britain and France encouraged a succession of complex mergers, seeking to create "national champions" in the civilian and military sectors of the industry. In the process, the British and French governments took equity positions in a number of key firms, provided extensive financial support for R&D programs, and followed heavily preferential policies in the purchase of aircraft. Japan and West Germany followed similar policies.[5]

The technological performance of some of the favored firms was impressive. The first turbojet-powered commercial transport, the Comet, was introduced by the British DeHavilland Corporation in 1952, six years before Boeing introduced the 707. In the civilian aerospace sector, however, efforts to sustain national champions proved very difficult, as soaring development costs gave the advantage to countries with the largest domestic markets. As development costs increased, France and Britain encountered mounting problems in lining up the advance orders and amassing the development funds needed to launch each new generation of aircraft.[6]

Despite continued attempts to support their national champions with subsidies and buy-at-home policies, the problems of the French and British industries continued to grow. In the 1950s and 1960s, only one of Britain's twelve commercial aircraft projects, the Viscount, proved commercially successful. The competitive position of Britain's major airlines, BEA and BOAC, was undermined by the pressures to buy national products and to forego better and cheaper aircraft. French government policy scored a partial success with the short-range turbojet Caravelle during the 1950s, exploiting the gap left by the longer-range 707 and DC-8; however, the Caravelle was displaced by the Boeing 727 when it appeared in 1962.

The Japanese government also discovered the drawbacks of a limited domestic market during this period. The Ministry of International Trade and Industry (MITI) supported the development in 1959 of a sixty-seat turbo-prop aircraft, the YS-11, by a consortium of domestic producers. The aircraft was a technical success but a commercial failure. Production ceased in 1974 after a nine-year run, with delivery of only 182 planes, mostly to domestic carriers.[7]

Recognizing the limitations of small domestic markets for commercial aircraft, European policy makers developed a regional approach, characterized by heavy government participation and support. France and Britain collaborated in the development of the supersonic Concorde, which entered commercial service in 1976. Once again, however, the plane was a technological success but a disastrous commercial failure. With an eventual development cost that was ten times the original estimate of $450 million, production was terminated in 1979 after delivery of only sixteen aircraft, all of them sold to the state-owned French and British airlines.

In the 1960s, another major pan-European consortium, Airbus Industrie, was launched and experienced a rocky beginning. The British, French, and German participants each initially tried to use the project to sustain their own national aircraft industries. These pressures and a cumbersome management structure increased project costs, hindered decision making, and generated a design that had little appeal for prospective buyers, resulting in a lack of orders and a financial crisis.[8] The British government withdrew from the consortium in 1969, and Airbus was reorganized under the technical and managerial leadership of its French participants. The ambitious technical goals of the early designs were modified and non-European components were given a larger place in the production plans. In 1975, the completion of the A300 signalled the entry of Airbus Industrie as an important producer of commercial aircraft. And in 1979, the British rejoined the Airbus consortium.

US government sources estimate that since the consortium's creation, it has absorbed as much as $12 to $15 billion dollars in public funds but has yet to yield a net profit.[9] Nevertheless, Airbus has become a significant competitor to the existing US commercial airframe firms. In the period from 1986 to 1990, for instance, Airbus accounted for 15 percent of the deliveries of commercial jet aircraft to noncommunist markets, while the two surviving US firms—Boeing and McDonnell Douglas—accounted for 81 percent. But at the beginning of the 1990s, the order backlog of Airbus was considerably higher than its share of sales, running at about 30 percent, and raising the possibility that it might increase its share of sales in the future at the expense of its US competitors.[10]

Confronting a European consortium, US firms looked for alliances that might strengthen their financial position and technical resources. Their responses built on earlier international collaborations stretching back over three decades.

The Spread of International Alliances

International collaboration in the aerospace industry first appeared in the production of military aircraft, in arrangements among the NATO allies and with Japan. From 1947 to 1980, at least twenty-eight US aircraft, missile, or rotorcraft designs were manufactured by foreign firms in more than twenty nations under licenses granted by US producers. These coproduction agreements enabled European and Japanese firms to improve or sustain their aerospace production capabilities, but because these agreements did not include the design and development of aircraft, they resulted in the transfer of only a limited range of skills and technologies.

During the 1960s and 1970s, the governments of the larger Western European democracies occasionally explored the possibility of collaborating in the development and production of military aircraft in order to overcome some of the same financial constraints that were limiting their commercial industries. Trans-European collaboration included a French-British helicopter program, the German-French Transall transport aircraft, the British-French Jaguar fighter aircraft, and the British-German-Italian Tornado multirole combat aircraft.

Although these projects allowed for a sharing of costs and technology, the development and production costs of the military aircraft produced in trans-European programs tended to be higher, and their development schedules considerably longer, than comparable US programs. Even when compared with national military programs in Europe, the trans-European programs appeared to be generating somewhat higher costs and slower deliveries.[11] These disappointing results were due in part to disagreements over design and performance objectives, and to differences over the sharing of the benefits, that were endemic to trans-European projects. Still, the advantages of cost-sharing and of avoiding US domination seemed sufficient to justify the projects in the eyes of the participants.

During the 1970s and 1980s, European governments also demanded a greater role in the development of the military aircraft they were purchasing from the United States. Pressure from foreign allies for codevelopment was not confined to European governments; the agreement between the US and Japanese governments to collaborate in developing a new fighter, the FSX, arose out of the same trend in policy. Codevelopment agreements allowed Japanese and European enterprises to collaborate with US aerospace firms on the "upstream" activities of R&D and design. These demands intensified at a time when the United States itself was eager to reduce the development costs of its weapons systems and wished to encourage standardization in the myriad weapons systems deployed by NATO. In 1986, the drive for codevelopment received an additional impetus in the form of congressional legislation that encouraged multinational cooperation in weapons development in an effort to reduce military expenditures.[12]

Another strategy adopted by foreign governments to increase their share of the business generated by military aircraft production was to demand a greater role in the production of the components for the aircraft they were purchasing from US sources. These demands led to the development of numerous offset agreements between US producers and foreign firms in Europe and elsewhere. One of the most celebrated examples of the use of offset agreements involved the F-16, a product of US-based General Dynamics. At stake was "the sale of the century," a huge prospective order from NATO forces. Faced with the prospect that several European governments might try to develop an indigenous military fighter to rival the F-16, General Dynamics agreed to assign a major production role to domestic firms in prospective purchaser nations. This role included the production of components not only for the aircraft sold to European nations but also for the aircraft sold to the US Air Force. For instance, European producers in Belgium, Norway, the Netherlands, and Denmark, in addition to being offered control of 40 percent of the production expenditures for planes sold to their respective governments, were also offered control of 10 percent of the cost of the planes delivered to the US Air Force and 15 percent of the cost of planes sold elsewhere. Aided by such arrangements, with the backing of leading Belgian and Dutch aircraft firms, General Dynamics was able to win the contract over strong competition.

Another celebrated example of the role of offsets in the sale of sophisticated military equipment involved Boeing's sale of AWACS aircraft to NATO. Boeing's strategy of seeking partners throughout NATO enabled it to defeat the competing entry, the all-British AEW Nimrod.[13] On paper, the initial Nimrod proposal—advanced by the British team of national champions, composed of Hawker Siddeley Aviation, Marconi-Elliot Avionic Systems, and Rolls Royce—seemed to promise distinct technological and price advantages over AWACS; however, the Nimrod aircraft could not match the technical performance of the Boeing AWACs, illustrating the weaknesses of limiting an aerospace company to suppliers from a single nation. Moreover, without allies among manufacturers in other countries, the marketing of the Nimrod proved a failure. After spending $1.6 billion, the British government was forced to terminate the project in recognition of the fact that Boeing's ability to draw on technology and marketing assistance from allies and partners around the world gave it a giant edge over a purely national aircraft.

For the US government and aerospace industry, offset agreements have always evoked a mixed reaction. Their desire to penetrate foreign markets for both political and economic reasons has struggled with a desire to limit foreign access to some of the technologies contained in military and civilian high-technology products like aircraft. Before 1978, offset agreements in military aircraft sales were largely negotiated on a government-to-government basis, indicating the mix of economic and political motives underpinning them.[14] By the 1990s, they had become a mainstay in sales of both military and civil aircraft to foreign governments and foreign firms and in sales to both industrialized and industrializing countries. As foreign producers have improved their technological capabilities, the products and technologies subject to offset agreements have increasingly involved highly advanced US technologies in both military and civil applications.[15]

The strategy of building multinational support among suppliers to ensure market penetration has become even more critical in the commercial sector, in part as a result of the intense competition between Boeing and Airbus. In the manufacture of the A300, for example, Airbus procured over 50 percent of the plane's components from US manufacturers, thereby capturing both their technology and their political support. At the same time, Boeing's choice of Rolls

Royce for engines in the 757, and of Aeritalia for airframe production in the 767, aided sales in the European market, even as the participation of Japanese firms in the manufacture of the 767 has helped Boeing to dominate the Japanese commercial aircraft market.[16] As Boeing's president noted, "If we were to bleed off all of the aerospace production, we'd get a backlash that would cause more trouble than sharing to a degree."[17]

By the 1990s penetration of foreign markets had become more important than ever for US producers of commercial aircraft. Industry executives were projecting that the demand for commercial air transport would grow more rapidly abroad than in the United States, consistent with trends that were visible in the 1980s.[18] In prospect, therefore, was an increasing emphasis on foreign partnerships. Complex consortia like General Electric's partnership with France's SNECMA, as well as Pratt & Whitney's partnership with Rolls Royce and an array of Japanese and other European firms, appeared to offer a preview of the future structure of the industry.

Prime contractors in civil airframes and engines have been driven not only by a desire to penetrate foreign markets but also by an interest in expanding the array of suppliers that compete for contracts and in spreading a share of the development costs and risks. Higher development costs create stronger incentives for risk-sharing; broad corporate alliances reduce the need to "bet the company" on each new generation of products. Boeing's arrangements with Mitsubishi, Kawasaki, and Fuji Heavy Industries have enabled it to reduce its risks and to maintain a near monopoly on sales to Japanese airlines. The V2500 engine consortium, by including Japanese firms, reduced the financial exposure of Rolls Royce and Pratt & Whitney, allowing them to continue to offer a "full line" of new engines for commercial airframes. The costs of the V2500 engine project were particularly onerous because it had no military counterpart that could defray a share of the development and testing expenses, illustrating the changing relationship between military and civil technologies in the industry.

Although the consortium approach has served to create a foreign presence in national aerospace industries, firms in the industry have been far less prone to establish multinational networks of subsidiaries than have firms in other technology-intensive industries. Aerospace firms have sometimes offered to produce their products through subsidiaries on foreign soil, but only as a last resort; the lure of China's market, for instance, led Boeing and McDonnell Douglas to offer to produce aircraft in that country.[19] But the cost penalties of operating multiple production facilities in commercial aircraft, combined with the pressures from their home governments to maintain a national defense base, have led firms in the industry to resist a multinational structure.

Nonetheless, because military and commercial aircraft involve the integration of so many complex subsystems and components, and because many of them are sourced internationally, the "nationality" of the final product has become increasingly difficult to establish, creating complex implications for policy. For example, the US government provides Export-Import Bank subsidies for the sale of Boeing 757 airframes to foreign buyers, even though many of them specify that British Rolls-Royce engines must be incorporated in the aircraft. The US government also has protested the excessive generosity of European government subsidies for the sale of the Airbus A300, despite the fact that this aircraft often employs General Electric engines. Which policy more effectively supports US income and employment growth? In the modern commercial aircraft industry, it is hard to know.

TRENDS AND PORTENTS

Although every country with an aerospace industry identifies that industry as critical to its defense planning, the aerospace industry has not escaped the globalizing trends that have engulfed large segments of the world's industrial structure. In moving toward a global structure, however, the industry has exhibited some distinctive patterns reflecting its unique status in national defense, its heavy reliance on technological change, and its strikingly concentrated industrial structure.

Leading firms have employed a number of tactics to maintain a technological edge while collaborating with erstwhile rivals. US firms, for instance, have limited the transfer or disclosure of critical elements of their technology to their foreign partners. In the development of its 767 with Japanese partners, Boeing has sought to safeguard its testing processes and software needed for redesign as well as many of the "black boxes" of the aircraft used in the cockpit navigation systems. General Electric took similar precautions in its joint development of an engine with SNECMA, although some of its restrictions arose from the fact that the engine involved drew part of its technology from a military engine developed for the Department of Defense. Pratt & Whitney also imposed tight restrictions on technology transfer within the V2500 engine venture, albeit with costly consequences. Although the V2500 was designed so as to minimize the need for exchanges of proprietary technology among participants, problems in integrating the separately developed engine components led to severe delays in the testing and introduction of the engine. Bolstering these efforts at secrecy, leaders of some international consortia have routinely obtained commitments limiting their partners' independent use of any acquired technologies for some stated period in the future.

US aerospace industry leaders also have sought to maintain their competitive advantage by a variety of devices: achieving scale economies through the standardization of components and designs across different types of aircraft and engines, developing a global network for providing services and spare parts, phasing in the introduction of new products so that the learning processes and cash flows of earlier products could support those that followed, and so on. Boeing has been particularly assiduous in pursuing such strategies, but other leading US enterprises have diligently applied such strategies as well.

The defenses of leaders against the entry of rivals, however, have been less than perfect. Both McDonnell Douglas and Airbus have courted the Japanese, hoping to capture support for their attempts to end Boeing's dominance of sales to airlines in Japan. An open-ended agreement in 1990 between Mitsubishi Heavy Industries, the largest Japanese aircraft company, and Daimler Benz, West Germany's largest industrial group, raised the possibility of a link between the Japanese aerospace consortium and the Airbus consortium. This prospect has increased the pressure on Boeing to be more forthcoming to its Japanese partners.

Well before the Daimler-Mitsubishi agreement was announced, the president of Boeing Commercial Airplanes observed that the Japanese "are going to become involved in a commercial jet program one way or another. We sure don't want them to get involved with Airbus."[20] Consistent with his statement, Boeing was already expanding the role of its Japanese partners in the development and manufacture of its commercial aircraft. In the 767 project, the Japanese consortium, comprised of Mitsubishi Heavy Industries, Fuji Heavy Industries, and Kawasaki Heavy Industries, provided low-level design and advanced manufacturing services and skills. The Japanese consortium planned also to play a more prominent role in the development of the successor 777, as well as becoming involved for the first time in marketing and sales finance. Clearly, the Japanese were making some progress toward MITI's long-term goal of developing a domestic commercial aircraft industry.[21] Similarly, in the V2500 joint venture for aircraft engines among Pratt & Whitney, Rolls Royce, and others, Germany's MTU and Italy's Fiat were assigned a more important role than they had previously occupied in such projects.

In military aircraft, Japanese firms have improved their manufacturing skills through coproduction partnerships with the United States. The FSX project with General Dynamics builds on a series of coproduction agreements that include the F-3, F-4 and F-15, all of which were manufactured by Japanese firms under license from US firms. The role assumed by the Japanese in the FSX, however, includes overall system design, development, and integration, going beyond any previous US-Japanese agreement in military aircraft. This expanded role notwithstanding, the FSX project is devoted to modifying a fighter airframe design that is at least twenty-years old, while the FSX engines will be US designs that are manufactured under license in Japan.

Yet, despite the fact that a globalization trend has been visible in both military and civilian aerospace throughout the postwar period, the supportive links that existed between the two sectors during much of that period appeared to decline in the 1980s. As was noted above, the technological and commercial support that military developments had provided to civil aircraft, such as the boost that the KC-135 had given to the B-707, seems unlikely to occur again in the future. Moreover, the viability of the fifteen hundred firms that supply military and civil aerospace firms increasingly depends on their fortunes in the commercial segment of the aerospace industry.[22] These US supplier firms are especially vulnerable to intensified competition resulting from the international joint ventures of US producers of military and civilian aircraft.

By the 1990s, the prospect of a sharp decline in expenditures on conventional and strategic weapons systems, coupled with the apparent existence of considerable excess capacity among the subcontractors who supply both the commercial and military sectors, pointed to the strong likelihood of shrinkage in the industry.[23] Faced with increased pressure on their domestic aerospace industries, foreign governments may well try to stiffen their buy-at-home requirements, especially in the acquisition of military products. As they do so, however, they will run head-on into the technological and financial imperatives that have obliged enterprises to develop their cross-border alliances. The resulting tensions will fuel national debates in the United States, Europe, and Japan over the policies to be pursued in maintaining a military and civilian capability in aerospace.

This struggle is likely to take a familiar form, a battle between those who see advantages in the government's taking an aggressive promotional role in the development of key industries and those who prefer to leave the field to market forces. Among political scientists and economists, the debate will array those who espouse a liberal approach against those who prefer more neomercantilist attempts to construct an active national industrial policy.

In the case of the aerospace industry, the industry's distinctive characteristics are likely to make this debate especially intense. The large economies of scale and important "first mover advantages" in this industry provide powerful pressures toward the domination of world markets by a handful of firms. A market structure of that sort would create incentives for governments to resort to strategic, predatory, or preemptive policies.[24] Moreover, with such domination, the leading firms in the industry will increase their ability to delay, deny, exploit, and extort; when the leading firms are located abroad, they will present a potential for foreign *diktat*.[25] Faced with such a threat, critics of conventional laissez-faire economics in Europe and Asia, as well as in the United States, will argue that national security planners can hardly afford to be agnostic about the nationality of suppliers and the location of production.

Public officials in Europe have already emphasized the point that extraordinary barriers exist to the entry of new firms into the industry, a consequence of the complexity of the technology, the size of the requisite financial commitments, and the early lead of American firms. Both the Europeans and the Japanese are fully aware that overcoming such barriers may entail extraordinary levels of public subsidy and protection.[26]

Observing the long-term policies of the United States, industrial planners in Europe and Asia may be excused for feeling that the exhortations from US policy makers for all nations to embrace a noninterventionist approach are disingenuous. In the end, Europe and Japan are unlikely to respond to such exhortations by reducing their efforts of the past few decades to develop an indigenous aerospace capability.

On the US side, both the military and the commercial considerations for resisting the spread of the industry outside US territory will have great persuasiveness in terms of jobs and exports and in terms of national defense. The debate over aerospace policy will be intertwined with ideological struggles over the appropriate use of public power. Arguments as to whether the United States should consciously adopt an industrial policy for the aerospace industry and the phalanx of related industries that support it are embedded in the larger question of governmental intervention in the structure of industry and the conduct of foreign trade. The arguments on all sides have already been so thoroughly developed that it is easy to envisage their structure.[27]

On one side, US proponents for an active industrial policy will argue that the aerospace industry, by virtue of the required scale and the critical importance of learning-by-doing, cannot be expected to respond to market forces in the constructive ways that Americans usually associate with competitive industries. In this view, the need for continuity and momentum is so critical for the survival of the industry that its fate cannot be left to the vicissitudes of supply and demand. Moreover, observing the likely policies of other countries in promoting an independent aerospace industry, proponents will argue that the United States cannot anticipate that an open competitive market or level playing field will be available in international markets.

In rejoinder, those in the United States who resist the idea of formulating an industrial policy for the industry will point to what they regard as a dismal and costly record of the governments that have attempted it. They will emphasize that government intervention for economic and national security reasons in other US industries, including steel, machine tools, and semiconductors, has burdened the

US aerospace industry with much heavier costs than those borne by European and Japanese competitors.[28] They will insist that the US federal structure of checks and balances, when coupled with the standard US requirement that bureaucrats must operate under close supervision and with limited discretion, is incompatible with granting the extensive powers to the bureaucracy that are implied by a supple industrial policy, such as choosing technologies and managing the distribution of benefits among winners and losers.

Another ideological issue that is likely to figure in the US debate is whether the trade and investment of US aerospace firms should be supported by the policies explored in the new literature on strategic trade theory. Under this theory, governments may be able to use domestic protection and export subsidies to establish and retain the critical advantages of first mover and dominant producer, thereby establishing international supremacy for their own national firms.[29] With scale economies and learning-by-doing occupying so critical a role in the international aerospace industry, the temptation for any government to follow such a course is evident.

Equally relevant, however, is the likely reaction on the part of governments exposed to the threat of dependence on concentrated foreign suppliers in key industrial sectors. Concerns about finding themselves at the mercy of foreign monopolists have motivated the efforts of governments in Europe and Japan to build up their own aerospace sectors. In the United States, the same fear exists: a fear that foreign firms, backed by their governments, might try to use cross-border relationships with US firms, such as the FSX and Boeing-Mitsubishi arrangements, as the first step in an effort to dominate the field.

Applying the principles of the prisoner's dilemma, theorists have recognized that in the end, the efforts of governments to seize and hold a dominant position could lead to stalemate. In order for the policy to succeed, rival governments must remain passive, accepting the existence of blocked markets and continuing to keep their own markets open. The most likely outcome of the application of strategic trade theory in a given sector, it was concluded, would be retaliation by the governments in that sector or some other sectors in which they enjoyed an advantage.

What could easily be overlooked in these debates about industrial policy and strategic trade theory, however, is the extent to which the evolution of the technology and industrial structure of the industry itself circumscribes the choices for future public policy. By the 1990s, the United States no longer possessed an internal market large enough to provide a protected national environment for the technological development and production learning required for a new family of aircraft. National requirements in the civilian market were beginning to appear insufficient to sustain the giant risks that any innovating firm would have to take in order to launch such an undertaking. At the same time, lacking a protected home market large enough to support new generations of aircraft, the costs to Europe or Japan of providing subsidies large enough to maintain an aerospace champion firm were becoming prohibitive. Given the costly example of Airbus, a repetition of that kind of undertaking seemed increasingly improbable. Moreover, neither the United States nor Europe nor Japan could count on a national lead in all of the major technologies required for the launching of a new family of aircraft.

Thus, although one cannot altogether rule out the long-term possibility of the emergence of a new national aerospace champion, supported by one or more governments, a more likely pattern of development will be the continuation and extension of cross-border consortia, composed of a number of firms of different nationalities. That pattern, if it developed, would serve to reduce the ability of any one country to engage in predatory behavior.

On the other hand, the effects of governmental policies on the distribution of the ancillary industries supporting the aerospace industry are less clear. In this arena, a government's aggressive use of subsidies or other devices associated with industrial policy and strategic trade theory could well provide it with some leverage. As we have already observed, aircraft manufacture entails the integration and assembly of an array of complex components. Moreover, the components frequently are employed in both military and civilian applications, so that the threat of a foreign government's control over supply could be seen as a major problem.

As for major airframe and engine producers, the policy problems they present may well prove to be of a very different kind. In their case, the networks that they have developed to deal with the problems of scale and risk have begun to create conditions in which the discipline imposed by market competition may be losing its bite.

Until the early 1990s, governments were prepared to tolerate cross-border partnerships, coproduction arrangements, and joint ventures whose basic purpose was to ensure vigorous penetration of each others' markets. Ultimately, however, the trend toward international partnerships could be used by firms and governments alike to freeze the structure of the industry with a global market-sharing arrangement. It could well be that the most pressing problems for the United States, Europe, and Japan in the decades ahead, therefore, will be to find ways of preserving the technological drive and the incentive for efficiency in the industry that competition would ordinarily be expected to provide.

ACKNOWLEDGEMENTS

We would like to thank Michele Shannon who assisted in the preparation of this paper. Support for the second author's research on this topic was provided by the Alfred P. Sloan Foundation and the Consortium on Competitiveness and Cooperation.

ENDNOTES

[1] Edward Constant, *Origins of the Turbojet Revolution* (Baltimore: Johns Hopkins Press, 1980), 198.

[2] D. C. Mowery, *Alliance Politics and Economics: Multinational Joint Ventures in Commercial Aircraft* (Cambridge: Ballinger, 1987), 41.

[3] S. L. Carroll, "The Market for Commercial Airliners," in R. E. Caves and M. J. Roberts, eds., *Regulating the Product* (Cambridge: Ballinger, 1975), 162. See also D. C. Mowery and N. Rosenberg, "The Commercial Aircraft Industry," in R. R. Nelson, ed., *Government and Technical Progress* (New York: Pergamon, 1982), 113.

[4] See A. March, "The U.S. Commercial Aircraft Industry and Its Foreign Competitors," *Working Papers of the MIT Commission on Industrial Productivity,* vol. 1 (Cambridge: MIT Press, 1989), 87.

[5] For additional discussion, see K. Hayward, *Government and British Civil Aerospace* (Manchester, U.K.: Manchester University Press, 1983); Mowery; and M. S. Hochmuth, "Aerospace," in R. Vernon, ed., *Big Business and the State* (Cambridge: Harvard University Press, 1974). Although dated, Hochmuth's discussion provides useful historical detail; however his favorable verdict on French aerospace policy has not been borne out by subsequent developments.

[6] See Hochmuth, "Aerospace," 150; Mowery.

152   *Theodore H. Moran and David C. Mowery*

See D. C. Mowery and N. Rosenberg, "Competition and Cooperation: The U.S. and Japanese Commercial Aircraft Industries," *California Management Review* 27 (1985): 70–82.

See the discussion of Airbus in Mowery; or K. Hayward, *International Collaboration in Civil Aerospace* (London: Frances Pinter, 1986).

For an estimate of Airbus subsidies, see P. Krugman, "The Effects of Foreign Industrial Targeting," *Brookings Papers on Economic Activity* (Washington, D.C.: Brookings Institution, 1987); or Gelman Research Associates, *An Economic and Financial Review of Airbus Industrie*, report prepared for the International Trade Administration, US Department of Commerce (Washington D.C.: Department of Commerce, 1990).

See "Zoom! Airbus Comes on Strong," *Business Week*, 22 April 1991, 48–50. Data on order backlogs often include options of varying degrees of firmness in addition to firm commitments and therefore are much less reliable than deliveries data as indicators of market share.

K. Hartley, *NATO Arms Co-operation: A Study in Economics and Politics* (London: Allen and Unwin, 1983); M. Rich, W. Stanley, J. Birkler, and M. Hesse, *Multinational Co-production of Military Aerospace Systems* (Santa Monica, Calif.: RAND, 1981). E. Kolodziej's account is revealing: "A former senior French official suggested a formula for estimating the costs of a cooperative program. These are equal to the cost of a national program times the square root of the number of participants. . . . Delays can be measured by multiplying the length of time of a national program by the cube root of the number of cooperating members." (E. Kolodziej, *Making and Marketing Arms* [Princeton: Princeton University Press, 1987], 150.)

See E. Kapstein, "International Collaboration in Armaments Production: A Second Best Solution," *Political Science Quarterly* (Winter 1991/1992).

Daniel Todd and Jamie Simpson, *The World Aircraft Industry* (London: Croom Helm, 1986); Arnold Lee Tessner, *Politics of Compromise: NATO and AWACs* (Washington, D.C.: National Defense University Press, 1988); "Airborne Early Warning: Two Major Systems for Europe," *Interavia: World Review of Aviation* (September 1980); and "Boeing Makes Final Bid for British Contract, Offers to Plow Profits Back into Nation," *New York Times*, 12 November 1986.

J. Cole, "Evaluating Offset Agreements: Achieving a Balance of Advantages," *Law and Policy in International Business* 19 (1987): 765–809.

J. Gansler, *The Defense Industry* (Cambridge: MIT Press, 1980), 205.

See Hayward or Mowery.

"Boeing Takes a Bold Plunge to Keep Flying High," *Fortune*, 25 September 1980.

See National Research Council, *The Competitive Status of the U.S. Civil Aviation Industry* (Washington, D.C.: National Academy Press, 1983); and V. Lopez, *The U.S. Aerospace Industry and the Trend toward Internationalization* (Washington, D.C.: Aerospace Industries Association, 1988).

S. Carey, "China Seen Set to Decide on Aircraft Job," *Wall Street Journal*, 19 February 1991, 11A.

[20]George Tibbits, "Boeing Sees 767-X Talks as Latest in Long Term Relationship with Japanese," The Associated Press, 1 November 1989.

[21]See Industrial Bank of Japan, *The Vision of MITI Policies in the 1980s* (Tokyo: Industrial Bank of Japan, 1980), 291.

[22]In the 1985 report of the National Research Council the US Civil Aviation Manufacturing Panel noted, "The 15,000-company supplier base is an important key, since these firms supply critical materials and parts to both the civil and military aircraft industry. Frequently, in the case of smaller second- or third-tier suppliers, the military and civil production outputs are sufficiently common that the same facilities and labor pools produce both." *The Competitive Status of the U.S. Civil Aviation Manufacturing Industry* (Washington, D.C.: National Academy Press, 1985), 99.

[23]"If procurement spending in defense declines over the long-term, there will not only be fewer new project starts in this sector, but the ability of these firms to get well will decline too. The resulting squeeze between increasing risk taking by contractors and declining compensation should force some firms to leave the business (or move into other lines of defense work), bringing supply into line with demand." (T. McNaugher, *New Weapons, Old Politics* [Washington, D.C.: Brookings Institution, 1990], 175); see also J. Gansler.

[24]Some sense of the magnitude of scale and learning-based cost improvements is conveyed by the calculation that the per unit cost of a hypothetical 150-seat commercial airliner drops 70 percent by the two hundredth sale before leveling off. This estimate was prepared by the US Department of Commerce in cooperation with McDonnell Douglas and is cited in Richard Baldwin and Paul Krugman, "Industrial Policy and International Competition in Wide Bodied Jet Aircrafts," in Robert Baldwin, ed., *Trade Policy Issues and Empirical Analysis* (Chicago: University of Chicago Press, 1988).

[25]Theodore H. Moran, "The Globalization of America's Defense Industries: Managing the Threat of Foreign Dependence," *International Security* 15 (1) (Summer 1990).

[26]See Mowery and Rosenberg, "Competition and Cooperation."

[27]See, for instance, testimony of Arden Bement, Pat Choate, Stephen Cohen, and Robert Kahn: US Congress, US Senate, Committee on Governmental Affairs, *Government's Role in Economic Competitiveness* hearings, 100th Cong., 1st sess., 25 March–7 April, 1987 (Washington, D.C.: US Government Printing Office, 1987); US Congress, US Senate, Committee on Governmental Affairs, *Economic Competitiveness, International Trade, and Technology Development Act of 1987*, report, 100th Cong., 1st sess., 23 June 1987 (Washington, D.C.: US Government Printing Office, 1987); and US Congress, House, Subcommittee on Economic Stabilization, Committee on Banking, Finance, and Urban Affairs, *Defense Production Act Amendments of 1988*, hearings, 100th Cong., 2d. sess., 30–31 March 1988 (Washington, D.C.: US Government Printing Office, 1988). See also, Stephen S. Cohen and John Zysman, *Manufacturing Matters: The Myth of the Post-Industrial Economy* (New York: Basic Books, 1987); and Clyde V. Prestowitz, Jr., *Trading Places: How We Allowed Japan to Take the Lead* (New York: Basic Books, 1988).

[28]The Stern Group, *Rebuilding American Manufacturing in the 1990s: The Case against Steel VRAs* (Washington, D.C.: The Stern Group, February 1989); US International Trade Commission, Investigation No. 332–149 under sec. 232 of the Tariff Act of 1930, *Competitive Assessment of the U.S. Metalworking Machine Tool Industry* (Washington, D.C.: ITC, September 1983); report to the US Congress by the Secretary of Defense in July 1989, *The Impact of Buy American Restrictions Affecting Defense Procurement* (Washington, D.C.: Department of Defense, 1989); and Stuart Auerbach, "U.S. Chip Industry Rivals Wire Together an Alliance," *Washington Post*, 14 August 1988, H6.

[29]See, for example, James A. Brander and Barbara J. Spencer, "Export Subsidies and International Market Share Rivalry," *Journal of International Economics* 18 (February 1985); Paul R. Krugman, ed., *Strategic Trade Policy and the New International Economics* (Cambridge: MIT Press, 1986); J. David Richardson, "Strategic Trade Policy," *International Organization* 44 (1) (Winter 1990); and Avinash Dixit, "International R&D Competition and Policy," in A. Michael Spence and Heather A. Hazard, eds., *International Competitiveness* (Cambridge: Ballinger, 1988).

J. Nicholas Ziegler

Semiconductors

The semiconductor industry figures prominently in any effort to map the limits of national control in a global economy. Given its promise for miniaturizing electrical equipment of all kinds, semiconductor technology was of immediate interest to defense agencies. Over time, however, commercial markets rather than military markets came to drive the industry's technological frontiers. Even though electronics assumed a growing part of the procurement budget of armed forces everywhere, military orders accounted for a declining fraction of the world's semiconductor output. The preponderant weight of commercial markets reduced the direct influence of defense agencies over the technological capabilities of the industry.

This dependence on commercial markets has created particularly severe problems for national security planners as the industry has spanned national boundaries. Leading semiconductor firms have entered overseas markets, disseminating their technology and building global organizations. Yet, the process of globalization has not been uniform. In critical parts of the industry, a complementary trend toward regional agglomeration has become evident.[1] Because competition in this industry has hinged on steady innovation, semiconductor producers have had to work closely with specialized suppliers and demanding customers, creating agglomerations that stimulated further learning and innovation. This essay examines how defense planners have dealt with each of these complex trends in their efforts to maintain an adequate defense industrial base.

J. Nicholas Ziegler is Assistant Professor of International Management, Sloan School of Management, M.I.T.

DEFENSE AND THE EMERGENCE OF AN INDUSTRY STRUCTURE

In retrospect, it is clear that defense priorities helped shape the semiconductor industry quite differently in different countries. In the United States, military orders provided early markets for new products and enabled American firms to gain technological leadership. With abundant research funds, American firms emphasized the generation of new products in their commercial strategies as well. In Europe, defense planners encouraged national firms to keep pace with American product innovations. In Japan, however, military priorities exercised a much lesser role; instead, Japanese officials encouraged firms to invest in a more gradual process of internal technology development.

The US example focused popular attention on the scientist-entrepreneur. Semiconductor materials, such as germanium and silicon, were known for the unusual property of conducting electrical current when "doped" with certain impurities. In 1947 researchers at Bell Laboratories demonstrated this effect by producing a tiny germanium device that amplified an electrical current. By controlling the impurities in a semiconductor's crystalline structure, scientists soon learned how to create devices that could perform all the functions of vacuum tubes in radios and early computers.[2]

Despite the import of these basic discoveries, the industry's evolution has also depended on innumerable incremental improvements that have facilitated the practical application of scientific knowledge outside the laboratory. After forty years of development, the semiconductor industry has come to include hundreds of companies, which collectively generate annual revenues of over $50 billion. But there have been some critical differences in the industry structures of the various countries that were developing the new technologies.

In the United States, the private sector and the military cooperated in disseminating semiconductor technology. The transistor patents gave Bell Labs, then a subsidiary of the American Telegraph and Telephone Company, a commanding position, and the company invited other firms to help develop the technology. During these early years, the military contributed generously to AT&T's research budget and encouraged Bell Labs to disseminate technical information to its licensees.[3] For three decades thereafter, procurement officers in the

US military could virtually always obtain state-of-the-art components from national suppliers.

The new technology drew three types of firms into the industry. Equipment producers such as AT&T and International Business Machines, used semiconductor devices as components in their products. Established companies that had been producing receiving tubes for radios and other products, such as General Electric, RCA, Raytheon, and Sylvania, recognized transistors as a substitute technology that could threaten their market, and they took up production as well. Newcomers such as Texas Instruments, Fairchild, Transitron, and Motorola, entered the business as specialized producers, selling their output on the open market.[4]

In the succeeding decades, all these producers would move beyond transistors to increasingly complex products. In the late 1950s, electrical engineers learned how to emplace several transistors or other elements in a single piece of semiconducting material, giving rise to the "integrated circuit" (soon known more colloquially as a "chip"). Since they allowed engineers to design numerous electrical functions into a single tiny circuit, these integrated circuits ushered in an entire new applied discipline known as "microelectronics."[5] Another development of consummate importance was the introduction in 1971 of the so-called microprocessor, single chips containing all the electronic functions found in a digital computer.

In these developments, the newer firms selling their semiconductor products on the open market—the so-called merchant producers—would take a central role. Yet military procurement clearly shaped the industry's technological frontiers.[6] Through 1963, defense-related purchases absorbed over 35 percent of the country's semiconductor output and over 90 percent of the market for integrated circuits. By the late 1970s, defense-related purchases of semiconductors were almost entirely comprised of integrated circuits, but accounted for only about 10 percent of the country's output.[7]

The military's early priorities led, fortuitously, to components that were well suited to commercial markets, especially for digital computers. The availability of integrated circuits lowered the technological barriers for firms wanting to enter the computer industry and sales of such products mushroomed. Between 1963 and 1973 the American market for integrated circuits grew from $16 million to roughly $2 billion.[8]

Powered by such growth, the merchant business in these products became fiercely competitive and the industry gained its legendary reputation for continual innovation. The complexity of integrated circuits doubled every year. By the early 1970s, the industry entered the era of large-scale integration, developing the capacity to pack thousands of electronic functions on a single chip.

As such chips found ever more applications, commercial markets began to overwhelm military markets. Procurement officers discovered that video-game manufacturers could wield more clout with their suppliers than could the major defense contractors.[9] In addition, military procurement procedures made the acquisitions cycle so lengthy that chips produced expressly for military systems were often outmoded before the systems could be deployed.

In 1980 the Pentagon sought to regain its leverage as a lead customer by launching a program for the production of very high-speed integrated circuits. Destined to receive almost $1 billion over an eight-year period, the newer program was intended to speed up the design, production, and deployment of components, thereby to interest merchant firms in redirecting their attention to the defense market.[10]

It gradually became clear, however, that the technology goals of the new program had been captured by the Pentagon's customary suppliers, that is, by the firms which specialized in military hardware. Such firms, following their usual bent, preferred to design specialized circuits for use in radars and other military systems rather than to develop capabilities applicable to semiconductor production in general. Instead of working with the merchant firms and equipment suppliers on incremental improvements in the manufacturing process, the prime defense contractors tended to keep development in-house and aimed at innovations in the form of powerful new products. Striving for major product breakthroughs had yielded great commercial payoffs when US firms were isolated innovators in an open field. As subsequent developments were to show, however, they were not nearly as well suited to the more crowded competitive conditions of the 1980s.

European efforts in chip making took root in a more variegated landscape. In Britain and France, defense planners followed the American example of encouraging domestic companies to enter semiconductor production. In other countries, public officials promoted the industry for nonmilitary purposes. In neither case, however, did European conditions favor fast-moving merchant producers on the American model. For one thing, the national defense markets of each of the European countries were uncomfortably small for risky ventures. In addition, most European countries lacked the private institutions for committing venture capital in small high-tech undertakings. European scientists and engineers also seemed unwilling to risk their careers in such ventures. Finally, since American merchant firms had already assumed technological leadership in the industry, it was exceedingly difficult for small European firms to get started.

Instead, European officials induced the older electrical conglomerates to enter the semiconductor field. Though often well supported by their governments, these enterprises had never been organized to compete in an ever-moving technological frontier. Accordingly, a division of tasks emerged whereby US merchant firms provided the latest components and European conglomerates used them in consumer and industrial products.

For a time this arrangement worked well. As long as the required electronics emphasized discrete devices, such as transistors, without requiring fundamental redesign of the equipment in which they were used, such time-honored firms as General Electric Corporation of Britain, Philips of Holland, and Siemens of Germany retained their traditional markets. As the electronics grew more elaborate, however, European firms experienced longer lags in mastering the US-authored innovations and therefore grew increasingly dependent on US chip makers for timely delivery.[11]

Needless to say, not all European defense planners were content to rely on American firms for critical military components. Forced to choose between using state-of-the-art components and investing in domestic suppliers, European governments developed a variety of policies to overcome the perceived "technology gap" that separated them from the United States. In Britain, the armed forces paid premium prices for specialized components to defense contractors such as Ferranti Electronics and the Plessey Company, but such firms had limited success in commercial markets. In France, the state supported a semiconductor firm, Sescosem, as part of its *plan calcul* in computers, but also without much success. In West Germany, the government's aim in promoting a semiconductor industry was commercial rather than military; the objective, therefore, was to broaden

German know-how enough to promote the rapid assimilation of new components.[12]

The Japanese case displayed a third pattern in the development of the semiconductor industry, in which defense needs were thoroughly subordinated to commercial goals. As in Europe, Japan developed no equivalent for the US merchant industry. But unlike their European counterparts, Japanese firms were under less pressure to keep pace with the latest US innovations. With no reason to explore the military ramifications of each change in the technological frontier, Japanese firms were freer to concentrate on strengthening their internal reservoir of know-how.

In the early stages of the industry's development, the integrated Japanese producers fabricated their own semiconductors, relying heavily on technologies licensed from the United States. Japanese officials were not content to allow continued technological dependence, however, and producers were encouraged to develop their own technological capabilities. The Ministry of International Trade and Industry (MITI) provided protection for Japanese firms in the domestic market and carefully limited foreign ownership of Japanese firms. It took years of bargaining before Texas Instruments, a major source of technology for Japanese firms, could obtain a 50 percent share in a joint venture with Sony. To acquire that interest, the firm was required to license important patents to Nippon Electric Corporation (NEC), Hitachi, Mitsubishi Electric, and Toshiba, in addition to Sony, and to limit its production to 10 percent of the Japanese market.[13]

The structure of the Japanese electronics manufacturers helped them to begin the in-house production of their own semiconductor components. As diversified companies, they all sold a range of consumer electronics, computers, and communications or industrial equipment, which provided an internal market for their semiconductor output.[14] In addition, the older firms received support through their membership in *keiretsu* groups. Each group included a range of manufacturing companies, a lead bank, and a trading company. In each *keiretsu*, members owned a considerable share of the equity of other members and favored other members in their purchasing practices. Such arrangements allowed Japanese firms to pursue much longer-term development objectives than the US merchant producers.[15]

The clearest evidence of Japan's policy preferences came from MITI's launching of a program in 1976 to anticipate the appearance of new generations of more powerful chips, in the range known as very large-scale integration, or VLSI. The VLSI project was a four-year effort budgeted at about $320 million, of which 42 percent came from public interest-free loans. The project elicited a noteworthy degree of cooperation from its members—Fujitsu, Hitachi, Mitsubishi Electric, NEC, and Toshiba. A single cooperative laboratory was established for the investigation of the generic technologies required for VLSI production, and all five industrial firms supplied personnel to each of the research teams in the cooperative lab. The actual designs of specific chips were regarded as proprietary information, however, and were developed within company laboratories.[16]

That cooperative project appeared to provide the springboard by which Japanese chip makers in the early 1980s penetrated the world market for memory chips. As a category distinct from microprocessors, which are used to process information, memory chips are used for the storage of information. By the late 1970s, they represented the largest market in the semiconductor industry. As memory chips went swiftly through several generations of development, the "yield," or percentage of defect-free chips, became the new arbiter of commercial success. With their great production expertise, continuously refined through feedback from in-house users, Japanese firms achieved new quality levels in mass-produced chips and swiftly took increasing shares of the global market. By the mid-1980s, many of the US merchant firms retired from the memory-chip business and concentrated increasingly on microprocessors and more specialized devices.

By the early 1980s, the process of globalization had markedly transformed the semiconductor industry. By then, at least one-third of the world's semiconductor output was sold across national borders. Once a heavy importer of semiconductor devices, Japan had moved from a trade deficit to a surplus with both the United States and Western Europe. In addition, a pronounced pattern of cross-national specialization was emerging. While Japanese firms claimed as much as 70 percent of the US market for memory chips in 1981, US firms remained dominant in microprocessors and other logic devices.[17] European firms ran a trade deficit in semiconductors with both Japan and the United States, but remained strong in certain components with niche applications in manufacturing settings.

By the early 1980s, the pool of technology on which the industry drew had been widely internationalized. The liberal licensing policy of Bell Labs had helped to shape early patterns. And the insistence of customers that the devices they used should be available from more than one source had reinforced the tendency toward globalization. But the geographical spread of the enterprises in the industry was far from symmetrical.

Owing to Japan's historical restrictions on foreign direct investment, US producers had established many more subsidiaries in Europe than Japan. By 1980, Motorola was the only US-based firm other than Texas Instruments to have operations in Japan.[18] By that time, US-based producers and their subsidiaries had captured only 12 percent of the Japanese semiconductor market, even though they had managed to obtain 56 percent of the European market.[19]

Meanwhile, enterprises were moving across the Atlantic in both directions. Earlier in the 1970s, Philips and Siemens had made a number of acquisitions in the United States. In 1979, the French company Schlumberger acquired the progenitor of all Silicon Valley firms, Fairchild Semiconductor.

The practice of direct investment in foreign countries was much slower to spread among Japanese firms. Japanese managers preferred to maintain control over manufacturing processes by automating their plants at home. By 1980 a few Japanese plants had appeared in Southeast Asia and a NEC plant was established in the United States; but for the most part, these were exceptions to a stay-at-home pattern.[20]

These diverse national developments set the stage for a struggle that became especially acute in the 1980s. In the first few decades of the semiconductor industry's development, its course closely approximated the well-documented product cycle model by which US-based firms innovated in the United States and then disseminated new products to world markets.[21] Such a pattern posed few problems for defense planners in the United States, as long as US firms made their technology available to the Pentagon before they licensed it overseas.

During the 1970s, however, the patterns of technology diffusion grew more complex.[22] US-based firms developed their global networks, allowing more rapid diffusion of new products. In addition, the emphasis in innovation began to shift from distinct chips to the entire production process. As the density of circuit lines increased, ever smaller defects could ruin an entire chip. Each of the hundreds of steps in the production process required new degrees of precision. It became progressively more difficult for any single firm to master—or to transfer—all the relevant technologies involved in chip fabrication. More and more, chip producers came to depend on outside suppliers for essential know-how involved in the fabrication of the devices they produced.

For defense planners, this development posed the risk of losing access to some important capabilities essential for defense production. For firms, it became advisable to pursue a two-track strategy of preserving access to markets around the world while producing in an environment that could provide all the complementary inputs needed to produce complex chips at a competitive price.

During the 1980s, these changes in technology created opportunities for a number of different business strategies. At the new levels of integration, chip producers could fabricate general-use components of much greater power. But the same technology also enabled producers to put an entire information system on a chip that was specially designed for—or dedicated to—a single customer. Firms that chose to compete in high-volume, standard product lines such as memory chips required large capital investments and access to global markets. By contrast, firms that chose to concentrate on customized chips needed close and continuous relationships with the firms for whom they were designing and fabricating chips.

The merchant producers of the United States fitted uncomfortably into the emerging market structure. In Japan, they faced integrated electronics manufacturers whose chip-producing divisions, with the help of their affiliated end-user divisions, had become major competitors on the open market. In Europe, the US merchants fared much better, but increasingly by working with entrenched conglomerates, which enjoyed close ties to their traditional customers and home governments. The proclaimed vulnerability of the US merchant producers soon concerned defense agencies, which began to see commercial competitiveness as a condition for self-sufficiency. As the industry became more politicized, officials in all countries looked for new ways to bolster the commercial vitality of their domestic chip firms.

The 1980s produced a series of significant changes that reflected the great travail in the industry. These included the development of a bilateral agreement between the United States and Japan governing the sale of memory chips, the funding of Sematech in the United States, the progressive maturing of Japanese firms, and the acceleration of official efforts in Europe to avoid falling hopelessly behind the technological frontier.

The US-Japan Agreement

In 1977 several US-based merchant producers, supported by "captive" producers that manufactured their chips internally, had founded the Semiconductor Industry Association. This organization took the lead in showing that Japanese firms were gaining market share in the United States by selling their chips at prices under cost.[23] With increasing pain apparent in the US industry, the United States and Japan concluded a bilateral agreement on semiconductor trade in July 1986.

The agreement illustrated the difficulties caused by the asymmetrical industrial structures of the two countries. The Japanese producers of chips absorbed a good portion of their output inside their vertically integrated firms; finding an unambiguous measure for the cost of production was therefore close to impossible. Consequently, the chip agreement specified that the Commerce Department and MITI should establish a series of floor prices at which Japanese firms would be permitted to sell in the US market.

The provision had several unintended consequences. For Japanese producers, it virtually guaranteed a windfall by boosting profit margins. For the US firms that purchased chips, the pact threatened to double or triple the cost of such components. US-based computer makers said the pact might make it impossible for them to compete against Japanese producers, and one US manufacturer quickly announced plans to build a computer plant in Singapore to circumvent the new pact.

Besides creating floor prices for Japanese-produced chips, the agreement specified that MITI would encourage Japanese firms to purchase US-made chips. But by early 1987 US officials became dissatisfied with MITI's implementation of the agreement and in March of that year, the executive branch announced its intention to impose retaliatory sanctions on imports from Japan. It is ironic that the sanctions further illuminated the country's dependence on Japan's electronics firms. Raising the price of the offending Japanese chips would disadvantage the US computer makers who used them; accordingly, retaliatory tariffs were instead placed on finished items sold by the Japanese firms that contained the offending chips—laptop computers, power tools, and various other consumer products.[24]

Birth of Sematech

As trade measures were being debated, US firms and policy makers alike contemplated collaborative responses to the manufacturing strengths of the Japanese chip producers. The Semiconductor Industry Association proposed the creation of a joint institute for research on manufacturing technologies for chip fabrication. In early 1987, a special task force of the Defense Science Board recommended that the Department of Defense fund such an institute, to be called Sematech. Public funding of $100 million per year commenced in 1988, with equal or greater contributions from the fourteen industrial participants.[25]

Sematech's operating objectives evolved over time. Initially, the new institute was to respond directly to Japanese competition in memory chips by building a pilot line in Austin, Texas, which would jointly supply developed process technology to all consortium members. But this plan quickly foundered on the customary practices of US-based chip producers, whose relations with the equipment suppliers had traditionally been "project-specific, cost-driven, and litigious." Sematech therefore shifted its emphasis toward linking chip makers and their equipment suppliers on the basis of "long-term cooperative relationships involving substantial and continuous cost- and information-sharing."[26] Toward this end, the consortium settled on more flexible outside research contracts that entailed collaboration between chip makers and their equipment suppliers.[27]

By 1989 the concern over Japanese dominance in memory chips had declined somewhat because Siemens in Germany and Samsung in South Korea had managed to master the large-scale production of memory components. At the same time, the supply of chips from

Japanese producers was also increasing. Since a closely held supplier of such chips no longer seemed essential, several US-based firms abandoned discussions for a jointly financed source, provisionally named US Memories.

Nonetheless, the US government still found it advisable to reinforce the industry's technology base by supporting equipment suppliers through Sematech. Prompted partly by the concerns of IBM, US policy makers were brought to the realization that Japan's competitive advantage lay not only in the fabrication of chips but also in the development of the equipment used in the process. In addition, Japanese equipment manufacturers were being bolstered by the broad experience of Japanese chip producers. That development was seen as particularly threatening by US-based computer firms, which depended on such equipment for the in-house production of their own chips.

The Sematech experiment illuminated some of the limitations of the approach that it represented. It was expected that consortium members would give other US-based firms priority access to Sematech-funded results. Still, with IBM, Texas Instruments, Motorola, and others maintaining a production network all over the world, Sematech could not realistically hope to keep the results of its research within territorial borders. In addition, with technological advances emanating from far-flung sources, it was not clear from one year to the next where the technological choke points of the industry were likely to be.

Nevertheless, Sematech signalled a clear shift in the way US officials defined the defense industrial base. By supporting generic manufacturing technologies, the initiative implied that a secure defense industrial base required robust commercial chip makers. Rather than simply buying the Pentagon's access to US merchant firms, Sematech sought to bolster the capabilities of those firms. Moreover, by attempting to strengthen links among chip makers and suppliers, Sematech clearly shifted the goal from that of securing military components from dedicated sources to that of deepening the reservoir of know-how available to the industry.

Maturation in Japan

The technological cooperation among Japanese chip producers that MITI had encouraged in the 1970s through its VLSI project proved its value in the 1980s. One illustration of that value was the central role of Nikon, the camera maker, in developing a second-generation chip-making machine for the five-firm consortium of Japanese chip producers that had participated in the VLSI project.

Japanese chip makers had customarily purchased a central piece of chip-making equipment—known as a stepper—from US firms. When the Japanese consortium contracted with Nikon to develop a second-generation machine, the firm was already supplying lens components to the leading US manufacturer of such machines. Once chosen for the task by one of the joint research teams in the cooperative VLSI laboratory, Nikon had rare access to the technical performance of all five firms. By comparing technical results from consortium members, Nikon was able to refine its machine far more effectively than would otherwise have been possible.[28]

More important than perfecting any single piece of machinery, however, the VLSI project helped to establish the area around Tokyo as the new center for advanced chip production. Mass production of these extremely dense circuits required exacting work at each step. The entire process had to be enclosed in specially equipped, dust-free "clean" rooms. Seemingly mundane tasks—from polishing silicon wafers to characterizing the gases and fluids with which they were treated—became limiting factors that required the support of highly specialized suppliers. As Japanese suppliers gained experience, their complementary capabilities generated an "industry infrastructure" that could not be readily replicated.[29]

As a result, it became easier to assemble the numerous specialties required for chip production in Japan than elsewhere; however, some of this know-how was able to be extended across national boundaries. Shimizu America, the subsidiary of a Japanese construction firm experienced in building clean rooms, was chosen by IBM, for example, to design IBM's newest chip facility in East Fishkill, New York.[30] Still, hiring a Japanese general contractor did not fully overcome the handicaps of operating outside Japan. Japanese managers began to report that it took roughly twice as long to build a state-of-the-art plant in the United States as in Japan—an estimate that was borne out in NEC's experience with a plant in Roseville, California.[31]

Strong evidence of the pull exerted by Japan's reservoir of semiconductor know-how also came from the changing distribution of the equipment-supplying industry. From 1984 to 1988, the share of worldwide shipments generated by US producers of semiconductor manufacturing equipment fell from 66 percent to under 50 percent, while the share of Japanese firms increased from 26 percent to 39 percent.[32] US and European equipment suppliers increasingly felt the need for a presence in Japan in order to keep pace. Although the breakthroughs achieved by Siemens and Samsung reduced the dominance of Japanese chip makers, they did little to stem the concentration of equipment-manufacturing expertise in the Tokyo area. While some US-based equipment firms were successful in Japan, US-based chip makers feared that they might not receive state-of-the-art machines on a timely basis.[33]

Western Europe

The recurring fears of enterprises and governments in Western Europe that they might slip hopelessly behind in the technological competition produced a variety of responses.

One response was to try to control the imports of Japanese semiconductors. Even with a tariff on imported chips, European producers had been attempting to develop an agreement with their Japanese competitors to keep Japanese prices high in sales to European home markets. When US producers reached such an agreement in 1986, the event filled the Europeans with dismay; yet, only in 1990 did the European Electronic Components Manufacturers' Association achieve a price-monitoring system for Japanese chips sold in Europe.[34]

The main objective of European initiatives, however, was to bolster the technological capabilities rather than the trade position of European chip makers. The persistent increase in the levels of chip complexity posed a severe problem for the integrated European electronics manufacturers. For a time, it had been sufficient for such producers to wire together a series of commodity chips in order to provide the electronic controls for their industrial and consumer products. As chip makers learned to cram increasing amounts of electronic intelligence on a single integrated circuit, however, it became possible to include all the electronic requirements of a product on a single specially designed chip.

Government officials quickly recognized how important it was for their firms to master the new levels of chip integration. In France, the chief of telecommunications decided in the late 1970s that a new "components plan" was necessary to help make France the world's third "electronic superpower."[35] On behalf of several firms in France, the state negotiated a series of agreements with US chip makers for the transfer of technology. The state eventually concentrated its support, however, on a national champion, Thomson. To execute the state's goals, Thomson sought to achieve "world scale" through a program of mass production and acquisitions. In 1985, the firm acquired the nearly bankrupt US merchant chip maker, Mostek Corporation. But France's plan for an autonomous chipmaking firm soon collapsed. The desired combination of research and development and commercial success did not take hold. By 1987, Thomson had merged its semiconductor operations with those of its Italian rival, Società Generale Semiconduttori (SGS).[36]

The West German government took a rather different tack. By the early 1980s, German officials felt it was essential to have at least one German company that could supply the new generations of large complex chips to industrial users. As in earlier years, the objective was international competitiveness rather than technological autarky. Since German officials wanted to avoid creating a French-style national champion, the technology ministry opted for a development program in which Siemens would coordinate its research with the Dutch firm Philips.[37]

Siemens proved particularly resourceful in upgrading its chip capabilities. In addition to its partnership with Philips, Siemens entered into a licensing arrangement with Toshiba to acquire its technology for the new generation of powerful memory chips. Since the goal of the program was increased technological capability rather than blanket self-sufficiency, there was no reason for Siemens engineers to renounce licensed technology as long as it promised to bolster the firm's internal capabilities over the long term. By 1987 and 1988, Siemens was showing impressive evidence of its ability to keep within reach of the latest innovations in the production of such chips.[38]

As the Europeans settled on further plans for supporting their chip makers through the Joint European Submicron Silicon (JESSI) program, the German approach of promoting cooperation rather than the French approach of establishing a national champion proved to be the dominant strategy.[39] Instead of concentrating resources on a few specific firms or products, JESSI established financial incentives and a set of rules for strengthening the delicate technological linkages that seemed increasingly important in the semiconductor industry.[40] Some support went to materials and equipment suppliers, aimed at strengthening linkages of a kind that had proved central in the emergence of Japan's industry infrastructure. Some support went also to so-called software tools that had become essential in the designing of customized chips for particular users, thus building up the linkages between chip producers and chip users. All told, the JESSI framework demonstrated a clear appreciation of the need to deepen the reservoir of know-how from which all firms in the European industry could draw.

International Interaction

By the 1980s, it was evident that firms in the semiconductor industry were struggling to maintain their access to global markets while participating in a number of well-defined, geographically distinct technology pools. The challenge, however, produced a number of very different structures and strategies in the semiconductor industry.

One strategy, evident among US firms, was to emphasize flexibility and specialization. During the 1980s, more than eighty-five new firms sprang up in Silicon Valley, most of them involved in networks manufacturing specialized chips for products in small and quickly changing markets.[41] Cooperating with other nearby firms, member firms in the network specialized in one or two aspects of the chip production process. Because frequent communication among specialized producers and users was indispensable, geographical proximity became an important competitive advantage. Variations on the Silicon Valley pattern could be seen in other regional agglomerations in the United States such as Austin, Texas, and a few other areas in the Southwest.

Some of the merchant chip makers that had established their positions in an earlier generation emphasized a very different strategy, aimed at protecting their earlier lead in the high-volume mass manufacture of standard chips. One aspect of that strategy was to attempt to enforce patent and copyright claims more vigorously and to refrain from licensing their new technologies, a decided change from prior industry practices.[42]

The result was a visible split in the US semiconductor industry. The "new-wave" firms prided themselves on perpetuating Silicon Valley's open and innovative ethos, while claiming that the old guard had grown rigid and closed. According to a few younger entrepreneurs, the older firms were vastly exaggerating the US industry's plight in order to obtain unwarranted trade protection and technology funding from the federal government.[43]

While the established US merchant firms were trying to protect their technology base at home, they also invested in Japan, hoping not only to sell chips in that market but also to gain access to Japan's infrastructure for chip fabrication. Motorola exchanged key technologies with Toshiba and opened up a jointly owned manufacturing venture in Sendai City, north of Tokyo. The new venture gave Motorola access to the equipment suppliers that had built Toshiba's most advanced plants. Texas Instruments and LSI gained new production capacity in Japan, by joining with well-established Japanese manufacturing firms that were diversifying into the chip market.[44]

Meanwhile, Japanese producers displayed a different balance between global market objectives and local technology commitments. Trade tensions made it prudent for high-volume Japanese producers to establish plants in the United States. As they began to manufacture end products in the United States, most of the leading Japanese chip makers also set up facilities in the United States to provide chips for those end products.[45]

Although the threat of import restrictions was one cause of Japanese investment in the United States, the desire for entry into US technology networks was another. For this purpose, the most promising mode of participation was through acquisition of US firms involved in the expanding market for specialized chips. The market for application-specific integrated circuits required intensive design and specialized fabrication capabilities that gave many US firms an advantage over their foreign competitors. Although Japanese firms managed to increase their share of the US market in such chips, they still had not approached the capabilities of the US specialists.[46]

Fujitsu's attempt to buy Fairchild Semiconductor in October 1986 was widely seen as an effort by the firm to bolster its capabilities for this segment of the market. Despite US worries, it was not easy for the federal government to find grounds for blocking such a sale. The

Defense Department expressed concern because Fairchild was one of the very few suppliers for certain highly specialized military components. Yet, unless the merger fell afoul of US antitrust laws, the administration had no clear basis for preventing it. The issue was only resolved when Fujitsu found the controversy too damaging to its image and withdrew the offer in early 1987.[47]

Officials in the Defense Department also opposed European acquisitions of military chip makers. When the British firm Plessey sought to purchase Harris Semiconductor in 1987, national security concerns were again voiced and the bid fell through. As it turned out, the Pentagon's threat that it would not buy from these firms if they fell under the control of foreign shareholders appeared sufficient to discourage such acquisitions.[48]

As cross-investments among US and Japanese firms grew, European firms also displayed a range of strategies for building to global scale and consolidating their place in local technology networks. The big three—Philips, Siemens, and Thomson-SGS—all committed themselves to substantially expanding their share of the US market. Meanwhile, European firms also entered the business of designing customized chips for Europe's industrial firms. Yet Europeans continued to worry over the ability of their leading electronics firms to compete in such an innovative and quickly changing industry.[49] At the same time, US and Japanese firms responded to the movement toward a single European market in 1992 by trying to build their images as part of the local business and technology communities.[50]

Developments in all industrialized countries showed that firms were increasingly sensitive to local concentrations in a global technology pool. To be sure, firms learned over time to use teleconferencing and other modes of communication to relieve the need for face-to-face interactions. For semicustomized components, for example, buyers eventually were able to transmit huge sets of design parameters over long distances.

For other purposes, however, physical proximity remained important. The task of debugging production equipment continued to hinge on so-called sticky data that could only be conveyed on site. Moreover, the number and the sophistication of the supply inputs needed for chip fabrication made it desirable for specialist suppliers to be located near one another. Particularly in constructing state-of-the-art fabrication facilities, it was virtually impossible that problems could be anticipated well enough to make remote consultation among numerous parties practical. For such tasks, the degree of organizational complexity was as important a limiting factor as the capacity for face-to-face communication.

IMPLICATIONS

The record of competition in the semiconductor industry shows how the trend toward globalization can be accompanied by a very different tendency toward regional agglomeration of technological capabilities. Together these two processes have created novel challenges for policy makers concerned with defining an adequate defense industrial base.

Neither process can be said to dominate the other. For governments as well as companies, there appears to be a growing tension between the need for access to global markets and the emergence of local concentrations within the technology pool. Despite a growing preoccupation with the issue, none of the governments concerned has clearly articulated what the concept of national security means for this industry.

In the United States, public policy makers have taken several approaches in response to these changes. For officials who see globalization as the primary force in the semiconductor industry, national security has meant regulating transactions that cross national borders. For those who see local concentration as the salient trend in the industry, national security has meant creating and preserving technological capabilities. For each definition of the problem, both inward-looking and outward-looking responses have been tried.

One inward-looking response to globalization has focused on assuring the supply of components with critical military applications. Stressing this approach, the US military has arranged for the manufacture of certain circuits in captive US facilities that operate under the military's tightest design and test specifications.

Taken alone, this approach has clearly become insufficient. By 1990, so many components were being produced abroad—whether in foreign-owned or US-owned factories—that the task of returning all production to US territory had become technically as well as financially overwhelming. Some of these components were highly specialized—including certain guidance circuits for the "smart" weapons used in the Gulf War.[51] Where mass-produced chips were involved, it became even more difficult for the Pentagon to avoid the use of foreign-sourced components since such chips were routinely embedded in subassemblies and then incorporated in military hardware. Including such embedded components, the semiconductor purchases of the US military were estimated at roughly $5 billion in 1989, of which as much as 30 percent may have been sourced offshore.[52]

A more outward-looking response to the cross-border problem has focused on market shares and trade practices. In the 1980s, many US firms and public officials found it congenial to define the semiconductor problem in terms of the shrinkage of the US share. By pointing to Japanese pricing practices, US firms diverted attention from the fact that Japanese firms were sometimes producing superior semiconductors.

Despite the unintended drawbacks of the 1986 chip agreement between the United States and Japan mentioned above, US firms pressed for an extension of the pact in 1991. This time, by emphasizing provisions to increase their share in the Japanese market rather than worldwide price regulation, the Semiconductor Industry Association gained better backing from US computer makers and also won some support from the smaller US-based chip producers.[53]

Still, there has been growing recognition in the industry that trade policies alone could not stem the concentration of production capabilities in Japan. Unless measures were taken to improve the technology base for semiconductor manufacturing within US borders, US chip makers were likely to grow more dependent in the 1990s on foreign suppliers for manufacturing equipment and materials. If US defense contractors had to rely on a semiconductor industry with inferior production technology, US defense planners could find themselves without access either to critical components or to the know-how to develop them.[54]

The inward-looking initiative that most directly responded to weaknesses in the technology pool has been Sematech. Sematech undoubtedly has improved relations between consortium members and some of their numerous small suppliers. But it has also shown how much US firms and policy makers still need to learn about managing collaborative research programs. The unique strength of the US semiconductor industry, distinguishing it from the Japanese industry, has been its ability to generate firms such as those that made up the new wave in Silicon Valley during the 1980s—firms with great expertise in producing specialty chips and customizing designs for particular customers. Yet Sematech's mode of operation and its high membership fees have offered little chance for the participation of these smaller and highly innovative chip makers.

Sematech's scope has also been reduced by its approach to the foreign-owned subsidiaries of enterprises operating in the United States. The Japanese leader, NEC, was said to share the interest of Sematech's members in ensuring "that a healthy network of equipment makers and suppliers remains in the United States."[55] European firms such as Thomson and Philips argued that their extensive investment in US-based research and production justified their participation. But Sematech's representatives feared that participation of subsidiaries of foreign firms would be seen in Washington as "giving away American technology" and as inconsistent with national security objectives.[56] The issue showed that the Sematech initiative had no forceful concept for eliciting contributions from foreign-owned firms to the local infrastructure.

While discouraging foreign participation, the existence of Sematech has not prevented its members from establishing their own private alliances with foreign firms.[57] In addition to the private Japanese-American alliances mentioned earlier, transatlantic collaboration was dramatically strengthened in 1990 and 1991 when Siemens and IBM announced ambitious plans for cooperating on future generations of memory chips. The Siemens-IBM arrangement showed that the technical complexity involved in the new production technologies was so challenging that even the largest firms were being obliged to pool their capabilities.[58]

A more outward-looking response to the problem of preserving the US technology pool has concerned the regulation of foreign direct investment in the United States. The issue is best illustrated by the case of Gazelle Microcircuits, a firm that specialized in the design of gallium-arsenide circuits for high-speed applications. Like many of the smaller Silicon Valley firms of the 1980s, Gazelle got some of its important early orders from Japanese firms. When it needed a capital infusion, foreign investors were ready to provide the required funds.

Defense planners viewed such firms as particularly vulnerable to foreign acquisition, and an agency of the Defense Department, the Defense Advanced Research Projects Agency (DARPA), provided a $4 million reimbursable grant to strengthen Gazelle's position. When the agency's director, Craig Fields, was eased out of his position shortly thereafter, the move was widely interpreted as the administration's way of reemphasizing its stand against interventionist industrial policies.[59]

The dilemmas faced by US policy makers in the new environment for semiconductor production were qualitatively more complex than those of earlier decades. Given the country's concern for open international markets, it has been easy for US policy makers to define the defense industrial base in terms of cross-border transactions. Subsequent worries about the domestic technology pool gave rise to the Sematech experiment, while also prompting unusual efforts to restrict foreign direct investment. The latter, however, have remained highly contentious, while also exposing the inexperience of US agencies in managing programs for commercial technology promotion.

By comparison, Japanese policies have appeared more successful. The near absence of military procurement meant that Japanese firms were encouraged by officials to concentrate their resources on long-term strengthening of internal capabilities rather than on short-term efforts to keep pace with a relentless succession of new products. In addition, the Japanese industrial structure, including the extensive sharing of know-how with suppliers and the support provided by *keiretsu* affiliations, proved to be particularly well adapted to achieving the steady improvements in process technologies that became decisive in semiconductor operations.

Meanwhile, Europe was in a position to draw lessons from a number of different national approaches. France's state-imposed strategies proved poorly suited to the semiconductor industry; it became clear that the national-champion approach was limited because it obstructed the interfirm linkages that were becoming so important for building technological capabilities. The German approach relied much more on establishing a framework of incentives than on imposing a single national strategy. These looser, framework-setting policies gave firms more discretion in combining technologies from several sources, including foreign firms. However, such an approach could not, by its very nature, guarantee the supply of particular parts for military systems. Instead, the German approach aimed at increasing know-how, on which the state might draw for more specific projects at a later time.

It once was thought that public agencies could call technological capabilities into being simply by making the necessary investments in the industries chosen for development. This view was borne out in the earlier decades of the chip industry, when military procurement powered successive innovations in semiconductor devices and designs. As the technology for producing chips grew more complex, however, it became apparent that technological evolution was being shaped by linkages among specialized firms that permitted them to build upon shared know-how. It became clear, too, that process know-how was becoming more important than product design, and that improvements in process were likely to be achieved by incremental refinements rather than by spectacular breakthroughs.

Of course, even process know-how can eventually be diffused across borders, as the achievements of Siemens and Samsung in mastering the mass production of memory chips has made abundantly clear. But the leads and lags involved in that diffusion have remained a concern for defense planners.

The daunting complexity of the activities involved in semiconductor production means that firms must search intensively for their know-how in far-flung pockets of expertise and innovation. In response, national governments have clearly had to begin improvising on their customary approaches to the defense industrial base. Rather than focusing on the particular mix of production that needs to be retained within their national territories, public officials are increasingly seeking ways of building the long-term organizational capabilities of firms in their national jurisdictions. For public policy, the key task seems to be the design of institutional frameworks in which suppliers, manufacturers, and users can contribute to a common technology pool. The task is delicate because the evolution of the technology pool hinges on innumerable exchanges of know-how and experience among very different types of enterprises. These are processes that can surely be enabled and encouraged—but not directly controlled—by public agencies. As a consequence, efforts to maintain the defense industrial base in this industry will continue to depend as much on the imagination and the political skills exercised by public officials as on the financial resources or the administrative clout available to them.

ACKNOWLEDGEMENTS

I am grateful to John Alic, Jürgen Häusler, Rebecca Henderson, Don Lessard, Richard Locke, Annalee Saxenian, Steve Weber, Eleanor Westney, and Jerry Ziegler for insightful comments and suggestions.

ENDNOTES

[1] Charles Sabel, "Flexible Specialisation and the Re-emergence of Regional Economies," in P. Hirst and J. Zeitlin, eds., *Reversing Industrial Decline?* (Oxford: Berg, 1989); Michael Porter, *The Competitive Advantage of Nations* (New York: Free Press, 1990); and Lester Thurow, "1992: The End of the Line for the Current World Economy," in D. Lessard and C. Antonelli, eds., *Managing the Globalization of Business* (Milan: Scientifica, 1990).

[2] Especially helpful sources on the semiconductor industry include Ernst Braun and Stuart Macdonald, *Revolution in Miniature: The History and Impact of Semiconductor Electronics* (New York: Cambridge University Press, 1978); and Michael Borrus, *Competing for Control: America's Stake in Microelectronics* (Cambridge: Ballinger, 1988).

[3] Thomas J. Misa, "Military Needs, Commercial Realities, and the Development of the Transistor, 1948–1958," in M. R. Smith, ed., *Military Enterprise and Technological Change* (Cambridge: MIT Press, 1985), 265–7, 273.

[4] The standard account remains John E. Tilton, *International Diffusion of Technology: The Case of Semiconductors* (Washington, D.C.: Brookings Institution, 1971).

[5] Robert Noyce, "Microelectronics," *Scientific American* 237 (3) (September 1977).

[6] James Utterback and Albert Murray, "The Influence of Defense Procurement and Sponsorship of R&D on the Development of the Civilian Electronics Industry," Center for Policy Alternatives Working Paper, No. 77–5 (Cambridge, Mass.: Center for Policy Alternatives, MIT, 1977).

[7] Richard C. Levin, "The Semiconductor Industry," in Richard R. Nelson, ed., *Government and Technical Progress* (New York: Pergamon, 1982), 62; and Integrated Circuit Engineering, *ICE Status* (Scottsdale, Ariz.: various years).

[8] Giovanni Dosi, *Technical Change and Industrial Transformation* (New York: St. Martin's, 1984), 150.

[9] Jay Stowsky, "Beating Our Plowshares in Double-Edged Swords: The Impact of Pentagon Policies on the Commercialization of Advanced Technologies," BRIE Working Paper, No. 17 (Berkeley, Calif.: BRIE, April 1986).

10On the VHSIC program, see "Microelectronics: Two Industries, One Technology," in John Alic et al., *Beyond Spinoff: Military and Commercial Technologies in a Changing World* (Cambridge: Harvard Business School, 1992); and Glen Fong, "State Strength, Industry Structure, and Industrial Policy: American and Japanese Experiences in Microelectronics," *Comparative Politics* 22 (3) (April 1990): 273–300.

11This lag is investigated in Dosi, *Technical Change*.

12Franco Malerba, *The Semiconductor Business: The Economics of Rapid Growth and Decline* (Madison: University of Wisconsin Press, 1985); and John Zysman, *Political Strategies for Industrial Order: State, Market, and Industry in France* (Berkeley: University of California Press, 1977).

13Tilton, *International Diffusion*, 147.

14M. Therese Flaherty and Hiroyuki Itami, "Finance," in Daniel I. Okimoto, Takuo Sugano, and Franklin B. Weinstein, eds., *Competitive Edge: The Semiconductor Industry in the U.S. and Japan* (Stanford: Stanford University Press, 1984), 159.

15For contrasting accounts, see Michael Borrus, James Millstein, and John Zysman, "Trade and Development in the Semiconductor Industry: Japanese Challenge and American Response," in J. Zysman and L. Tyson, eds., *American Industry in International Competition* (Ithaca, N.Y.: Cornell University Press, 1983); and Daniel Okimoto, *Between MITI and the Market* (Stanford: Stanford University Press, 1989), 132 ff.

16Kiyonori Sakakibara, "From Imitation to Innovation: The Very Large Scale Integrated (VLSI) Semiconductor Project in Japan," Sloan School Working Paper, No. 1490–83 (Cambridge: Sloan School of Management, MIT, October 1983); and Marie Anchordoguy, "Mastering the Market: Japanese Government Targeting of the Computer Industry," *International Organization* 42 (3) (Summer 1988): 509–43.

17Organization for Economic Cooperation and Development, *The Semiconductor Industry: Trade Related Issues* (Paris: OECD, 1985), 31, 103, 105, 113.

18Franklin Weinstein, Michiyuki Uenohara, and John Linvill, "Technological Resources," in Okimoto et al., eds., *Competitive Edge*, 35–77.

19Dataquest figures cited in OECD, *The Semiconductor Industry*, 117; and Semiconductor Industry Association, *The Effect of Government Targeting on World Semiconductor Competition* (Cupertino: SIA, 1983), 74.

20Yui Kimura, *The Japanese Semiconductor Industry: Structure, Competitive Strategies, and Performance* (Greenwich, Conn.: JAI Press, 1988), 166.

21Raymond Vernon, "International Investment and International Trade in the Product Cycle," *Quarterly Journal of Economics* (May 1966): 190–207; and "The Product Cycle Hypothesis in a New International Environment," *Oxford Bulletin of Economics and Statistics* 41 (4) (November 1979): 255–67.

22John Cantwell, *Technological Innovation and Multinational Corporations* (Oxford: Blackwell, 1989).

23For a contemporary account, see "Fallout from the Trade War in Chips," *Science*, November 22, 1985.

[24]Clyde Prestowitz, *Trading Places: How We Are Giving Our Future to Japan and How to Reclaim It* (New York: Basic Books, 1990), 171–4.

[25]Defense Science Board Task Force, *Defense Semiconductor Dependency* (Washington, D.C.: Department of Defense, 1987); and "US Chip Makers Plan $1 Billion Collaboration," *Financial Times,* 24 October 1986, 1.

[26]Advisory Council on Federal Participation in Sematech, "A Report to Congress by the Advisory Council on Federal Participation in Sematech," (Washington, D.C.: Advisory Council on Federal Participation in Sematech, May 1990).

[27]US General Accounting Office, "Federal Research: Sematech's Efforts to Strengthen the U.S. Semiconductor Industry," No. RCED-90–236 (Washington, D.C.: General Accounting Office, September 1990).

[28]William F. Finan and Jeffrey Frey, "Study of the Management of Microelectronics-Related Research and Development in Japan," No. T89065 (Washington, D.C.: Semiconductor Research Corporation, November 1988).

[29]For these and other examples of the Japanese industry infrastructure in semiconductors, see Kazuhira Mishina, "Essays on Technological Evolution," Ph.D. diss., Harvard University, Graduate School of Business Administration, Cambridge, Mass., September, 1989.

[30]*New York Times,* 6 January 1987, D7.

[31]Mishina, 31–32.

[32]VLSI Research, cited in Advisory Council on Federal Participation in Sematech, "A Report to Congress."

[33]"U.S. Semi Equipment Makers Must Move the Earth to Survive," *Electronic Business* 16 (9) (14 May 1990): 44. For arguments by Senator Lloyd Bentsen of Texas that Japanese equipment manufacturers were withholding technology from US chip makers, see the *Financial Times,* 7 May 1991, 20.

[34]Kenneth Flamm, "Semiconductors," in Gary C. Hufbauer, *Europe 1992: An American Perspective* (Washington, D.C.: Brookings Institution, 1990).

[35]This was the goal put forth in Giscard d'Estaing's presidency in a famous report by two civil servants, Simon Nora and Alain Minc, *L'informatisation de la société* (Paris: Documentation française, 1978).

[36]Christian Stoffaes, *Politique Industrielle* (Paris: Cours de Droit, n.d.), 463–511; *Le Monde,* 5 November 1985; and *Le Monde,* 30 April 1987.

[37]"Siemens Gears Up for Super-Chip Era," *Financial Times,* 10 July 1985, 13.

[38]*Financial Times,* 11 July 1988, 32; and *Electronic Business* 14 (20) (15 October 1988): 52.

[39]For example, "Go-Ahead for European Superchip Project," *Financial Times,* 13 September 1988, 2.

[40]"JESSI soll mittelständische Wirtschaft an die Mikroelektronik heranführen" (JESSI to lead small- and medium-sized enterprises to microelectronics), *BMFT Journal* (Bonn: Federal Ministry for Research and Technology, June 1990), 12.

[41] For this view of Silicon Valley's industrial development, see Annalee Saxenian, "Regional Networks and the Resurgence of Silicon Valley," *California Management Review* (Fall 1990); for a contrasting perspective, see Richard Florida and Martin Kenney, "Silicon Valley and Route 128 Won't Save Us," *California Management Review* (Fall 1990); and for authors' replies see "Letters to the Editor," *California Management Review* (Spring 1991).

[42] "A Chip Maker's Profit on Patents," *New York Times*, 16 October 1990, D1. Other intellectual-property cases are reported in *Financial Times*, 28 January 1986, 4; *Wall Street Journal*, 24 September 1986, 7; *New York Times*, 26 June 1990, D1; and *Electronic News*, 11 August 1986, 1.

[43] For example, the remarks of T. J. Rodgers, President of Cypress Semiconductors, in "Divisions in the Ranks of US Chipmakers," *Financial Times*, 8 August 1990, 4.

[44] "Motorola to Build Chip Plant in Japan," *Financial Times*, 1 May 1990, 4. See also, *Wall Street Journal*, 5 December 1986, 35; *New York Times*, 20 March 1990, D1; and *Washington Post*, 23 January 1990, D1.

[45] Kimura, 166–7; and *Wall Street Journal*, 26 December 1986, 26.

[46] "Doubt Cast on U.S. Chip Strategy," *International Herald Tribune*, 23 June 1986.

[47] For example, "Fujitsu Chip Deal Draws More Flak," *New York Times*, 12 January 1987, D1.

[48] *New York Times*, 23 September 1987, D1; and *Financial Times*, 4 November 1987, 28, 48.

[49] For instance, "National Champions become Laggards," *Financial Times*, 29 April 1991, 17.

[50] Mike Hobday, "The European Semiconductor Industry: Resurgence and Rationalization," *Journal of Common Market Studies* 28 (2) (December 1989): 155–86; and Michael Skapinker, "The Fashionable Place to Be Seen," *Financial Times*, 26 March 1991, 12.

[51] "American Smart Bombs, Foreign Brains," *Business Week*, 4 March 1991, 18.

[52] The estimate on foreign sourcing is from the Logistics Management Institute, cited in B. Rayner, "Foreign Firms Chip Away at the U.S. Defense Arsenal," *Electronic Business* 15 (2) (23 January 1989): 84. For estimating the military's annual semiconductor purchases, the Electronics Industries of America takes 10 percent of the Pentagon's procurement for all electronics equipment—$52.87 billion in 1989. Such estimates vary dramatically, according to methods of counting and types of chips included.

[53] "Japan and US both Take Firm Line in New Chip Talks," *Financial Times*, 19 February 1991, 5.

[54] For the downstream consequences of falling behind in semiconductor technologies, see Charles Ferguson, "America's High-Tech Decline," *Foreign Policy* 74 (Spring 1989): 123–44.

[55] "NEC Wants to Join U.S. Project," *New York Times*, 15 August 1988, D1.

[56] "U.S.-Europe Technology Union Urged," *New York Times*, 24 July 1989, D1.

[57]For more on this point, see David Mowery and Nathan Rosenberg, "New Developments in U.S. Technology Policy: Implications for Competitiveness and International Trade Policy," *California Management Review* (Fall 1989): 107–24.

[58]*Financial Times,* 25 January 1990, 26; *Washington Post,* 25 January 1990, C1; and *Financial Times,* 5 July 1991, 1.

[59]"Silicon Valley Investment by Pentagon," *New York Times,* 10 April 1990, D5; and "Transfer of DARPA Chief Draws Criticism in Congress," in *Aviation Week and Space Technology* (30 April 1990): 25–26.

David S. Painter

International Oil and National Security

W ITH THE 1991 GULF WAR STILL FRESH IN MIND, no one
has to be reminded that the problem of dependence on
foreign sources for products essential to national security
has had perhaps its most enduring expression in the oil industry. Oil
has been, and continues to be, central to the modern military
establishment and to modern industrial society. But for most of the
twentieth century the major industrial powers, with the significant
exceptions of the United States and the Soviet Union, have had
meager domestic oil production. And, with the same two exceptions,
the major oil producers have had very little industry. Although the
nature of the dependence has changed over the years, access to
external sources of oil has been both a key source of rivalry among
the great powers and a key factor in relations between the industrial
countries and the nonindustrial world.

OIL AND WORLD POWER

Oil became an important factor in military power in the decade
before World War I when the navies of the great powers, led by Great
Britain and the United States, began to switch from coal to oil as their
main source of power. The role of oil in World War I had a dramatic
and long-lasting impact on the way governments viewed the oil
industry. During 1917 severe shortages of oil threatened at different
times to immobilize the British navy and the French army; in both
cases, urgent requests to the United States for help led to the
provision of the needed supplies. Lacking such external assistance,

*David S. Painter is Assistant Professor of History in the School of Foreign Service at
Georgetown University.*

183

Germany found oil shortages curtailing its military operations at critical points. In addition, although the navies of the great powers played a relatively minor role in World War I, access to oil remained a prerequisite to sea power; and the major military innovations of the war—the tank, motorized transport, the airplane, and the submarine—were all oil-powered.[1]

In struggles over access to oil, Great Britain and the United States possessed significant advantages. After World War I, the British navy and the US navy were the most powerful in the world; both nations therefore had the ability to secure access to overseas oil-producing areas. In fact, both nations had already been firmly entrenched in oil-rich areas even before oil became a critical commodity—Great Britain in the Middle East and the United States in the Gulf-Caribbean region. The United States was also blessed with a thriving oil industry of its own, which produced more than enough oil for the nation's needs.

Moreover, US and British companies dominated the world oil industry. Five of the seven international majors (the so-called seven sisters) were the progenitors of today's four largest US oil companies—Exxon, Mobil, Texaco, and Chevron—the other two were British (although Royal Dutch/Shell, as its name indicates, also incorporated a major Dutch interest). In contrast, neither German nor Japanese companies had any significant stake or influence in international oil markets.

World War II underlined the crucial importance of oil to modern warfare. Fighting ships, seagoing freighters, tanks, airplanes, motorized troop transport, and submarines played a major role in the war. In addition to controlling much of the world's oil production, the United States was at the forefront of improving oil products for military use, including aviation gasoline and specialty lubricants needed for high performance in aircraft engines. In contrast, the failure of Germany and Japan to gain access to oil was an important factor contributing to their defeat.

The two superpowers that emerged after World War II were, not coincidentally, the two industrial powers with large domestic oil reserves. (The United States and the Soviet Union were also the only powers that possessed ample quantities of both coal and oil.) In addition, US oil companies were firmly entrenched in all the great oil-producing areas outside the Soviet Union.

The strong position of the United States in world oil brought multiple advantages. The rebuilding of Western Europe and Japan had emerged as a critical element in the US strategy of containing the Soviet Union; accordingly, assuring a supply of oil for these areas became a key US objective. Meanwhile, Soviet expansion into Eastern and Central Europe as a result of World War II left the Soviet Union in control of almost all of Europe's known indigenous oil reserves, as well as important sources of coal in Poland and the Soviet zone of Germany. A 1945 Joint Chiefs of Staff report warned that Soviet control of Europe's oil could become "another link . . . in the economic chain by which the Western European powers are becoming fettered to the Soviet Union." Adding to the danger, postwar Western Europe faced a coal crisis of alarming proportions.[2] With US and even Venezuelan production increasingly needed to satisfy burgeoning US demand, the Middle East was not only the logical place, but practically the only place from which to supply the growing needs of Western Europe and Japan.

Development of Middle East oil was also seen as contributing to US security interests in other ways. The expansion of oil revenues to the governments of the producing countries, it was thought, would promote prosperity and stability in the region. Western control of Middle East oil would also deny the region's resources to the Soviet Union, which for several years after World War II lacked sufficient oil supplies to carry out offensive military operations. Finally, US strategists did not overlook the fact that the Middle East contained the best defensible locations for launching a strategic air offensive against the Soviet Union in the event of global war.[3]

It is difficult to assess the importance of oil to military power in the nuclear age. On the one hand, the advent of nuclear-powered submarines, aircraft carriers, and guided missile cruisers has reduced the critical need for oil in maintaining sea power; indeed, concern over access to oil was a consideration in the decision to convert part of the US navy to nuclear power. On the other hand, each new generation of weapons has entailed a greater need for oil than the generation it replaced. And conflicts such as that in the Persian Gulf have demonstrated the continued relevance of conventional oil-consuming forces in a parlous world.

Apart from its military uses, however, oil's critical economic importance has been enough to give it a special place in the defense planning of industrialized countries. Cheap oil gave the US economy important advantages over its competitors from the 1920s to the 1960s. Cheap oil was also an important element in European and Japanese reconstruction and helped fuel the "long boom"—the extended period of sustained economic growth in the decades following World War II. By the same token, expensive oil was an important factor in the less dynamic performance of the industrial economies in the 1970s and early 1980s. Although oil may not be central to the current "third industrial revolution," which is built around high technology and the electronics industry, it still retains a dominant place in the energy sectors of both the industrial nations and the developing world.

NATIONAL RESPONSES: 1914–1945

Because of the strategic and economic importance of oil, the governments of the major industrial powers have been extremely reluctant to rely on market forces alone to determine its availability. Outside the United States, the military importance of oil became evident long before its economic role emerged as critical; indeed, as late as 1938, oil was but a secondary fuel in Europe and Japan, used mainly in transportation and accounting for only 10 percent of energy consumption.[4]

It was the military uses of oil therefore that sparked some of the early moves of Great Britain to secure sources in the Middle East. In 1914, Winston Churchill, then the First Lord of the Admiralty, persuaded the British government to acquire control of the Anglo-Persian Oil Company (APOC). APOC's holdings gave Britain access to concession rights in most of Iran, and through holdings in the Turkish Petroleum Company (TPC) to those areas of the Ottoman empire that later would become Iraq. Ever since, governments have used state-owned or state-sponsored "national champion" companies to gain assured access to oil.[5]

What governments have learned, however, is that ownership by itself guarantees little. Although APOC was a commercial success, it fell short of assuring Britain's access to oil. Iranian production never provided more than one-fifth of Britain's oil needs. And, although the British liked to think of Iran as a reliable source of supply, as almost a member of the empire, Reza Shah's aborted attempt to expropriate

APOC in 1932 demonstrated that Iran was not completely under British control.[6] Iraq was politically more reliable, but Great Britain shared its control of Iraqi oil with a number of partners, which jointly held production down in order to limit competition.[7] Moreover, the British government's ownership of APOC shares may have hampered the company in its efforts to develop a strong position in Latin America because many of the region's governments were reluctant to allow companies owned by foreign governments to participate in their domestic oil industry.

For a short time after the end of World War I, most governments anticipated a shortage of oil. As long as that prospect existed, British policy aimed at excluding US oil companies from the Middle East, in particular from Iraq's potentially rich fields, which it controlled under a League of Nations mandate. Instead of a shortage, however, international oil markets were soon glutted, and both British and US companies saw advantages in cooperating to manage the glut. Meanwhile, the British government concluded that participation by US oil companies in an international consortium to develop Iraqi oil would help stabilize a key link in its lines of communication to India. After considerable urging by the US government, the British also allowed US companies into Bahrain and Kuwait, which at the time were British protectorates that had agreed not to grant oil concessions without the approval of the British government.[8]

Seeking to increase the security of their oil supplies by diversification, British companies also developed oil fields in Mexico and Venezuela. In the early 1920s, Mexico was the world's leading oil exporter. But production declined sharply during the decade as the major oil companies, concerned over the course of the Mexican revolution, shifted their investment to Venezuela, which soon replaced Mexico as the world's leading exporter. In 1938, British holdings in Mexico were nationalized, along with those of the major US companies; by 1939, Venezuela was supplying almost half of Britain's oil needs.[9]

The Mexican nationalizations were traumatic for international oil companies and sobering for their governments, a dramatic affirmation of the fact that seeming ownership of the oil fields did not guarantee continued access to oil supplies. In both Britain and the United States, government officials and company managers feared the potential impact of Mexico's successful nationalization on Venezuela and smaller producers such as Colombia and Peru. To make matters worse, Mexico responded to a boycott imposed by the major oil companies by finding buyers in Germany and Japan. With World War II in the offing, Mexico's move was perceived as providing those countries not only with oil but also with a potential foothold in a strategically sensitive area.[10]

In November 1941, with war even more imminent, the US government reached agreement with Mexico on compensation for the expropriated US companies. (A British agreement with Mexico would not be concluded until 1947.) The US government also took the lead in defusing a potential crisis in Venezuela by supporting a 50/50 profit-sharing settlement between the Venezuelan government and the major oil companies. Pleased with the result, the Venezuelan government confirmed existing concession rights and opened new areas to the companies. Venezuelan production increased substantially and Venezuelan oil played an important role in fueling the British and US war efforts.[11]

There had been occasions during the 1930s when the British government seriously considered whether it could reduce its reliance on imported oil by using its ample coal supplies to generate synthetic fuel. In the end, however, that possibility was rejected on security grounds in favor of relying on the strength of the British navy to maintain the country's access to oil.[12]

In the final analysis, British access to foreign oil in wartime was dependent not so much on ownership of foreign oil reserves as on the ability to maintain control of the sea routes. Assisted by US forces, the British navy was expected to maintain British access to oil in the Western hemisphere. The British navy's control of the seas would also be essential to assuring access to Middle East oil. Moreover, from the viewpoint of Britain, it was vital to protect that area because it lay athwart land, sea, and air routes to India, the Far East, and the Pacific dominions.

In France, as in Britain, the government came out of its World War I experience concerned over its access to foreign oil. Before 1920 Germany had been one of Britain's partners in TPC, but in 1920 France acquired the German interest. In 1924 France established a national oil company, the Compagnie Française des Pétroles (CFP), to hold the French shares in TPC. With CFP's interests centered in Iraq, France was drawing nearly half its oil imports from that country by the outbreak of World War II. France's access, it was evident, was less than wholly secure since it depended on the assistance of the British to keep sea lanes open to the Middle East. But when supplemented by efforts to use alcohol as an alternative fuel and to extract oil from coal, France's efforts represented a serious though ultimately unsuccessful effort to achieve energy security.[13]

Germany had neither indigenous oil reserves nor major oil companies to acquire foreign concessions. This vulnerability, of which Germany's leaders, as well as its potential enemies, were acutely aware, left Germany with limited options in the acquisition of oil: It could try to buy needed supplies on international markets, which left it dependent on foreign companies and foreign governments; or it could seek by political pressure or force of arms to acquire direct control over foreign sources of supply. In any event, German access to oil in Latin America and the Middle East would always be threatened by British and US command of sea routes.[14]

To reduce its vulnerability, Germany opted to make oil from its ample supplies of coal. The Nazi government began encouraging the manufacture of synthetic fuels in 1934, and by the outbreak of World War II nearly half of Germany's peacetime requirements were being met by coal-derived synthetic fuels. Synfuel production turned out to be barely adequate for wartime requirements, however, and the massive installations required to produce them were vulnerable to air attack.

Oil figured heavily, therefore, in the war plans of the German military, as it looked for sources that did not depend on vulnerable sea routes. In November 1940, Germany's access to Rumanian oil was assured by Rumania's allying with Hitler and Mussolini. Germany also managed to receive large quantities of oil from the Soviet Union under the infamous agreement between Stalin and Hitler that preceded Germany's invasion of Poland; however Hitler's desire to gain control of additional oil for Germany's heavily mechanized armed forces remained very strong and contributed to his decision to invade the Soviet Union in June 1941. Yet, despite these efforts to achieve an adequate supply of oil, Germany suffered from oil shortages throughout the war.[15]

Oil was also a key factor driving Japan's decision to attack the United States. Japan's domestic oil industry had never been very large. Although Japanese companies had attempted to obtain concessions in major producing areas before World War II, they had been shut out by the international oil companies and by foreign governments. In 1939 Japan seemed utterly dependent on the United States for its oil, drawing 80 percent of its oil needs from the US West Coast. Most of the rest came from the Netherlands East Indies (NEI), which possessed the largest reserves in East Asia, but production in that area was almost completely controlled by Shell and by a joint venture of two of the US majors.

Control of the Netherlands East Indies became the consuming objective of the Japanese military. Seizing control of the NEI, it was clear, would lead to conflict with Great Britain and the United States. But after the United States, Britain, and the Netherlands imposed an oil embargo on Japan in the late summer of 1941, the Japanese saw themselves as having no choice. The value of NEI oil to the Japanese war effort proved limited: first because the retreating forces' sabotage of the oil fields left the Japanese with major repair problems, and later because US submarines became a menace to shipping. By late 1944, Japan was beset by severe oil shortages.[16]

In sum, Great Britain, France, Germany, and Japan all failed to find adequate solutions to the problem of dependence on foreign sources of oil in wartime. Neither British companies nor the British navy were, in the final analysis, able to assure Britain access to needed oil supplies. The other powers were in an even worse position. Only the United States and the Soviet Union, which were self-sufficient in oil, could be assured of adequate supplies.

THE ORIGINS OF US OIL POLICY

Access to foreign oil first emerged as an issue in US foreign policy following World War I. Concern was growing in the United States that US domestic reserves were approaching exhaustion, and that US oil companies would need additional sources of supply to serve their domestic and foreign markets. Eventually, as the threat of shortage turned into the reality of glut, the United States and Great Britain threw their support behind regulatory arrangements that had been worked out by the major international oil companies. Throughout the remainder of the interwar period, the US government largely limited its role in foreign oil matters to insisting on the principle of equality of opportunity for US oil companies. By the eve of World

War II, US oil companies had acquired concessions in all the major oil-producing areas. By that time, US companies accounted for nearly 40 percent of the oil production and about half of the reserves outside the United States and the Soviet Union.[17]

During the 1930s, blessed by plentiful supplies of oil on their own territory, US policy makers saw access to foreign oil more as a commercial than a military issue. During the depression, with international markets already under control, the federal government, several state governments, and the oil companies worked out a cooperative system of national production control centered around the state of Texas, which accounted for almost half of the country's total production. The central purpose of the control system was to ration production and to place a ceiling on total oil output so that marginal producers could survive in the face of considerable excess capacity. The system had a number of economic effects: it raised US prices and allowed some of the high-cost marginal wells to continue operating, thereby slightly reducing the levels of US consumption; accordingly, it may have helped to preserve lower-cost fields for future use. Texas authorities refused, however, to require producers to pool their extractive activities in each oil field, so that wasteful extractive processes were allowed to continue. With the Texas Railroad Commission as the balance wheel, the system remained in place until the early 1970s, when domestic production alone could no longer fill national demand.[18]

The World War II experience of the United States highlighted the potential importance of access to foreign oil. The United States entered World War II with a surplus production capacity of over one million barrels a day, representing almost 30 percent of total US production in 1941. This margin enabled the United States to fuel almost single-handedly not only its own war effort but also that of its allies. By 1943, however, US oil reserves were barely keeping pace with increased consumption.[19]

The possibility of running short of oil during wartime led to renewed concerns over the long-term adequacy of US reserves. In response to that concern, policy makers in the US government eventually focused their attention on the Middle East, especially on Saudi Arabia where two firms, SOCAL and the Texas Company, held concession rights. The Middle East not only contained one-third of the world's known reserves, it also offered better geological prospects for the discovery of additional reserves than any other area. The report of a US government-sponsored oil mission that surveyed the Middle East in late 1943 confirmed what was already an open secret: "The center of gravity of world oil production is shifting from the Gulf-Caribbean region to the Middle East—and is likely to continue to shift until it is firmly established in that area."[20]

Under wartime conditions, the Roosevelt administration contemplated creating a government-owned national oil company to take over US concession rights in Saudi Arabia. It also proposed having the US government construct and own an oil pipeline stretching from the Persian Gulf to the Mediterranean as a means of securing the US stake in Middle East oil. By the war's end, the US government had also worked out the text of an agreement with Great Britain that contemplated guarantees for existing concessions, equality of opportunity to compete for new concessions, and a binational petroleum commission to allocate production among the various producing countries. But the deep differences that existed between the interests of domestic and international producers in the United States, when coupled with the strong ideological opposition of Americans to government involvement in corporate affairs, derailed these initiatives. In the end, the United States turned to the major oil companies, as it had in the 1920s, to secure the national interest in foreign sources of petroleum.

In a series of private deals in 1946 and 1947, the major US companies managed to secure US concession rights in the Middle East, establishing a basis for holding down their production from higher-cost sources in the Western hemisphere. The reliance of the US government on private oil corporations to protect and promote US interests in foreign oil did not mean, however, that the government had no role to play. On the contrary, the US government became involved in maintaining an international environment in which private companies could operate with security and profit. The Truman Doctrine, with its call for the global containment of communism, provided the political basis for the United States to take an active role in maintaining the security and stability of the Middle East. US support for a Jewish homeland in Palestine complicated, but did not nullify, US efforts in this regard. The Marshall Plan also helped to solidify US ties to the Middle East by providing dollars for

Western Europe to buy the oil offered by US companies from their holdings in the Middle East.

The US government's policy of utilizing private oil companies as vehicles of the national interest served to strengthen its resistance to strongly nationalistic governments, especially when their policies posed a threat to US private interests and threatened to reduce oil production for export to world markets. US resistance to such tendencies had been visible before World War II, both in its official reactions to the Mexican oil nationalizations, and in its more successful efforts to maintain access to Venezuelan oil. The US response to the nationalization of the Iranian oil industry in 1951 provided another occasion for resisting economic nationalism. Although the principal dispute was between Britain and Iran, the US government, after trying for two years to mediate a settlement, involved itself in the ouster of Iranian prime minister Mohammed Musaddiq in 1953. To bolster the position of the major oil companies, it curtailed its pending antitrust proceedings against them, obtained their inclusion in an international consortium to run Iran's oil industry, and forged a special relationship with Iran's shah. These actions were important milestones in the process by which the United States replaced Great Britain as the main guardian of Western interests in the Middle East.

The United States looked to US oil companies and US military power to assure itself of access to foreign oil. Although the British, the French, the Germans, and the Japanese had been unsuccessful in similar efforts, the extremely strong economic and military position of the United States after 1945 made such a policy feasible. Indeed, building on that strength and reflecting its position as leader of the "free world," the US government set about ensuring that sufficient oil would be available not only for its own needs but also for the needs of its principal allies.

FUNDAMENTAL CHANGE: 1955–1979

The story of the demise of the postwar oil regime and the oil crises of the 1970s has been well told elsewhere and need not be repeated here. But accompanying these highly visible events and setting the framework for future change were two critical developments: change in the structure of the world oil industry; and change in the factors promoting oil consumption.

The oil industry, unlike many industries vital to national security, produces a nonrenewable resource, and the adequacy of existing oil reserves for national security is a function of demand as well as of supply. On the supply side, the dominance of Middle East and North African oil in world oil markets is largely due to geological accident. But the growing importance of these areas is also due in part to the rapid increase in levels of oil consumption in the United States, Western Europe, and Japan.

The geological and economic factors that gave producing areas their critical importance were abetted by a series of political events— the 1973 Arab-Israeli War and the 1978–1979 Iranian revolution. The impact of these events was all the greater because of the profound psychological and strategic consequences of the US involvement in the Vietnam War during the 1960s. By the early 1970s, the Soviet Union had achieved a massive military buildup which brought it to rough strategic parity with the United States; accordingly, both the ability and the disposition of the United States to take a strong position in defending its interests in the Middle East and elsewhere in the developing world were measurably reduced. To make matters worse, US relations with Saudi Arabia became increasingly strained by US support for Israel, and US relations with Iran sank to an all-time low after the fall of the shah and the subsequent hostage crisis.

Meanwhile, from the viewpoint of major oil companies, the golden age of the postwar oil regime had dramatically ended. At the peak of their influence in the 1950s, the seven major oil companies controlled over 90 percent of the oil reserves and accounted for almost 90 percent of oil production outside the United States, Mexico, and the centrally planned economies. Moreover, they owned almost 75 percent of world refining capacity and provided about 90 percent of the oil traded in international markets.[21] With Musaddiq's suppression serving as a warning to those who might challenge the international oil companies and their sponsors, the United States was actively involved in maintaining the security and stability of the great oil-producing areas in the Middle East and Latin America. In particular, the United States sought to cement close ties with the governments of the main oil-producing countries through economic and military assistance. All these measures, when added to the availability of US domestic oil reserves, gave the US government credibility as the guarantor of the oil needs of the Western alliance.

Despite these strengths, the system contained the seeds of its own demise. Beginning in the mid-1950s, a number of smaller, mostly US-owned companies challenged the majors' control over the world oil economy by obtaining concessions in Venezuela, the Middle East, and North Africa. Drawn by the lure of high profits, aided by the increasing standardization and diffusion of basic technology and the security provided by the Pax Americana, and unconcerned about reducing the generous profit margins available in international markets, the newcomers cut prices in order to sell their oil. Pressure from the production of these companies, coupled with the reentry of Soviet oil into world markets in the late 1950s, exerted a steady downward push on world oil prices. The imposition of US import controls in the 1950s put further pressure on world oil prices by limiting US demand for foreign oil.[22]

Declining oil prices led to a resurgence of economic nationalism in the producing countries, whose income was being reduced by the price cuts. In February 1959, and again in August 1960, the majors cut their oil prices, presaging further declines in the profits paid to host governments. In September, the oil ministers of Iran, Iraq, Kuwait, Saudi Arabia, and Venezuela met in Baghdad and formed the Organization of the Petroleum Exporting Countries (OPEC). OPEC was able to prevent further declines in posted prices. And fortuitously, persistent increases in the world demand for oil allowed the companies to increase production, thereby maintaining their overall level of profits. But as new sources of African production entered the market, market prices resumed their downward trend.

Between 1950 and 1972, total world energy consumption increased 179 percent—at a much faster rate than the population increase—so that energy consumption per capita more than doubled. Oil accounted for a large amount of the increase, rising from 29 percent of world energy consumption in 1950 to 46 percent in 1972, as Western Europe and Japan followed the United States in adopting patterns of economic activity premised on increasing levels of oil use. By 1973, oil accounted for 43 percent of US energy consumption, compared with 31 percent in 1941, and only 13 percent in 1920. Similar trends were to be seen in Japan and Western Europe.[23]

High levels of oil use were built into the US economy in several ways. As early as 1932, the so-called highway lobby had begun promoting public expenditure for highway construction. Between 1956 and 1970, the federal government spent approximately $70 billion on highways, as contrasted with less than $1 billion on rail transit. Between 1945 and 1973, US car registration increased from 25 million to over 100 million, and per capita gasoline consumption in the same period skyrocketed. Between 1950 and 1973, fuel efficiency actually fell by more than 10 percent, as gas-guzzling car models grew popular. The nation's truck population grew from 5 million in 1945 to around 21 million in 1973, and trucks increased their share of intercity freight traffic from 16 percent in 1950 to 21 percent in 1970.[24]

The restrictions imposed on oil imports by the Eisenhower administration in the 1950s meant that increases in US oil consumption were largely met by domestic production. The restriction program, pushed principally by domestic producers in the oil-producing states, has been criticized for undermining US security by "draining America first." Indeed, idle production capacity dropped sharply between 1959 and 1970. On the other hand, by maintaining higher prices, the restrictions may have somewhat dampened US demand and postponed for a time the onset of US import dependence.

The oil import question presented the United States with a strategic dilemma that persists to this day. If what would be needed in an emergency was a rapid increase in production, oil in the ground was of little use, and even proved reserves were not particularly helpful. The need could only be filled by spare productive capacity. Too high a level of imports would undercut such capacity by driving out all but "flush" producers. Moreover, reliance on oil imports, especially from the Middle East, was unwise from a security standpoint because of the chronic instability of the region and its vulnerability to Soviet attack. On the other hand, restricting imports and encouraging the increased use of a nonrenewable domestic resource would eventually undermine the goal of preserving a national defense reserve and maintaining spare productive capacity.

In any event, the dramatic rise in oil consumption decimated the US reserve position; the United States *was* drained first. The United States had dominated world oil production during the first half of the twentieth century, with US fields accounting for slightly more than 70 percent of world production in 1925 and over 50 percent in 1950. But by 1965 the US share of world production had fallen to about a quarter, and by 1972 to a fifth, of world production. Similarly, the US share of the world's proved oil reserves fell from about 46 percent on the eve of World War II to a little more than 6 percent in 1972. As the oil companies sought more profitable outlets for their capital in the Middle East and other overseas areas, oil imports skyrocketed: imports rose from 9 percent of US consumption in 1954 to 36 percent of US consumption by 1973.[25] The ability of the US spare productive capacity to underwrite Western oil security had ended.

With the erosion of the US oil position, a spectacular shift in the industry occurred, moving it toward the Middle East and North Africa. By 1972, those areas were producing 41 percent of the world's oil and accounting for almost two-thirds of the world's proved oil reserves.[26] The region's producing nations, led by Libya, began to take action to gain control over oil pricing and production levels. The Arab oil embargo of 1973–1974 accelerated these activities, leading not only to a sharp rise in oil prices but also to the nationalization of the companies' holdings in the member countries of OPEC. The equity participation of the international oil companies in OPEC production fell from about 94 percent in 1970 to about 12 percent in 1981.[27]

By the mid 1970s, differences among the Western countries in their reactions to higher oil prices plus their divergent views on the Arab-Israeli conflict had dissipated what little unity existed among them. There was some loose talk in the aftermath of the 1973–1974 embargo about military action to regain control of Middle East oil; but aside from the inhibitions created by the Cold War, it was already evident to the West that the use of force would probably lead to the destruction of the oil fields, a judgment that would be affirmed by the Gulf War. Instead, the United States sought to salvage the old petroleum order by organizing the Western consuming nations in a united front against OPEC. In February 1974, the US-initiated Washington Energy Conference laid the groundwork for the establishment later in the year of the International Energy Agency (IEA). The IEA called on member states to reduce their reliance on oil from the Middle East, to diversify their sources of energy, and to adopt policies promoting reductions in the consumption of oil.

Around the world, higher oil prices encouraged the development of alternative sources of oil, especially in Mexico, the North Sea, and Alaska. The use of coal and nuclear power also increased, although both turned out to have their own drawbacks, particularly those relating to the environment.

In the United States, however, the crisis failed to bring about a reduction in the absolute levels of oil consumption. Government-imposed restraints on the price of oil muffled the market's response to the rise in international prices. Initially imposed in August 1971 as part of a larger package of wage and price controls, the US government found oil price controls difficult to remove, owing to suspicions that the oil industry had profited unfairly from shortages and higher prices. Price controls not only encouraged consumption but also discouraged exploration and development in the United States. As a result, increased demand was met largely by imports. When the second oil shock hit in 1979, the United States was more dependent on imports than ever.[28]

MARKET FORCES AND MILITARY POWER: 1979–1991

The lack of success of the United States in achieving energy security encouraged a return to earlier policies based on reliance on world markets. In an influential article published in 1978, David Stockman (later Ronald Reagan's first budget director) called for a policy based on the free movement of market prices, supplemented by "strategic reserves and strategic forces."[29] Governmental measures to restrain demand and government financing of the development of synfuels and alternative energy sources would be terminated and market principles would be allowed free play.

In April 1979 President Jimmy Carter announced a phased decontrol of oil prices; full decontrol followed shortly after Ronald Reagan assumed the presidency in 1981. President Carter also reaffirmed the US interest in the security and stability of the Middle East in January 1980 when he announced that "an attempt by any outside force to gain control of the Persian Gulf region will be regarded as an assault on the vital interests of the United States of America, and such assault will be repelled by any means necessary including military force." The Carter administration followed up, soon thereafter, with steps to create the long-discussed rapid deployment forces for possible use in the region. That move had been planned from the time of the collapse of the shah's regime in early 1979, reflecting US recognition that the problems of the Middle East stemmed not only from the possibility of Soviet aggression but also from instability inside the region. In addition, in the wake of the collapse of the shah's regime, the Carter administration sought to strengthen the "special relationship" between the United States and Saudi Arabia, a policy continued by the Reagan administration.[30]

Finally, the United States established and began filling a Strategic Petroleum Reserve (SPR) to reduce the nation's vulnerability to oil supply interruptions. By 1990 the SPR held almost 600 million barrels of oil, somewhere between 80 and 90 days of net oil imports at then prevailing import levels. The other industrial nations also built up similar, and in some cases higher, levels of strategic reserves.[31] In oil security terms, strategic reserves, which were expensive to create and maintain, functioned as a substitute for the spare production capacity that the United States once possessed.

With increased prices and improving technologies of exploration and development, new sources of oil appeared outside the Middle East, primarily in Mexico, the North Sea, and the Soviet Union. Middle East oil production, which was 37 percent of world output in 1977, fell to 19 percent in 1985. But US production increased only for a brief period; by mid-1990 it was down to 7 million barrels per day.[32]

Higher oil prices also worked their way through the economies of the Western industrial nations and Japan to encourage significant increases in energy efficiency. The amount of energy required to produce a dollar of real GNP declined 26 percent between 1972 and 1986. The gains in efficiency in oil use were even more dramatic: by 1990, 40 percent less oil was used in producing a dollar of real GNP than in 1973. As a result, by 1990 oil played a less significant role in the economies of the Western industrial nations than it had before the two oil shocks of the 1970s.[33]

The continuing transformation of the world oil economy also increased the role of market forces in the pricing of oil. In the aftermath of the first oil shock, state-owned oil companies in the producing countries had begun to market increasing quantities of their production directly to downstream users, bypassing the international oil companies and increasing their world market share from

8 percent in 1973 to 25 percent by 1976. During the disruption of the second oil shock, state-owned oil companies greatly expanded their direct sales; by 1980 almost 45 percent of oil traded in international markets was sold directly by the national oil companies of the producing countries. Moreover, state-owned enterprises in producing countries began to acquire refineries and distribution networks in foreign countries, thereby enhancing competition among producing countries.[34] With the emergence and growth of an organized spot and futures market for oil, the differences that had distinguished the marketing of oil from that of other commodities began to disappear.

The success of the allied forces in the 1991 Gulf War could be viewed as a vindication of the so-called Stockman strategy. Oil prices, having climbed sharply after the invasion of Kuwait, subsequently returned to nearly preinvasion levels. The IEA also contributed to stability by calling on member countries to make simultaneous use of their respective stockpiles. The success of US diplomacy and military force in the Gulf War demonstrated that with the retreat of the Soviet Union from a world role and the parallel relaxation of East-West tensions in Central Europe, the capability of the United States to intervene in the Middle East had been significantly enhanced.

THE CONSERVATION ALTERNATIVE

The perverse but inevitable result of market-based, supply-side policies has been to renew the dependence of the United States and its allies on Middle East oil. Thus, the market-based solution to oil security may contain the seeds of its own undoing.

A major drawback generated by that line of policy since the early 1980s has been the devastation of the US domestic oil industry. After a short-lived revival of US production following the decontrol of US oil prices in 1981, oil producers in the United States were hit hard, as an increase in supply and a decline in demand led to a collapse in oil prices in 1986. The resulting shutdown of high-cost sources may present a problem for future US oil security because many marginal oil wells, having once been capped, will be permanently out of production.[35] Other high-cost producers will be similarly affected by the persistence of low prices for oil; according to reliable estimates, for instance, much of the production in the North Sea requires prices above $15 per barrel.

To make matters worse, price-driven conservation has slowed down as the real price of oil has fallen. In particular, the US attachment to an oil-based transportation system continues to drive US oil consumption to higher levels. Although US automobile fuel efficiency almost doubled between 1970 and 1990, this gain was partly eroded by a 40 percent rise in total motor vehicle use in the same period. In addition, the number of trucks on the roads tripled between 1970 and 1990, and their fuel consumption doubled.[36] Although Western Europe and Japan are geographically more compact and do not rely as heavily on gasoline-driven engines, it is doubtful that they will curtail their oil use significantly below the levels achieved in 1990.

Because production in North America and the North Sea reached close to capacity by the early 1980s, and because Soviet oil production peaked in 1988, producers in the Middle East captured most of the increase in demand during the late 1980s. By 1990 imports were making up nearly 50 percent of US oil supply, around 70 percent of West Europe's oil supply, and over 90 percent of Japan's oil supply; and 25 percent of US imports, 41 percent of Western Europe's imports, and 68 percent of Japan's imports were coming from the Middle East.[37]

Dependence on Middle East oil continued to represent a potentially dangerous situation in an increasingly complex world. The volatility of internal and international politics in the Middle East showed no sign of abating. And with the inexorable spread of military technology to regional powers, the possibility of large-scale lethal episodes continued to be high. Thus, despite the short-term success of the United States and its allies in the Gulf War, increased dependence on Middle East oil continued to present the United States and its allies with a major security problem.

As a result, several analysts have begun to reevaluate the costs and benefits of a more active government role in shaping the supply of and demand for oil. Noted oil analyst Melvin Conant, for example, has pointed out that large reductions in oil use would be difficult to achieve solely through market forces because Persian Gulf producers can, in effect, keep the West "hooked" on their oil by keeping prices just low enough to make alternatives economically unattractive.[38] Other analysts have argued that conservation, rather than increases in the production of oil or other sources of energy, would be the least expensive way to reduce US oil imports, and would generate environmental and social benefits. Increased reliance on nuclear energy, for example, misses the mark because the principal use of oil is for transportation, not for the generation of electricity.[39]

Although there is little prospect that the United States will end its dependence on imported oil in the short term, and it is even less likely that Western Europe or Japan will do so, significant reductions in US oil imports would make a major contribution both to US security and that of others in the Western alliance. The adoption of a public conservation strategy would not, of course, be easy. It would clash with well-organized political and economic interests, deep-seated ideological beliefs, and "the structural weight of an economic system in which most investment decisions are in private hands."[40] Domestic producers could be counted on to argue that greater incentives for exploration and development are the answer. Companies with access to overseas oil, though anxious to secure government protection for their oil, would not want to see government action that reduced demand.

Conservation also clashes with the still potent ideology of the need for growth as the least disruptive means to fulfill the rising expectations of all groups in a democratic society. Higher oil prices, which would be necessary to reduce consumption, would not be popular with consumers even if mechanisms were developed to compensate them for the increased costs. On the other hand, each one cent rise in the gasoline tax is estimated to bring in $1 billion in revenue, a potentially potent argument in a time of persistent budget deficits. Finally, limiting US demand for oil runs up against prevalent patterns of social and economic organization—in particular, public policies promoting automobile and truck use, the continuing neglect of public transportation, and the fact of dispersed housing patterns.

Yet, governments cannot hide from one ineluctable fact: the geological reality of the concentration of oil reserves in the Middle East. Given that fact, conservation, along with the diversification of energy sources and the maintenance of sufficient strategic reserves, will have to be a key element in the energy security strategy of the 1990s.

ACKNOWLEDGEMENTS

I would like to thank William Burr, Melvin Conant, Christopher Dlutowski, Allan Goodman, Max Holland, Ethan Kapstein, Melvyn Leffler, Robert Lieber, Theodore Moran, Anne Nisenson, Raymond Vernon, Peter Weinzierl, and the members of the Global Economy and National Security Study Group for taking time to read and comment on earlier drafts of this essay. Special thanks are due to David Hillon for his comments and his assistance in preparing the manuscript.

ENDNOTES

[1] See W. G. Jensen, "The Importance of Energy in the First and Second World Wars," *Historical Journal* 11 (1968): 538–45; and Daniel Yergin, *The Prize: The Epic Quest for Oil, Money, and Power* (New York: Simon and Schuster, 1991), chap. 9.

[2] "Significance of U.S. Oil Concessions in the Middle East," Records of the Joint Chiefs of Staff, RG 218, ABC 679 (5–2–43) sec. 1–B, (Washington, D.C.: National Archives, 18 July 1945). On the coal crisis, see Ethan B. Kapstein, *The Insecure Alliance: Energy Crises and Western Politics Since 1944* (New York: Oxford University Press, 1990), chap. 2.

[3] On US strategic plans, see Melvyn P. Leffler, "Strategy, Diplomacy, and the Cold War: The United States, Turkey, and N.A.T.O., 1945–1952," *Journal of American History* 71 (March 1985): 807–25.

[4] Joel Darmstadter, Perry D. Teitelbaum, and Jaroslav G. Polach, *Energy in the World Economy: A Statistical Review of Trends in Output, Trade, and Consumption Since 1925* (Baltimore: Johns Hopkins Press, 1971), 654, 679.

[5] APOC continued to operate as a commercial enterprise except that the British government gained the right to appoint two directors with veto power over the company's decisions, and the British navy received a large (and undisclosed) discount on its purchases. See G. Gareth Jones, "The British Government and the Oil Companies, 1912–1924: The Search for an Oil Policy," *Historical Journal* 20 (September 1977): 647–54; and Yergin, chap. 8.

[6] Marian Kent, "Developments in British Government Oil Policy in the Inter-War Period," in Klaus Jürgen Gantzel and Helmut Mejcher, eds., *Oil, the Middle East, North Africa and the Industrial States* (Paderborn: Ferdinand Schöningh, 1984), 68.

[7] US Congress, Senate, Committee on Small Business, *The International Petroleum Cartel: Staff Report to the Federal Trade Commission* (Washington, D.C.: US Government Printing Office, 1952), chap. 4; Theodore H. Moran, "Managing an Oligopoly of Would-be Sovereigns: The Dynamics of Joint Control and Self-Control in the International Oil Industry, Past, Present, and Future," *International Organization* 41 (Autumn 1987): 580–4.

[8] William Stivers, "International Politics and Iraqi Oil, 1918–1928: A Study in Anglo-American Diplomacy," *Business History Review* 55 (Winter 1981): 517–40; Michael J. Hogan, "Informal Entente: Public Policy and Private Management

in Anglo-American Petroleum Affairs, 1918–1928," *Business History Review* 48 (Summer 1974): 187–205; and Fiona Venn, *Oil Diplomacy in the Twentieth Century* (London: Macmillan, 1986), chaps. 3–4.

[9]Kent, 64; B. S. McBeth, *British Oil Policy, 1919–1939* (London: Frank Cass, 1985), 93–94.

[10]Clayton R. Koppes, "The Good Neighbor Policy and the Nationalization of Mexican Oil: A Reinterpretation," *Journal of American History* 69 (June 1982): 62–81.

[11]Ibid.; Stephen G. Rabe, *The Road to OPEC: United States Relations with Venezuela, 1919–1976* (Austin: University of Texas Press, 1982), chap. 4.

[12]D. J. Payton-Smith, *Oil: A Study of War-Time Policy and Administration* (London: H. M. Stationery's Office, 1971), 22–24; and McBeth, 141–2.

[13]This discussion of French policy is drawn from Richard F. Kuisel, *Ernest Mercier: French Technocrat* (Berkeley and Los Angeles: University of California Press, 1967), chap. 3; Andre Nousch, "Pétrole et politique: l'exemple français (1945–1962)," in Gantzel and Mejcher, 127–36; and Gregory P. Nowell, "The French State and the Developing World Oil Market: Domestic, International, and Environmental Constraints, 1864–1928," in *Research in Political Economy*, vol. 6 (Greenwich, Conn.: JAI, 1983), 225–70.

[14]Venn, 84–86; Helmut Mejcher, "The International Petroleum Cartel (1928), Arab and Turkish Oil Aspirations and German Oil Policy towards the Middle East on the Eve of the Second World War," in Gantzel and Mejcher, 27–59.

[15]Arnold Krammer, "Fueling the Third Reich," *Technology and Culture* 19 (July 1978): 394–422; Jensen, 548–54; David Deese, "Oil, War, and Grand Strategy," *Orbis* 25 (Fall 1981): 532–7; and Yergin, chap. 17.

[16]See the discussion in Irvine H. Anderson, Jr., *The Standard-Vacuum Oil Company and United States East Asian Policy, 1933–1941* (Princeton: Princeton University Press, 1975), app. B; Venn, 87–90; and Yergin, chaps. 16 and 18.

[17]Unless otherwise noted, the account of US foreign oil policy in this section is drawn from my book, *Oil and the American Century: The Political Economy of U.S. Foreign Oil Policy, 1941–1954* (Baltimore: Johns Hopkins University Press, 1986).

[18]See David F. Prindle, *Petroleum Politics and the Texas Railroad Commission* (Austin: University of Texas Press, 1981).

[19]See Harold F. Williamson, Arnold R. Daum, and Gilbert C. Klose, *The American Petroleum Industry: The Age of Energy, 1899–1959* (Evanston, Ill.: Northwestern University Press, 1959), chap. 21; and Yergin, 371–383.

[20]Quoted in Painter, *Oil and the American Century*, 52.

[21]International Petroleum Cartel, 21–33; on marketing see Brian Levy, "World Oil Marketing in Transition," *International Organization* 36 (Winter 1982): 114; and, in general, John M. Blair, *The Control of Oil* (New York: Random House, 1976).

[22]For a survey of the changes in the world oil economy in this period, see Neil H. Jacoby, *Multinational Oil: A Study in Industrial Dynamics* (New York: Macmillan, 1975).

[23]Joel Darmstadter and Hans H. Landsberg, "The Economic Background," in Raymond Vernon, ed., *The Oil Crisis* (New York: W. W. Norton, 1976), 16, 19; Steven A. Schneider, *The Oil Price Revolution* (Baltimore: Johns Hopkins University Press, 1983), chap. 2; and DeGolyer and McNaughton, *Twentieth Century Petroleum Statistics* (Dallas: DeGolyer and McNaughton, 1980), 104.

[24]Schneider, 60–61.

[25]Darmstadter and Landsberg, 30, 32–33; Painter, *Oil and the American Century*, 9, 218; Douglas R. Bohi and Milton Russell, *Limiting Oil Imports: An Economic History and Analysis* (Baltimore: Johns Hopkins University Press, 1978), 23.

[26] Darmstadter and Landsberg, 32–33.

[27]A convenient summary of these events can be found in US Department of State: "The Changing Oil Market," Bureau of Intelligence and Research Report, 1137–AR, 25 July 1985 (prepared by David H. Vance); and Ian Skeet, *OPEC: Twenty-Five Years of Prices and Politics* (New York: Cambridge University Press, 1988), chap. 3.

[28]See Benny Temkin, "State, Ecology and Independence: Policy Responses to the Energy Crisis in the United States," *British Journal of Political Science* 13 (October 1983): 441–62; and Hans H. Landsberg, "Let's All Play Energy Policy," *Dædalus* 101 (Summer 1980): 71–84.

[29]David A. Stockman, "The Wrong War? The Case against a National Energy Policy," *Public Interest* 53 (Fall 1978): 3–44.

[30]See Simon Bromley, *American Hegemony and World Oil: The Industry, the State System and the World Economy* (Cambridge, U.K.: Polity, 1991), chap. 6.

[31]*Economist* (22 September 1990): 24.

[32]*World Oil Trends: A Statistical Profile*, 1986–1987, ed., (n.p.: Arthur Anderson & Co. and Cambridge Energy Research Associates, 1986), 24–27; *Washington Post*, 26 September 1990.

[33]*Washington Post*, 26 September 1990; *Economist*, 11 August 1990, 12; and *World Oil Trends*, 22.

[34]Levy, "World Oil Marketing in Transition," 113–25; and "The Changing Oil Market," INR Report 1137-AR.

[35]US Department of Energy, *Energy Security: A Report to the President of the United States* (Washington, D.C.: US Department of Energy, 1987), chap. 2; *Washington Post*, 12 February 1986; and US Congress, House, Joint Economic Committee, *The U.S. Oil Industry in Transition: Causes, Implications, and Policy Responses* (Washington, D.C.: US Government Printing Office, 1986).

[36]Curtis Moore and S. David Freeman, "Kicking America's Oil Habit," *Washington Post*, 16 September 1990; and Daniel Lazare, "Why Good Gas Mileage Is Not Enough," *In These Times*, 7–13 November 1990, 11, 22.

206   *David S. Painter*

[37]Percentages are calculated from data in BP *Statistical Review of World Energy*, June 1991 (London: The British Petroleum Company, p.l.c., 1991).

[38]Conant's remarks are contained in "Symposium: American Foreign Policy in the 1990s," *SAIS Review* 10 (Winter/Spring 1990): 24–27.

[39]See, for example, Christopher Flavin, "Beyond the Gulf Crisis: An Energy Strategy for the '90s," *Challenge* (November/December 1990): 4–10; and Amory B. Lovins and L. Hunter Lovins, "Drill Rigs and Battleships Are the Answer! (But What Was the Question?): Oil Efficiency, Economic Rationality, and Security," in Robert G. Reed III and Fereidun Fesharaki, eds., *The Oil Market in the 1990s: Challenges for the New Era* (Boulder, Colo.: Westview, 1989), 83–138. See also Daniel Lazare, "The Green Taxing of America," *In These Times*, 8–14 May 1991; and Moore and Freeman.

[40]The quotation is from Temkin; see also the still relevant discussion in Leon N. Lindberg, "Comparing Energy Policies: Political Constraints and the Energy Syndrome," in Lindberg, ed., *The Energy Syndrome: Comparing National Responses to the Energy Crisis* (Lexington, Mass.: Lexington Books, 1977), 325–56.

James Kurth

The Common Defense and the World Market

THE TWENTIETH CENTURY HAS WITNESSED THE culmination of the tension between national security and the global economy. In the first half of the century, two world wars wonderfully concentrated the minds of governments on the primacy of national security. In the second half of the century, one government after another was persuaded to accept the primacy of the global economy. The collapse of the Warsaw Pact marked the decisive retreat of the last great power that had been resisting the spread of the global economy. As we enter the last decade of our century, it seems that the epic struggle between national security and the global economy may be coming to an end, with the decisive submission of the former to the latter.

The tension between national security and the global economy has been evident for many centuries, reflected in the Portuguese adventures in Asia and Africa and the Spanish adventures in the New World.[1] By the seventeenth century, national monarchies had developed a broad array of instruments—navigation acts, chartered monopolies, and state arsenals, among others—by which the state drew benefits from a growing global trade. By the eighteenth century, these had been institutionalized into a systematic theory and practice, which we know as mercantilism.

Mercantilism is usually seen as a systematic policy of favoring domestic producers in the interests of national security. Yet, as the chapter by Moravcsik illustrates, national monarchies normally engaged in a lively international trade in armaments. In many cases,

James Kurth is Professor of Political Science at Swarthmore College.

207

military security and international trade went together, linked by the search for economic efficiency. That link has persisted through the vast transformations brought on by the Industrial Revolution and by the globalization of the world economy.

RESPONDING TO THE INDUSTRIAL REVOLUTION

Over the centuries, national governments have framed their policies in response to their need for security and economic welfare. On the eve of the Industrial Revolution, all the great powers of the time—Britain, France, Austria, Prussia, and Russia—were under the control of monarchies and were dominated by mercantilist policies. In those circumstances, national security and economic welfare were indistinguishable, different aspects of a single objective. There were, however, great differences in degree among the five powers. The state in which the monarchy was least authoritarian and the parliament most autonomous was Britain; accordingly, Britain was also the state in which the economy was least controlled by the state, entrepreneurs were under the least restraints, and foreign trade was most prominent. As one moved eastward from Britain to France, Austria, Prussia, and Russia the monarchy became successively more absolutist and the economy successively more mercantilist.[2]

The Industrial Revolution reinforced the differences along the West-East continuum, according to a pattern that was first systematically articulated by Alexander Gerschenkron.[3] In the first industrializing state, Great Britain, business enterprises led the transformation. Having nothing to fear from international competition in industrial products, the British soon abandoned the mercantilist approach and developed the doctrine and policy of free trade. Industrialization also brought advantages in military competition, particularly in naval development. Global trade was seen, therefore, as contributing both to security and to economic welfare, which in any case were inseparably linked.

Later industrializing states faced more formidable economic and military problems. For one thing, lacking the shielding from enemies that Britain enjoyed from the sea, they were obliged to maintain large standing armies; but that was not enough. In order to compete in foreign markets or to prevail in military conflicts, they needed to catch up with the early industrializers. One urgent need was to find a way of mobilizing large amounts of capital in a short time for investment in modern plants. For France and Prussia, this meant a banking system closely linked to the state; and for Russia and Japan, the state itself. Meanwhile, until they achieved their goal of catch-up, these countries needed to provide protection for their infant industries. Consequently, eschewing free trade, they developed doctrines and policies for guiding the development of the national economy.

Inside Europe, therefore, the role of the state as the arbiter between national security and economic efficiency was at its lowest in Britain to the west, and at its highest in Russia to the east. Further to the west, in the United States, the role of the state was even more limited. And further to the east, in Japan, the state exercised extensive authority in bringing about economic development. In Japan, the necessity to build a strong navy reinforced the need for government support of rapid industrialization in heavy industry.

The first half of the twentieth century would be one of the most tumultuous eras in world history. During that period, national security in most countries became a dominant concern. But it was not until after the close of World War II in 1945 that the relative roles of governments changed in these countries, disturbing the West-East continuum.

With the defeat of Germany and Japan, and the exhaustion of Britain and France, four of the great powers were demoted from great power status to merely being major states. The remaining two, the United States and the Soviet Union, were elevated to the new rank of superpower. The new West Germany allowed for far less government direction of the economy for purposes of national security than had the old Germany. Conversely, the United States, now engaged in a long Cold War, tolerated somewhat more direction from the state than it had in the past. And Japan, while retaining strong government direction of its economy, developed a completely new definition of national security.

SECURING THE DEFENSE INDUSTRIAL BASE

When national policy makers have seen the global economy as a threat to the security of the national defense industrial base, they have employed a variety of policy responses. Borrowing from the analysis in the Friedberg essay, I see their responses as falling into three groups: providing measures of protection, such as import barriers; providing measures of promotion, such as subsidies; and developing measures of prevention, such as export controls.

Policies of protection in the narrow, traditional sense are familiar enough. It might seem that protection would be an obvious policy choice for governments to secure their defense industrial base. Yet, as the Moravcsik essay demonstrates, governments have often purchased weapons produced in other countries if these were demonstrably superior to those produced at home.

When choosing foreign weapons, the military services of course have been opposed by the domestic weapons producers. In conflicts between military and business organizations, national governments generally have supported the military. In such cases, the global economy has been seen as reinforcing national security.

But the willingness of governments to buy abroad has undergone cycles of change. In the immediate aftermath of great wars, including the Napoleonic Wars, World War I, and World War II, national governments have been more inclined to buy from national sources. In such periods, there has been an especially large defense industrial base left over from the wartime expansion. As a great war has receded into the past, however, the defense sector has tended to lose its economic importance, making it easier for the military services to return to the international market. Even in normal times, however, some governments have been more inclined than others to protect their defense industrial base. As Christopher Davis relates, the Soviet Union has represented the extreme case of government protection and promotion, even at the cost of ruining its civilian and commercial industry. But France and Japan have also been strongly disposed to protect their defense industry. These two countries, it is worth noting, are the two capitalist powers with the strongest tradition of government guidance of the economy, the "strong states" of the comparative politics literature. So it is not surprising to find that they are also the countries with the most explicit plans for developing a national structure appropriate for their national security.

Japan, as described in the Samuels essay, represents an especially remarkable case of linking national development to national security. In the first decades of Japan's industrialization, the Japanese government actively promoted the "indigenization" of technology, along with a national defense industry. This provided the model for an industrial policy that since World War II has promoted civilian and commercial industry. Indeed, by promoting commercial production from the 1950s to the 1980s, the government incidentally brought Japan's industry to a state that has served especially well in the contemporary era of high-technology, electronics-based weapons systems.

The leading example of a policy of prevention has been the development and implementation of national export controls. Governments have applied such policies only infrequently in peacetime. But as the Mastanduno essay recounts, the United States pushed such policies hard after World War II, persuading its allies to join in an elaborate system of multilateral controls directed against the communist bloc. These controls, "the American style of economic warfare," had their origins in World War II and were readily carried over into the Cold War. The intensity and duration of the Cold War institutionalized US export controls so that they persisted even into the era of economic globalization. Even before the Gulf War aborted Iraq's systematic attempt to develop weapons of mass destruction, systems of control over the proliferation of nuclear weapons were already on the books, and proposals for the control of chemical weapons were well advanced. There is evidence that the United States will continue to promote such controls long after the Cold War has been forgotten.

These disparate national policies, however, need to be seen in their larger national contexts.

THE UNITED STATES: THE LIBERAL STATE

The 1940s were the heroic age of US foreign policy. The United States first achieved an epic triumph in World War II and then set about to create a new world order in its own image. This new order was a splendid example of enlightened self-interest, of Gramscian "hegemony," in which a leading class or power creatively conceives of its own self-interest in terms so broad and so generous that it brings the willing assent of those that it leads. Even today, when much of this structure has fallen into ruins and its foundations have greatly eroded, the grandeur of the original architecture still inspires awe.

International Liberalism and Extended Deterrence

The new American order embraced two central concepts, one applying to the global economy, the other to global security. The global economy was to be based upon the idea of international liberalism: liberal states, particularly those in North America and Western Europe, would support market forces in an open international economy. This might be termed the GATT model, after the General Agreement on Tariffs and Trade, which was established in 1948. Global security was to be based upon the idea of extended deterrence, that is, a collective undertaking to respond with nuclear weapons if necessary to any Soviet attack on the United States or on the territory of its allies. This might be termed the NATO model, after the North Atlantic Treaty Organization, which was established in 1949.

The two concepts of international liberalism and extended deterrence, the two models of GATT and NATO, thus filled out the economic and security dimensions of the new international order. For more than four decades, Americans have taken them for granted, almost as if they were "self-evident truth."

But, in fact, these two concepts together have represented no more than an Atlantic perception of a world order. The concepts of international liberalism and extended deterrence developed out of the conditions in the areas within the US-led Atlantic alliance, areas that dominated the global economy and world politics after World War II. As we have seen, both concepts had been prefigured in the earlier economic and security policies of Britain, especially during the century of "the hundred years peace" between the Napoleonic Wars and World War I. True, Britain was already abandoning such policies before World War II. But as the United States assumed the British role after the war, it also assumed some of the ideas historically identified with the Pax Britannica; ideas that came readily to nations with commercial economies, liberal polities, and strong navies.[4]

The economic and military advantages that the United States enjoyed in the early postwar years reinforced these historical legacies. In the late 1940s, the United States accounted for 50 percent of the world's industrial output, and was the world leader in high-technology products and high-productivity processes. In addition, in 1945 the United States had a monopoly in nuclear weapons and an overwhelming preponderance of naval forces. For a country in such a happy condition, international liberalism and extended deterrence were policies of choice. Besides, no other country was in a position to press strongly for an alternative.

When globalization was extended from the Atlantic region to the Pacific, however, the American concepts of international liberalism and extended deterrence no longer received such willing assent. The restoration of Japan was led by a national bureaucracy that, supported by its trading complexes and banks, had retained and even strengthened its prewar position. Japan developed an alternative economic concept, one that can be termed international mercantilism, and developed an alternative security concept, one that the Japanese call "comprehensive security"—that is, security based principally on economic power and commercial competitiveness.[5]

Japan - International mercantilism) Comprehensive Security

From Economic Welfare to National Security

In the first few years after World War II, the United States hoped to support its new international order with its old national priorities, that is, with its prime emphasis being economic welfare and having minimal spending on national security. By 1949, US defense spending had fallen to 3 percent of GNP, and its massive defense industry had shrunk back to but a saving remnant.

Already by that time, however, the United States was taking official cognizance of the Cold War. Thereafter, the Soviet acquisition of nuclear weapons, the communist victory in China, and the Korean War elevated national defense once again to a dominant theme in US policy. For the first time in history, US military forces were permanently stationed abroad, notably in West Germany and South Korea. Military spending sprang back to high levels, ranging between 9 and 12 percent of GNP from 1954 to 1964. And the establishment of a large defense industrial base became a permanent object of US policy.

The US government also institutionalized, through CoCom, an elaborate system of controls on exports of weapons and technology to communist countries. Although export controls were a direct contradiction of international liberalism, and the CoCom model was the antithesis of the GATT model, both were to operate side by side in the four decades to follow.

From American Superiority to Global Competition

The extraordinarily competitive position of the US economy in the 1940s and the 1950s helped the country to pursue an active policy overseas. It provided a healthy base for federal taxes and federal spending, and it financed large-scale expenditures on extended deterrence, the deployment of US military forces overseas, and extensive foreign aid programs. Prosperity was underwriting peace, providing the Eisenhower administration with its familiar slogan, "peace and prosperity."

When West European countries and Japan reentered world markets in the 1950s, however, US industry felt their presence almost at once. At first they rebuilt their old industries, including textiles, steel, shipbuilding, and chemicals. Soon, however, they moved into newer areas, including automobiles and electronics. In these initial phases, countries such as West Germany and Japan employed the advantages of latecomers in their production processes, that is, lower wages and more modern equipment than their counterparts located within the United States. Especially during the 1960s and 1970s, US industry's share of global markets underwent a severe erosion. To US planners, global trade competition, the first dimension of the globalization process, now seemed to be undermining US national security.

Adding to the US sense of slippage in the postwar period was the Soviet Union's achievements in space travel and the expansion of its own formidable industries devoted to military production. That expansion was especially pronounced in tanks and tactical aircraft, the country's winning weapons in the land battles of World War II.

The conditions of extended deterrence and international liberalism brought about the second dimension of the globalization process, the spread of the multinational enterprise. The US alliance system, especially NATO, encouraged a massive flow of American direct investment into other countries, especially into Europe. Multinational enterprises operated in larger numbers, on a greater scale, and in more countries than ever before.

In terms of national objectives, however, that development was seen by policy makers as having equivocal results. The multinationals certainly benefited greatly from their freedom to roam the noncommunist world, but there was considerable uncertainty whether US national security or economic welfare did as well.[6]

The European subsidiaries of US-based multinationals eventually began to sell their output not only to members of NATO but also to members of the Warsaw Pact. European host governments resisted the efforts of the US government to extend its export restrictions to the subsidiaries of US firms established in Europe, generating such nasty quarrels as the struggle over the provisioning of the Soviet pipeline in 1982.[7]

Multinational enterprises helped to accelerate a third dimension of globalization, the spread of high-technology capabilities. US-based multinationals began to acquire components for US weapons systems not only from their US plants but also from subsidiaries and independent suppliers abroad. The new reality was summed up in 1987 by the commander of US military forces in the Pacific, Admiral James Lyons:

> All of the critical components of our modern weapon systems, which involve our F-16s and F/A-18s, our M-1 tanks, our military computers—and I could go on and on—come from East Asian industries. I don't see change in that, during the foreseeable future. Some day, we might view that with concern, and rightly so. Certainly, the East Asian industries have really become an extension of our own military-industrial complex.[8]

From Military Spin-offs to Commercial Drain-offs

The institutionalization of high military spending in peacetime that took place after the Korean War helped to establish a large defense industrial base,[9] and also had an important impact upon the commercial performance of the US economy as a whole. But this impact would change over time.

For the first decade or so, the impact of military spending upon economic performance seemed rather positive. First, there was the fiscal or macroeconomic effect: as long as fiscal resources were plentiful, military purchases could be sustained even in recessions, reducing their duration and severity. Besides, military spending on new weapons technologies seemed to be helping the US government to lift the national economy to higher stages of development; military innovations, for instance, were spun off to support aviation in the 1940s and 1950s, computers in the 1950s, and semiconductors in the 1960s.

By the early 1970s, however, the benefits of military spending upon economic performance had become dubious. The fiscal effect of the Vietnam War had been to drive the US economy into an era of sustained inflation. Military spending was beginning to divert innovators from products and processes most suited to commercial use to the more exotic and expensive needs of the battlefield. The diversion was evident in semiconductors, as the Ziegler analysis points out, and was also apparent in other key industries including machine tools.

By the early 1980s, the impact of military spending upon economic performance had become largely negative. The Reagan administration undertook a new military buildup, bringing military spending from 5 or 6 percent of GNP in the 1970s to 7 percent in 1985. Although the increase was modest in relation to GNP, it was piled up on top of high fiscal deficits, giving rise to the accumulation of more federal debt in the Reagan years than in the two preceding centuries. For a time in the 1980s, interest rates and a high valuation of the dollar contributed to a further weakening of US exports in the global market.[10]

One part of the Reagan administration's military program, however, seemed to give some promise of a different result. A few advocates of the Strategic Defense Initiative hoped that it could also serve as a US version of the industrial policies of foreign competitors, particularly those of Japan, thereby repeating the role that military contracts had performed earlier in the fields of aviation, computers, and semiconductors. But any hope for a new golden age of military spin-offs to commercial competitiveness was extinguished by the drive to hold down military spending in response to the fiscal deficit.

Meanwhile, through the four decades of the postwar period, the country's principal allies were spending far less for military purposes than the United States, exposing themselves to the charge that they were playing the role of the free rider. By the 1970s, a negative relationship became evident between the level of military expenditure and the change in industrial competitiveness: the lower the level of military expenditure, the stronger the competitive performance. The resulting array placed West Germany and Japan at the top of the growth league, and the United States and the United Kingdom at the bottom. Despite some recovery in the US performance in subsequent years, the array continued largely unchanged.

The United States, it was evident, was the linchpin in the security system on which other countries relied after World War II. Britain and France were reduced from great power status and military autonomy to merely being major powers within a US-led alliance. This condition of dependence upon a US defense was even more true of the defeated nation-states, Germany and Japan. But in all these countries, a new conception was developing of how its national security was related to the international economy.[11] This conception shaped the policies that each government would pursue toward its defense industrial base.

BRITAIN

At the end of World War II, Britain continued in many ways to give the appearance of a great power. It still governed the largest colonial empire in the world; was one of the big three at the Potsdam conference; was one of the four victors sharing in the occupation of Germany; and was one of the five permanent members of the United Nations Security Council. But the reality was quite different. Britain had been economically exhausted by its wartime efforts, as was revealed in July 1945, when the British government had to appeal for a large emergency loan from the United States. By 1947, economic necessity forced the British to withdraw from being the main support of the Greek government in its effort against communist insurgents. Britain's withdrawal led first to the Truman Doctrine and then the Marshall Plan.

For forty years thereafter, the essence of British security policy was an effort to sustain British interests with American power. From the British perspective, the ideal "special relationship" was one between British ends and American means, British brains and American brawn. This special relationship was bolstered by a number of different factors: a common language and culture, a liberal-capitalist economy, and a liberal-democratic polity as well as the shared experiences of resisting Germany in two world wars and the Soviet Union in a cold peace.

In 1952, Britain developed an independent nuclear deterrent and became a third nuclear power. But the independence of the deterrent was only nominal. Since 1962 the British nuclear deterrent has consisted of US-made ballistic missiles placed within British submarines.

The policies of the British government toward the British defense industry have generally conformed to the pattern suggested by the role of junior partner in a special relationship. The British defense budget percentage has been the second largest after that of the United States, running at 4 or 5 percent of GNP. But the British market has not been large enough to sustain an efficient defense industrial base. For many years, the British defense industry found a natural market in the former members of the Empire, principally the sheikdoms of the Persian Gulf. But this was still not enough to sustain an industry on the required scale. Accordingly, as the Moran-Mowery essay recounts, by the late 1960s the British were engaged in joint production arrangements with the military aircraft industries of other countries, including France and West Germany. By the 1980s the British government was sufficiently relaxed with regard to the need for military autonomy that it allowed US firms to take over the country's leading producer of military helicopters.[12]

FRANCE

At the end of World War II, the gap between the appearance of great power status and the reality of economic weakness was even greater for France than for Britain. France had also been exhausted by the war, but the reason lay in something far more demoralizing than what had happened to Britain, namely, France's defeat and occupation by Germany. For a time, the personality of Charles de Gaulle as commander of the Free French gave the illusion of a victorious France. Besides, with the close of World War II, France still governed the second largest colonial empire in the world; was one of the four powers sharing in the occupation of Germany; and was one of the five permanent members of the United Nations Security Council. But because of the reality of its defeat, France was even weaker than Britain in the essentials of economic and military power; and much of what remained would be consumed in the long and disastrous colonial wars in Indochina from 1945 to 1954 and in Algeria from 1954 to 1962. Balking at every step, France nevertheless had to take its place within the US security system.

Out of office during most of these years, de Gaulle perceived this reality clearly, and when he returned to power in 1958, he quickly set about to reverse it. De Gaulle's France represented a sort of Indian summer of the nation-state, a reminder of what it had been in the lost era before World War II and the ascendancy of the superpowers.

De Gaulle saw that the keystone of the nation-state was military autonomy; thus his insistence on an independent nuclear force, his *force de frappe,* as well as his withdrawal from the integrated NATO structure commanded by an American general.

An independent nuclear force, in turn, required a strong defense industrial base—a French military-industrial complex. The chief components of this were a large aerospace industry and a large nuclear industry; supporting it was a French defense budget that normally has been 3 or 4 percent of GNP. But economies of scale of course meant that these industries would not be efficient unless their markets were larger than what France alone could provide. This required a major emphasis on the export of weapons systems and nuclear power plants, which often went to Third World countries, including those in the former colonial empire and Iraq. But France still could not sustain a weapons industry on the required scale. Accordingly, like Britain, France was driven to engage in joint production arrangements with the weapons industries of other countries.

Since the de Gaulle era, French governments have continued to give a higher priority than have Britain and West Germany to maintaining a domestic aerospace industry and nuclear industry. But the differences have now shrunk to a matter of degree.

WEST GERMANY

Before World War II, Germany had been the extreme example of the "military-political" state in Europe, of the state applying military power to gain economic space.[13] After World War II, Germany was reduced first to being an occupied country and eventually to a nation with restricted sovereignty.

As a military state, Germany had been distinguished by the superb organization of its military into an effective force. After its defeat, the country redirected its national capacity for organization and discipline and instead became an exemplary "trading state."

For a number of reasons, the allies did not leave a centralized bureaucracy to lead the new West Germany as they did in Japan. In West Germany, the powers of the federal government were held in check by some basic structural changes, including an expansion of the powers of state and local governments and the development of a central bank insulated from the federal government's authority. What was left of the national leadership were the same forces that had led German industrial development in the past, the major banks and corporations. These great organizations returned to become leading forces in the German economy, devoted to economic efficiency and commercial success.

When the West German army was reestablished in 1955, it was integrated into a NATO framework under an American commander. The West German armed forces acted as if they were part of the US army, and had no independent political purpose or strategic doctrine. With so limited a role, West German governments succeeded in holding down military spending to only 3 percent of GNP.

During its first decade, the West German military bought many of its weapons systems from the United States. Eventually, West Germany reestablished its own defense industry, but it was one that remained relatively modest in comparison with that in the United States, Britain, and France. Being too small for efficient production and not having available an ex-colonial market into which to expand, the German defense industry moved even more quickly and more completely than its British and French counterparts into joint production with the defense industries of other NATO allies.

Having made its peace with the rest of Europe, in West Germany no institution developed a concept of national identity or even of national security as they normally would be defined. The military had a NATO orientation; the banks and corporations had a Common Market or European orientation; and the bureaucracies had a number of diverse orientations—European, federal, and state. This absence of a German orientation was of course reinforced by the fact that East Germany lay outside its orbit. With the advent in 1990 of a unified German state, one condition for the development of a distinctly German orientation was again in place. A question for the future will be what institution or interest is likely to provide the leadership for a German concept of national security.

JAPAN: THE MERCANTILIST STATE

Japan offers some striking parallels to the West German experience: a state that had been defeated in its efforts to use military force to gain economic space; a nation with a high propensity for organization and discipline, turning that capacity to economic ends; and a nation prepared to live comfortably with less than the full trappings of national sovereignty.

Even more than West Germany, Japan has been the exemplar of a trading state, spending only 1 percent of its GNP upon defense. In Japan's transformation from military state to trading state in the postwar years, a crucial role was played by the US Occupation. The Americans dismantled some of the central institutions of the old Japan—the army, the navy, and the *zaibatsu*, or industrial conglomerates. Unlike in Germany, however, the occupying powers did not dismantle the centralized bureaucracy.[14]

The Japanese armed forces were replaced by the US armed forces, which assumed some of the roles that the Japanese military would have performed. US forces bolstered the military security of Japan in the Korean War and guaranteed safe passage for Japanese goods going to Southeast Asia, as well as Indonesian and Middle Eastern oil coming to Japan.

Without its own army and navy, Japan no longer had its own military strategy. By dismantling the industrial *zaibatsu*, if only in part, the occupation had also reduced a second pillar of authority. Yet another pillar remained from the earlier order, the bureaucracy. By relying on the bureaucracy for the actual administration of Japan during the occupation, the United States had further enhanced its role. With remnants of the conglomerates still in existence, an industrial structure existed that could interact effectively with the bureaucracy. At the conclusion of the occupation, the Japanese state was in an even better position than it had been before World War II to lead the Japanese society with a particular vision. That vision was a modern form of mercantilism.

The only power that could have opposed the mercantilism of Japan was the United States. But it chose not to do so. Why the United States did not, when it was promoting liberalism and opposing mercantilism so vigorously in Europe, has been the subject of considerable scholarly analysis. One reason was evident: in Asia, the United States had only one major ally to help it confront the communist regimes of China and the Soviet Union, and that was Japan. In any event, mercantilism remained intact in Japan, not showing any significant signs of change until the 1980s.

The Japanese bureaucracy has conceived of the state as guiding society toward effective competition in the global economy, for the purpose of increasing the power and wealth of the state and society. It has also regarded this competition as taking place within the context of a dynamic comparative advantage. Responding to the changing environment, the state's role has been seen as helping society to move progressively higher on the ladder of technology, abandoning low-wage industries for those with higher productivity.

Because Japan could no longer provide for its national security with its own military, it had to construct a functional equivalent, using US military power and a style of low-posture diplomacy in the application of its economic power. This combination provided the forces supporting the Japanese concept of "comprehensive security."

For Japan, then, national security has required the US military umbrella; but it has also required economic efficiency in the global market, an objective to which the state has been committed. In economic terms, this has meant returning to the policies of the national monarchies of two centuries ago, that is, to mercantilism; but it has required a much greater identification with the international market than was required two centuries ago, producing what I have chosen to call international mercantilism.

THE SOVIET UNION: THE MILITARY-POLITICAL STATE

The most consistent example of a military-political state in modern times has been the Soviet Union. Before the Bolshevik Revolution, Russia had provided an extreme example of the pattern of late development, relying on state direction of the economy. After the revolution, as the Davis essay demonstrates, it became even more so. In the view of some observers, the entire Soviet Union was one gigantic defense industrial base or military-industrial complex.

However, the Soviet system represented an unstable equilibrium. Undermining the apparent stability of the structure was a steady decline in its economic performance. Each successive decade from the 1950s to the 1980s saw a decline in the rates of economic growth of the Soviet Union and its East European allies. And although the Soviet Union was a military-political state, rather than one committed to increasing trade and consumption, this economic failure undermined its political legitimacy.[15] As it turned out, even an exemplar of the military-political state could not avoid the test of the global economy.

For the Soviet bloc, the 1950s were a decade that perfectly fit the Stalinist formula, resonating with a personality that had chosen "steel" for a pseudonym. It was a decade of forced-draft industrialization, of rapid growth in heavy industries such as steel, chemicals, electricity, shipbuilding, and, of course, weapons of all sorts. It brought into being a large class of industrial workers, which was supposedly the suitable mass base for communist rule.

Producing annual growth rates that often exceeded 6 percent, the Soviet state's impressive economic performance gave great legitimacy to the Soviet model. But the great project of steel communism was already reaching its limits, unable to deal effectively with the next demanding stage of development.

The 1960s might be called the decade of Sputnik communism, after the dramatic success of the Sputnik space program in 1957. Now the emphasis was on high-technology industrialization. There was also a vast expansion of higher education and the creation of a large class of managers and professionals. Growth rates remained high in this period, 4 to 5 percent annually, but they were lower than they had been in the earlier decade and were not much above the growth rates in Western Europe.

The 1970s might be called the decade of goulash communism, after Khrushchev's description of Kadar's Hungary, which he saw as something of a model. Now, the emphasis was on consumer-goods industrialization. In order to bring this about, the Soviet bloc opened itself to Western loans, investments, joint ventures, and licensing agreements, the first beachheads of the global economy. A prime example was the arrangement with the giant Italian enterprise, Fiat, to reorganize and expand Soviet production of the Lada automobile.

By the 1970s, the annual growth rates of the Soviet bloc had fallen to 3 or 4 percent, and the new standard of legitimacy was virtually identical to one of the central values of the West, namely, that of consumerism. On this standard, the Soviet bloc was obviously at a marked disadvantage.

Finally, the 1980s might be called the decade of yuppie communism. By then, the annual growth rates of the Soviet bloc economies had fallen to 1 or 2 percent, or even less. The communist regimes were no longer able to fulfill the promise of mass consumption, and they retreated to the promise of elite consumption, that is, consumption by the "new class" of bureaucrats, managers, and professionals.

Throughout these four decades, the Soviet government continued to spend 15 to 20 percent of its GNP on the military, or what Khrushchev called the "metal-eaters." It maintained and expanded a massive defense industrial base at the cost of having only a feeble industrial base for producing competitive goods for the global market. But the standards of both political legitimacy and military efficiency were steadily shifting away from what the Soviets did best, building a steel economy without regard for consumer interests. The move from low-technology, mechanical, mass-produced armaments to high-technology, electronic, and precision weapons systems represented a shift from what the Soviets did best to what the Japanese and the Americans did best.

As the Davis essay recounts, these developments led to crisis in the Soviet military-political state and to Gorbachev's unsuccessful efforts at reform. Finally, in 1989, the communist governments in Eastern Europe collapsed with a suddenness and completeness that astonished the world.

Each of the three dimensions of globalization—markets, technology, and the structure of enterprises—contributed in some way to the crisis of the Soviet state and the collapse of the Soviet bloc.

The globalization of markets increased the benefits of participating in an open economy and the costs of maintaining a closed bloc. With foreign trade, however, came a need for Western loans and investments, and a need to be attentive to Western economic advice.

The globalization of high-technology capabilities widened the margin by which Soviet technologies lagged behind those of the United States and Western Europe, a condition that was disagreeable but familiar. But it also placed Soviet technology behind that of Japan and East Asia, a condition that was unprecedented and unacceptable. If even South Korea could surpass the Soviet bloc in technological achievement, the Soviet system was obviously in deep trouble.

The globalization of enterprise structure did not mean the spread of multinational enterprises into the Soviet bloc, at least not at first. It did mean, however, the creation in capitalist countries of a class of corporate managers with international, even global values and styles, a class that the bureaucratic managers and professionals in the Soviet bloc were increasingly eager to join.

Thus it was that the greatest military-political empire that the world has ever seen was overcome in the cresting tide of globalization.

AFTER THE COLD WAR

Gorbachev's efforts to end the Cold War appeared to mark the transition to a new stage in the tension between national security and the global economy. The globalization trend had been seen by some US planners as creating a serious problem for US national security. But with the collapse of the Warsaw Pact, the need for a US defense base also seemed greatly reduced. By undermining the Soviet military-political state along with the US national defense industrial base, globalization appeared to provide a solution to the very problem it had created.

Nevertheless, with the prosecution of the war in the Persian Gulf and the turmoil in Russian leadership, some of the problems of globalization have returned in even greater strength. Although the Russian capacity for conventional warfare is much impaired, Russian nuclear capabilities cannot be ignored. Nor can the possibilities be disregarded of the appearance of new petty tyrants in the developing world. A critical question for the future is to identify what will be needed to maintain and strengthen the capabilities for dealing with such potential threats.

Part of the answer is crystal clear. A national defense base can no longer suffice to provide that capability. During the Cold War era, only the two superpowers, the United States and the Soviet Union, were able to maintain enough control within and beyond their borders to claim the existence of a national defense base. But both have been losing their coercive influence on other countries.

In the future the Russian defense industrial base may continue to be national in important ways, but it will have to depend upon large-scale imports of technology from the global market if it is to have any acceptable degree of efficiency. The US defense base seems destined to follow the trend toward progressive international involvement.

The new era, therefore, will not be the era of the national defense industrial base, or even of the continental, European one. Rather, it will be the era of the global defense industrial pool. This pool will be fed by streams flowing in from many sources, from many nations. And national governments will have to be satisfied with access to, rather than control of, the pool.

How will national governments respond to this new era of the global defense industrial pool? For the European governments, the new era will not be so different from the old. Centuries of experience have inured them to some measure of dependence on foreign technologies, foreign products, and foreign firms. For the US government, the new era will indeed be a new experience, to be endured with great reluctance.

Will any nation have real powers of coercion over other governments by virtue of its contributions to the global pool? The remnants of such power will probably continue to reside in the United States for some time to come. Beyond the United States, the only other candidate is Japan. There has been some recent speculation that Japan for political purposes might try to exploit its monopoly in some components that are especially desired by the US military. But the bargaining relationship between the Japanese and US governments covers many points of vulnerability for both economies. From the perspective of planners in the US Defense Department, who concentrate on the weapons procurement relationship, the relative bargaining power between themselves and their counterparts in the Japanese government may seem troubling at times. But from the perspective of the US president, and from the perspective of most Japanese officials, many bargaining components are involved in the relationship beyond those involving weapons procurement. These include Japan's heavy dependence on US and European markets, Japan's heavy financial stake in the industries and capital markets of those areas, and Japan's continued traditional vulnerabilities as a crowded island without natural resources. The capacity of either country to effectively threaten the other over vital issues continues to decline.

ENDNOTES

[1] Immanuel Wallerstein, *The Modern World System: Capitalist Agriculture and the Origins of the European World-Economy in the Sixteenth Century* (New York: Academic, 1974); also his *The Modern World System II: Mercantilism and the Consolidation of the European World-Economy, 1600–1750* (New York: Academic, 1980); and William H. McNeill, *The Pursuit of Power: Technology, Armed Force, and Society Since A.D. 1000* (Chicago: University of Chicago Press, 1982).

[2]Perry Anderson, *Lineages of the Absolutist State* (London: NLB, 1974); and E. J. Hobsbawm, *The Age of Revolution: Europe 1789–1848* (London: Weidenfeld and Nicolson, 1962).

[3]Alexander Gerschenkron, *Economic Backwardness in Historical Perspective* (Cambridge: Harvard University Press, 1962).

[4]Karl Polanyi, *The Great Transformation: The Political and Economic Origins of Our Time* (Boston: Beacon, 1957); Paul M. Kennedy, *The Rise and Fall of British Naval Mastery* (New York: Cambridge University Press, 1976); also his *The Rise and Fall of the Great Powers* (New York: Random House, 1987).

[5]Clyde V. Prestowitz, Jr., *Trading Places: How We Allowed Japan to Take the Lead* (New York: Basic Books, 1988); Chalmers Johnson, *MITI and the Japanese Miracle* (Stanford: Stanford University Press, 1982); and Richard J. Samuels, *The Business of the Japanese State: Energy Markets in Comparative and Historical Perspective* (Ithaca: Cornell University Press, 1987).

[6]Raymond Vernon, *Sovereignty at Bay: The Multinational Spread of U.S. Enterprises* (New York: Basic Books, 1971); also his *Storm over the Multinationals: The Real Issues* (Cambridge: Harvard University Press, 1977); Raymond Vernon and Debora Spar, *Beyond Globalism: Remaking American Foreign Economic Policy* (New York: Free Press, 1989); and C. Fred Bergsten, Thomas Horst, and Theodore H. Moran, *American Multinationals and American Interests* (Washington, D.C.: The Brookings Institution, 1978).

[7]Theodore H. Moran, "The Globalization of America's Defense Industries: Managing the Threat of Foreign Dependence," *International Security* 15 (1) (Summer 1990): 65; and Bruce W. Jentleson, *Pipeline Politics: The Complex Political Economy of East-West Trade* (Ithaca: Cornell University Press, 1986).

[8]"Interview with James A. Lyons, Jr.," *Proceedings, U.S. Naval Institute* 113 (July 1987): 67. Comprehensive accounts of the globalization of the US defense industry and of competing proposals for policy responses are Moran, "The Globalization of America's Defense Industries"; and Ethan B. Kapstein, "Losing Control: National Security and the Global Economy," *The National Interest* 18 (Winter 1989/1990): 85–93.

[9]James R. Kurth, "The Military Industrial Complex Revisited," in Joseph Kurzel, ed., *American Defense Annual 1989–1990* (Lexington, Mass.: Lexington Books, 1989); 195–215; Thomas McNaugher, *New Weapons, Old Politics: America's Military Procurement Muddle* (Washington, D.C.: The Brookings Institution, 1989); and Jacques Ganzler, *The Defense Industry* (Cambridge: MIT Press, 1981).

[10]A comprehensive overview of this issue and debate is Aaron L. Friedberg, "The Political Economy of American Strategy," *World Politics* 41 (3) (April 1989): 381–406.

[11]James R. Kurth, "The United States and Western Europe in the Reagan Era," in Morris H. Morley, ed., *Crisis and Confrontation: Ronald Reagan's Foreign Policy* (Lanham, Md.: Rowman and Littlefield, 1988), 46–79.

[12]Andrew Pierre, *The Global Politics of Arms Sales* (Princeton: Princeton University Press, 1982); and David C. Mowery, *Alliance Politics and Economics: Multinational Joint Ventures in Commercial Aircraft* (Cambridge: Ballinger, 1987).

[13]Richard Rosecrance, *The Rise of the Trading State: Commerce and Conquest in the Modern World* (New York: Basic Books, 1986).

[14]James R. Kurth, "The Pacific Basin versus the Atlantic Alliance: Two Paradigms of International Relations," *The Annals* 505 (September 1989): 34–36.

[15]"Eastern Europe. . . Central Europe. . . Europe," *Dædalus* 119 (1) (Winter 1990); and James R. Kurth, "Economic Change and State Development," in Jan F. Triska, ed., *Dominant Powers and Subordinate States: The United States in Latin America and the Soviet Union in Eastern Europe* (Durham, N.C.: Duke University Press, 1989), 85–101.

The technology of modern warfare and communications has made overall development of heavy industries an indispensible element of national power. . . . It is inevitable that the leading industrial nations should be identical with the great powers, and a change in industrial rank, for better or for worse, should be accompanied or followed by a corresponding change in the hierarchy of power.

Hans Morgenthau
Politics Among Nations, 1968

The expense of war crippled states. . . . The inglorious and costly Irish wars ruined Elizabeth's finances toward the end of her brilliant reign and, more than any other single factor, prepared the way for the truce of 1604. The cost of war in the Mediterranean was so great that bankruptcy often followed. . . . War fleets devoured money and supplies.

Fernand Braudel
The Mediterranean and the Mediterranean World, 1973

Wealth is an absolutely essential means to power, whether for security or for aggression. . . . Power is essential or valuable as a means to the acquisition or retention of wealth. . . . There is a long-run harmony between these ends, although in particular circumstances it may be necessary . . . to make economic sacrifices in the interest of military security and therefore also of long-run prosperity.

Jacob Viner
The Long View and the Short, 1958

A country trying to make the most out of its strategic position with respect to its own trade will try precisely to create conditions which make the interruption of trade of much graver concern to its trading partners than to itself.

Albert O. Hirschman
National Power and the Structure of Foreign Trade, 1945

Index